Housing Dynamics in Korea

BUILDING INCLUSIVE AND SMART CITIES

OECD
BETTER POLICIES FOR BETTER LIVES

This document, as well as any data and any map included herein, are without prejudice to the status of or sovereignty over any territory, to the delimitation of international frontiers and boundaries and to the name of any territory, city or area.

Please cite this publication as:
OECD (2018), *Housing Dynamics in Korea: Building Inclusive and Smart Cities*, OECD Publishing, Paris.
http://dx.doi.org/10.1787/9789264298880-en

ISBN 978-92-64-29886-6 (print)
ISBN 978-92-64-29888-0 (PDF)

Photo credits: Cover © Sean Pavone Photo 2012/ iStock / Getty Images Plus

Corrigenda to OECD publications may be found on line at: *www.oecd.org/about/publishing/corrigenda.htm.*

Foreword

Housing policies have a significant role in promoting inclusive growth, boosting economic development, and enhancing well-being. For those reasons, housing policies should have a central role in national urban policy agendas to achieve quality and inclusive urbanisation. Housing in Korea has been part of the national government's strategic policy development agenda for the past three decades, helping to reduce the historical housing shortage and improve the quality of dwellings. Despite these achievements, Korea now faces a housing affordability problem as housing prices are too high for several social groups (i.e. youth, the newly wedded, and the elderly), while rental housing and social housing are insufficient to meet the demand.

This report analyses Korea's response to the housing affordability crisis. It notes that Korea has a complex social housing system that, although largely focused on low-income households, such households still suffer from housing poverty in terms of housing stability, affordability and quality. The report argues that the national government alone will not be able to overcome the current housing challenge, which requires expanding the network of public housing providers by including the private and community sectors. The report also analyses the relationship between housing and urban regeneration strategies where Korea has moved to a more integrated approach to respond to the more complex challenges of social inclusion, job creation, housing and economic revitalisation. Finally, the report analyses Korea's smart cities strategy. Korea is a global leader in smart city development which has brought benefits to Korean cities (e.g. integrated transport systems) and the national economy.

The findings and recommendations of this report build on the discussions with a diverse range of researchers, national and local policy makers and civil servants in Korea during an OECD study mission in September 2017. The report incorporates the experiences of other OECD countries from where lessons have been drawn on housing, urban regeneration and smart cities. This report may contribute to the discussion of housing policies in other OECD member and non-member countries as they face similar challenges and develop their national housing policy frameworks, some of them for the first time.

This report was prepared as part of the programme of work of the OECD Regional Development Policy Committee. It was approved by the Committee on 19 January 2018 under the COTE CFE/RDPC(2017)13. The Committee seeks to enhance well-being standards from cities to rural areas, and improve their contribution to national performance and more inclusive and resilient societies.

Acknowledgements

This report was prepared by the OECD Centre for Entrepreneurship, SMEs, Regions and Cities led by Lamia Kamal-Chaoui, Director, with the financial support of the Korean Ministry of Land, Infrastructure and Transport (MOLIT).

Special thanks are extended to Gyu-Hyeon Kim (Director General), Seongkyun Cho (Director), Seung-Hee Yi (Deputy Director) and Byung-Chul Hwang (Assistant Director) from MOLIT for their continuous and valuable support throughout the project.

The OECD Secretariat is grateful to the numerous representatives from the national and local authorities and institutions who shared their insights with the OECD team during the study mission to Korea: Se Eun Hwang (Deputy Director), Jihun Roh (Deputy Director), Soo-Min Lee (Deputy Director) and Taeheung Kim (Assistant Director) from MOLIT; Hyun-Wuk Park (Deputy Director) and Su-ah Lee (Deputy Director) from the National Agency for Administrative City Construction (NAACC); Hee Seon Jin (Deputy Mayor), Jong Ik Kim (CEO of Urban Regeneration Center Seoul), Changgyu Kim (Team Leader) and Chang Gu Lee (Team Leader) from the Seoul Metropolitan Government; Mina Kang (Director), Sehil Byeon (Director), Minho Seo (Managing Director), Hyeseung Kim (Senior Research Fellow), Wanggeun Lee (Senior Research Fellow), Sungsoo Kim (Research Fellow), Sehoon Park (Research Fellow), Eunran Kim (Research Fellow), Yun Sang Lee (Associate Research Fellow), Jae Choon Lee (Associate Research Fellow), Gil Jae Lee (Associate Research Fellow) and Jin Hee Lee (Associate Research Fellow) from the Korea Research Institute for Human Settlements (KRIHS); Young-Soon Kim (Executive Research Fellow), Joon-Young Park (Executive Research Fellow), Mee Youn Jin (Research Fellow), Young Eun Lee (Research Fellow), Shinwon Park (Research Fellow), Seungyeon Cho (Research Fellow), Jeong-Ik Oh (Research Fellow) and Sang-Hun Lee (Research Fellow) from the Korea Land and Housing Corporation (LH); Jin Young Lee (Executive Director), Gong Soo Lim (Director), Doowon Bang (Research Fellow), Ki Tae Kim (Team Head), Jong Moon Huh (Deputy Director), Seungryul Ma (Team Head) and Jung Hoon Park (Manager) from the Korea Housing and Urban Guarantee Corporation (HUG); Seong Soo Kim (Executive Director), Ha Won Jeong (General Manager), Jae Hoon Hwang (Team Head), Hyun Gi Yun (Manager) and Sang Soo Park (Assistant Manager) from the Korea Housing Finance Corporation (HF); Jung Ho Yun (Team Manager) from the city of Anyang; Sung Hun Kim (Director) from the Sooyu Urban Regeneration Support Center; and Jae Goun Jeon (Manager) from the Busan IT Industry Promotion Agency.

This report was co-ordinated by Oscar Huerta Melchor. It was drafted by Baesung Kim, Debra Mountford and Oscar Huerta Melchor under the supervision of Rudiger Ahrend, former Head of the OECD Urban Programme; and subsequently Aziza Akhmouch, Acting Head of the OECD Cities, Urban Policies and Sustainable Development Division. This study draws on valuable contributions from Se-Hee Lim from Seoul Cyber University, Miseon Park from KRIHS, Junghoon Lee from Yonsei University, and Baku Kawai from OECD/CFE. Karen Maguire provided valuable comments on the draft. Kay Olbison edited the report. Special thanks are also extended to Pilar Philip and Cicely Dupont-Nivore for preparing the report for publication and to Pauline Arbel for preparing the cover page.

Table of contents

Tables

Figures

Boxes

Executive Summary

Korea's record for improving access to quality housing has been significant. This has been due, in part, to the introduction of minimum standards (e.g. number of rooms and floor space differentiated by size and composition of households) and the direct government support for housing construction. Korea has a wide set of planning, financial, legal and institutional instruments to implement its housing welfare policy contained in the Comprehensive Housing Plan (CHP). However, although the long-term public rental housing inventory has been steadily rising over the last decade, its share (5.5%) of total housing is still below the OECD average (8%). The government's housing welfare strategy focuses on direct financial assistance through a number of financing instruments (e.g. subsidies, mortgages, tax relief) managed by national and in some cases municipal government. The strategy also includes specific programmes intended to facilitate access to private rental housing such as the jeonsei deposit loan.

Tackling housing deficits while fostering social cohesion requires integrated urban policies and programmes. Thus, Korea has made housing a core component of the "Urban Regeneration New Deal". The five year programme aims to reduce socio-economic disparities across regions, and create shared opportunities in cities to realise inclusive growth. Korea's strategy is to provide public rental housing in central urban areas through urban regeneration programmes. Indeed, the current administration intends to supply 170 000 housing units annually for public rental of which 70 000 will be provided through urban regeneration programmes.

In parallel, Korea has launched a New Deal for Smart Cities. Korea is a global leader in smart city development which has brought benefits to Korean cities (e.g. integrated transport systems) and the national economy. National government now seeks to make smart cities an opportunity for all and to be a core component of inclusive growth and urban regeneration strategies. Smart cities in Korea utilize cutting-edge ICT infrastructures to effectively resolve urban problems such as transport, energy and environment, education, and health.

Notwithstanding this performance, Korea faces an affordable housing problem mostly in urban areas, and in particular in Seoul. For a long time, the government has been trying to control prices with anti-speculation measures (e.g. Housing Stability Measures known as the "8.2 measures"), but the problem persists. One of the challenges is that urban areas have geographical constraints for expansion. Moreover, a strong demand for housing that no longer originates only from low-income groups, a rigid supply of land due to the large number of government regulations, and low interest rates are issues behind the increased speculation. The financial sustainability of housing construction is another problem as, for instance, the Korea Land and Housing Corporation (LH) is responsible for approximately 50% the construction and long-term management of public rental housing, but lacks the administrative flexibility to change rent levels due to existing rent setting rules for low-income tenants.

Adapting the Korean public housing system to a new socio-demographic context of an ageing population, low fertility rates, and shrinking households requires a plurality of housing policies that respond to increasingly detailed and complex needs. The public rental system has over 20 different types of houses, each with specific eligibility criteria, varying levels of government subsidies and financial support, and different lease periods, but it lacks cohesion and co-ordination.

Consequently, to improve the housing welfare system and enhance its relationship with urban regeneration and smart city strategies, Korea may consider the following recommendations:

Housing welfare

- Build a network of housing providers to alleviate government's financial burden. Subnational governments and the community sector (e.g. local NGOs) could be gradually given a more active role in housing provision to design and manage tailored and localised housing programmes.
- Ensure relevance to regional housing needs when designing housing solutions.
- Simplify the different types of public rental housing and waiting lists to improve the management of the public housing provision.
- Use land-use planning regulations as instruments to stabilise house prices while permitting housing construction and preventing the externalities of urban sprawl.
- Perform periodic assessments of the effectiveness of the housing sector programmes and instruments (benefits, tax relief and subsidies) to verify they are meeting their social objectives.

Housing finance

- Modernise and upgrade the private housing rental sector to alleviate the burden on the public rental sector and boost the dynamism of the housing market. Better regulation of the private rental market that includes the compulsory registration of private landlords will both safeguard their rights and property and protect tenants.
- Promote a wider range of innovative financial schemes for mortgage holders (e.g. monthly amortisation loans) which includes options to finance public housing construction (in particular for social housing) to increase the supply of affordable housing.

Urban regeneration

- Align labour market, business development, transport, inward investment and social policies to reinforce the Urban Regeneration New Deal and ensure sustainable outcomes beyond the five-year programming period. Investments from across the public sector which impact urban regeneration should also be aligned.
- Build a rigorous evidence base against which programmes, policies and actions can be monitored and continue using housing as a catalyst for urban regeneration.

Smart city actions

- Use smart city developments to promote service innovation through integrating and diversifying smart city services such as health and social care, transport and energy and thus achieving a balance between the public and private sector-driven projects. Smart urban regeneration should be underpinned by robust business cases for smart renovation, using smart technology and sustainable building materials and constructing denser housing, to revive deprived areas of cities.

- Construct interoperable Internet of Things (IoT) networks to enable cities to leverage new sets of urban data and capture new value from consolidating a variety of data. This will be critical for enhancing infrastructure integration in smart cities of the next generation.
- Boost smart city governance through strong leadership and the delivery of citizen-centred services using civic engagement platforms. Create programmes to support start-up ICT businesses that would lead to innovation ecosystems.

Assessment and Recommendations

Korea has made significant progress in improving housing conditions. The government's efforts to bridge the housing stock gap and to improve quality have paid off. However, the Korean experience shows that housing construction per se does not necessarily mean people will have easy access to decent housing. Korea's current housing challenge is to ensure access to good quality and well-located housing to low-income households to reduce inequality. Over the last three decades, Korea focused on housing construction but did not invest enough in building an attractive and secure public housing sector nor in modernising the private rental market and financial options for likely home buyers. This led to stagnant homeownership levels and house price volatility. Korea has to address its housing affordability challenge in the context of a rapidly ageing population, low fertility rates, and shrinking households. As such, the elderly, newlyweds, and young people are also part of the target population of social housing policies.

The state of housing

Korea has bridged the housing stock gap and improved its quality

Korea managed to close the housing gap that had emerged as a consequence of the industrialisation and urbanisation processes. This was the result of the implementation of different governmental housing construction programmes since the 1970s, for example the "Two Million Housing Drive". The number of housing units built passed from 4.36 million in 1970 to approximately 16 million in 2014. The housing supply ratio grew from 71% in 1980 to 103% in 2014. The number of dwellings per thousand inhabitants had increased from 141 in 1970 to 383 in 2015.

Since the 1990s, Korean authorities have placed the emphasis not only on the quantity but also on the quality of housing. In 2000, the national government introduced the minimum housing standards which mostly referred to the number of rooms and floor area with different criteria depending on the size and composition of households. The share of substandard housing also decreased from 16.6% in 2006 to 5.4% in 2016. For instance, less than one in ten households had adequate bathroom facilities in 1980, but it soared to 96.9% in 2010; similarly, the proportion of dwellings with running water rose from 56.1% in 1980, to 97.9% in 2010.

Although housing conditions have improved, further efforts are needed to raise the levels of housing welfare to that of other OECD countries regarding floor space per person, owner-occupancy rate, and public rental housing as a share of total housing. In Korea the average number of rooms per person is approximately 1.43, lower than OECD average of 1.7. The average share of people without basic sanitary facilities in Korea was 4.16% in 2013, which is higher than OECD average of 1.16%.

A looming housing affordability challenge

Although Korea has achieved a balance between demand and supply, it does not necessarily mean that the housing stock is enough nor that all households have easy access to decent housing. Moreover, housing demand no longer originates from low-income groups (the traditional recipients of social housing). Therefore, affordable housing is currently the Korean government's top social policy priority. Despite heavy investment in housing construction (7% of GDP) and the increases in the housing stock, the access to affordable rental housing is still poor and home ownership levels have stalled. The government has adopted a number of financial measures to deal with house price speculation such as heavy taxes on multiple homeowners. The house price to income ratio (PIR) and the rent to income ratio (RIR), which are normally used in Korea to measure housing affordability, have both steadily increased since 2006, suggesting a deterioration of housing affordability. For instance, the RIR rose from 18.7% in 2006 to 20.3% in 2014. Although the housing affordability index suggests that housing affordability is comparable to most OECD countries, there is a growing concern that housing prices are too high for ordinary households in Korea, especially in Seoul metropolitan area. Moreover, low- to middle-income households still experience heavy financial burden due to the cost of housing. Housing costs typically take up a sizeable proportion of household budgets. In addition, limited financing options and negative perception towards public rental housing complexes accommodating low-income people is making it difficult to meet housing welfare demand with the supply of public rental housing alone. Korea needs a more ambitious and co-ordinated approach to urban housing that can embrace land use, land value, taxes and sustainability strategies.

Owner occupancy levels are decreasing

There are at least three types of housing tenure in Korea: owner-occupied, jeonsei, and monthly rent. Owner-occupied is the main housing tenure type in Korea but its level is decreasing. The national level of owner occupancy fell from 58.6% in 1980 to 53.6% in 2014, lower than in some advanced OECD countries. In the rental housing market, the share of jeonsei, the traditional Korean rental system, has dropped from 23.9% in 1980 to 19.6% in 2014, whereas the share of the monthly rental scheme (23.9%) has been rising to even surpass jeonsei levels. This signals a new trend in the rental housing market; traditionally, the share of jeonsei is higher than that of monthly rent.

There is a large discrepancy between homeownership and owner occupancy

Despite the government's focus on home purchase and the extensive house building projects conducted over decades, the level of homeownership is just above 60% which is comparable with other countries such as France, Japan, the United Kingdom and the United States. However, the owner-occupancy level is significantly lower at 53% according to MOLIT. The reason for this discrepancy is the separation of residence and ownership in Korea. It is not uncommon in Korea to own a property but actually live in a rented one for economic reasons or for the convenience of being closer to the work place. There has also been a rapid growth of multiple property ownership among wealthier homeowners as well as volatile house prices.

Seoul Metropolitan Area has the lowest levels of housing welfare in the country

Across Korea's regions, the housing supply ratio has improved over the last decade following the national trend. However, Seoul Metropolitan Area (SMA) - composed of

Seoul, Incheon, Gyeonggi - lags behind the rest of the regions despite having the highest levels of construction. This may be due to the fact that approximately 50% of the country's population lives in the SMA and thus demand is higher. Furthermore, provinces and other metropolitan areas have relatively better housing conditions than SMA. People living in the provinces have comparatively larger floor space than those living in predominantly urban areas. Indeed, SMA had a smaller floor area per person (30.7m^2) than the national average (37.1m^2) in 2016. One possible explanation is that the average number of household members in SMA is higher (2.58) than in other metropolitan areas (2.51) and provinces (2.42). Although the share of substandard housing has decreased across the country, in predominantly urban areas, and particularly in Seoul, there is an upward trend. The reason for this may be the increase in small-sized housing for single person households in urban areas that does not meet the minimum floor area requirement.

Housing and rent prices in Seoul are significantly higher than in the rest of the country. In 2016, the average housing price in SMA was double the average prices in the rest of the country. High housing prices may be a threat to local and national economic growth, placing increasing pressure on existing infrastructure, raising business costs, exacerbating skill shortages, and preventing people from moving to metropolitan areas like Seoul.

Within functional urban areas, households in urban cores have the lowest share of owner-occupied floor area per household and per person. This suggests that living conditions in cities, especially for urban cores, are costlier and therefore accessing decent housing requires more efforts and investment.

Regional characteristics largely determine housing welfare

Housing welfare largely depends on the quality of regional well-being levels such as access to public services and jobs. When choosing accommodation, people tend to consider elements such as access to public services, schools, jobs and commuting. In Korea, as regions provide more public rental housing, the probability of living in substandard housing significantly decreases. However, the probability of living in unaffordable housing increases as the median price or rent within an area rises. Statistical analysis suggests that an increase in public rental housing is helpful to solve the problem of inadequate housing. The supply of public housing helps to solve the problem by expanding the stock of affordable housing in regions, and it also indirectly contributes by keeping a lid on private rent prices. Policy intervention is needed to prevent housing prices rising much faster than wages.

The housing welfare system

Korea has a complex social housing system…

Public rental housing refers to the housing units that are built, purchased, or leased with funding from the government, the National Housing and Urban Fund (NHUF), or the assistance of public land acquisition and subsidised by the government; rentals are below market rates and target low-income households. Public housing has two tenure types: public for-sale and public rental. Korea's social housing system operates separately from the private rental market and only households for which the market is deemed unable to deliver housing benefit from it. Housing is allocated to eligible tenants based on income thresholds via a waiting list system with consideration given to the priority rating of tenants.

The Korean public rental system is a complex modality as it has different types of houses each with different eligibility criteria, varying levels of government subsidies and financial support, and different lease periods. The reason for the diversity of schemes is to effectively tackle the housing needs of socially vulnerable groups of different income levels (mainly disabled, low-income households, and welfare-dependent families). There are more than 20 types of public rental housing and each of them has a different policy target group with a different income level (e.g. permanent rental housing, national rental housing, 5-year rental, 10-year rental, jeonsei rental housing, purchased rental housing, "Happy Housing").

...*focused on low-income households and specific groups*

Despite efforts to improve the housing conditions of low-income households, they still suffer from housing poverty in terms of housing stability, affordability and quality. This is why the major concern of housing policy is placed on housing welfare for the underprivileged and the emerging target groups such as young people, single-person households, the elderly and newlyweds. Public rental housing has played a significant role in providing decent units with affordable rent, particularly for the extremely low- to low-income households. Among the lowest-income group, almost 20% live in public rental housing, 33% borrow a jeonsei deposit loan, and over 50% receive the housing benefit. However, although the long-term rental housing inventory has been steadily rising over the last decade, it represented only 6.3% of total housing in 2016, below the OECD average (8%). This is why Korea's housing welfare policy involves the diversification of support measures such as private rental and expanding housing benefits.

Housing programmes in Korea have been evolving over the last decades. They have been providing direct financial assistance to tenant households from low and middle-income households and home buyers. Korean authorities have typically utilised three types of subsidies for different income groups to provide homes and/or to relieve rent burdens by providing: i) public housing for renting and owner occupation, ii) housing benefits as demand-side assistance, and iii) low-interest loans for jeonsei support. The lowest income group is eligible for at least one of the subsidies.

Moreover, the housing agenda aims to alleviate the housing cost burden for young people, newlyweds, and multi-child families by: i) supplying and providing maintenance of public rental housing (200 000 units for public rental housing annually), ii) enhancing the coverage of housing allowance, iii) improving the regulation of the private rental market; and iv) increasing loans for both rental housing and housing for purchase. Homes will be customised for newlyweds (tailored housing design and proximity to childcare centres).

Korea has outlined a strategic vision for housing policy

The Comprehensive Housing Plan (CHP) and the Housing Welfare Roadmap (HWR) are Korea's main housing policy documents that set medium and long-term housing plans in consideration of the housing market conditions as well as the economic situation. The CHP sets housing policy goals, dictates the sectoral strategies to achieve the objectives and allocates public rental units across the country based on the estimated demand. The CHP projects that long-term rental units will increase from 930 000 in 2012 to 1.9 million units in 2022, housing units per thousand inhabitants will rise from 364 units in 2010 to 422 in 2022, and the percentage of households residing within substandard units will drop from 10.6% in 2010 to 5% in 2022.

The 2017 HWR intends to create a housing ladder to improve social mix among inter-generational and inter-income groups. It provides housing options according to households' income levels, and divides the target groups into would-be owners, renters, and vulnerable groups. The HWR aims to increase the share of public rental housing from 6.3% to 9% of total housing by 2022.

To enhance their effectiveness, the public rental housing schemes and waiting lists need to be consolidated

Korea's large number of public housing modalities is disjointed as each new administration tends to introduce a new type of public rental unit to differentiate itself from previous governments, which makes the system more complex. Moreover, authorities require innovation on the types of public rental housing, rent setting rules, and waiting lists. Instead of formulating brand new types of public rental, Korea could consolidate and simplify the types of public rental housing and rearrange them by the income group of recipients. In addition, it would be important to prepare a consistent waiting list for public rental housing across different providers. Currently, the frequency of the opening and management of waiting lists differs by type of public rental housing and by local municipality. It is crucial to reform the waiting list system to enable a systematic operation and make it user-friendly and easily accessible for all public rental housing types and regions.

Moreover, the rent setting rule may be reformulated based on the tenants' income level in a way that encourages upward mobility. Since living in public housing contributes to enhancing residential satisfaction, relieving rent burden, and tenure stability, turnover rates stay relatively low (4%-8%) in permanent rental and national rental housing. The Public Housing Act establishes the rent level of public rental housing in consideration of the target groups and their income levels. However, the rent level should also consider all relevant construction costs such as land price, financial assistance from the NHUF, repair and maintenance expenses, insurance, loan interest, taxes and public utilities charges.

Building a network of public and private housing providers could alleviate the government's financial burden and ensure sustainability

The Korean government takes a heavy financial burden for the provision of social housing as it is the main financial source and provider of public housing. Providing public rental housing requires government contributions that range from direct subsidies in the form of budget allocation to indirect subsidies such as low-interest loans through the NHUF. For instance, in the case of permanent rental housing units, the government provided up to 85% of financing (and tenants covered the remaining 15%) because of the belief that permanent rental units should go to the most underprivileged households in society. The Korea Land and Housing Corporation (LH) - a public housing provider - is responsible for constructing and supplying good quality, affordable housing units to the vulnerable segments of the population; developing housing land, new towns; and managing land reserve, rental housing and land. LH is the largest provider of long-term public rental housing with a 74.4% share, whereas local governments and the private sector contribute only 19.3% and 6.3% respectively. Until 2015, LH had built 1.2 million long-term public rental houses (5.9% of total housing stock). LH had a financial loss of about USD half a million per unit of national rental housing provided as newly-built units.

As such, Korea's central government may need to devise innovative tools and incentives to encourage the participation of diverse players in supplying public rental housing with different types of leasing terms, and different target groups. Some OECD countries have encouraged the participation of the non-profit sector for public housing provision, for instance, the housing associations (UK), housing corporations (Netherlands), limited-profit housing organisations (Austria), and organisations providing housing at moderated rents (France). Some others like Italy have even created public private partnerships, although with mixed results.

Subnational governments could be gradually given a more active role in public housing provision

The Ministry of Land, Infrastructure and Transport (MOLIT) is responsible for leading the formulation and implementation of housing policy. So far, centralised initiatives and policy management have been effective in the case of Korea; however, a more effective and tailored provision of public rental housing requires a more active role of local governments. Regions, cities, and villages have particular housing needs that require a flexible and localised response. The national housing policy needs to be much more flexible and cities need to be given much more freedom to respond to their particular circumstances if they are to make the most of housing's potential to deliver economic growth and meet people's social needs. Local governments are in a better position to identify the specific needs of the different target groups.

The role of central government could be shifted from controlling every detail to managing and supervising high-level matters, while providing block grants to give more discretion to local governments. At the same time, local governments should be expected to be more responsible for tackling their local needs and be more proactive in mobilising local resources such as housing inventories, funds, and local activists.

Local governments can use strategic land use planning to stabilise house prices

Local governments play an essential role in ensuring equitable access to an adequate supply of affordable and good quality housing for their entire population. There are two main channels to address housing affordability at the local level. First, local governments can provide public or social rental housing at below market rents to low-income and particularly vulnerable households through, for example, local housing associations. Second, local governments can implement measures that reduce house prices and rents in the private housing market. Local governments can influence house prices and rents through land use regulations and the building approval process. If land use regulations prevent housing supply from adjusting to growing demand, house prices will rise. Local governments can require from developers that a share of newly built housing is made available to low-income residents at below market rents. Decisions on where to locate public and social housing can also contribute to inclusion by promoting mixed-income neighbourhoods and preventing the risks linked with spatial segregation by income.

In cities and regions with fast-growing populations, such as Seoul and Sejong, land use regulations need to permit sufficient housing construction to meet growing demand for housing while preventing the negative externalities of urban sprawl, for example by encouraging the densification of the existing housing stock. This would be in addition to the anti-speculation measures adopted by the government.

Local governments, with the support of national government, should integrate housing policy objectives within their urban planning responsibilities to support sustainable urban development. The reason is that local governments influence public and private housing markets through their planning and development control decisions, have strong connections to the local community, and are well positioned to facilitate a whole of government approach to housing outcomes. Korean local authorities could formulate "local housing strategies" incorporating an analysis of local housing supply, expected demand, socio-demographic and market trends as well as recommendations for planning processes, land use plans and development regulations. Local housing funds should be set up by local governments to provide tailored programmes for local needs.

Social housing programmes and instruments need to be assessed periodically and the target group broadened

The experience of OECD countries suggests that it is important to assess periodically the effectiveness of housing programmes and instruments at national and local levels so as to detect any negative impact, and make the necessary adjustments. This evaluation should show how effective national policies and local strategies have been in addressing defined housing needs and meeting objectives. For this, it is important that local governments produce the necessary data and define measurable objectives and indicators for performance monitoring, as the national government does. The evaluation should be in relation to the defined housing needs and objectives and should try to identify legislative, institutional and even political constraints that may exist in every local government, as well as factors that have contributed to the success. It is also important to assess whether the taxes, tax reliefs and subsidies in the housing sector are achieving their social objectives or whether they are destabilising the housing market and the wider economy. It is essential that, while diversifying the mechanisms for facilitating access to housing, Korean authorities consider the perverse effects some of them may have on the wider economy as has happened in other OECD countries.

In 2018, Korea expects to implement the housing benefit reform which aims to broaden the group of recipients who are not considered in the current regulation. The new housing benefit is expected to cover an additional 30% of current beneficiaries. This is a positive step; however, the second lowest decile group will still receive relatively less benefits compared to the lowest group, such as the opportunity to reside in public rental housing and receive housing benefit. Housing policy could place more emphasis on how to address the needs of the income groups in the second and third lowest deciles who do not qualify for the same benefits as the lowest income households.

Housing finance

Government provides direct financial assistance for housing projects…

Korea has adopted a number of housing financing instruments managed by the national government and in some cases the municipal authorities. Some of the existing instruments are subsidies mortgages and mortgage guarantees for home buyers, tax relief for access to home ownership, housing allowances provided by municipalities with funding from the national level, subsidies for development of affordable rental housing, and social rental housing provided by both national and municipal governments. Instruments such as grants to home owners, mortgage relief for over-indebted home owners and subsidies for the development of affordable home ownership are not available in Korea. In Korea, the provision of guarantees by the state or local authorities on loans taken on the private market is another increasingly used form of public support.

The National Housing and Urban Fund (NHUF) and other government funds run by different ministries provide low-cost and stable financing support for homebuyers and renters. The NHUF has a housing account that provides funds to private consumers who wish to purchase or lease housing and to housing providers for the construction of low-income rental housing and affordable pre-sale housing by raising capital through national housing bonds, subscription savings of prospective homebuyers, and loan collection. It also intends to supply rental houses through urban regeneration projects. The aim is to diversify the methods to supply rental housing, improve the housing environment for small-size housing residents through the rehabilitation of run-down private houses and financial assistance for small-size rental housing construction, improve the landscape of commercial facilities and vitalisation of community groups formed by residents, and revitalise economic activities.

… however, low and middle-income households have inadequate access to housing loans

Inadequate access to housing loans has been a stumbling block preventing low and middle-income people from house ownership. To facilitate access to housing, Korea needs to innovate in mortgage markets, but with carefully designed regulatory oversight and prudent banking regulations. To improve the access to finance one option for Korean authorities and financial institutions may be to switch the loan repayment structure from interest-only bullet loans to monthly amortisation loans, support the adoption of long-term fixed-rate mortgages provided by commercial banks, and introduce innovative mortgage schemes like the local programmes that provide property tax relief particularly to low-income households and older homeowners. Since household income in Korea tends to significantly decrease after retirement, the government needs to induce households not to defer their debt burden until the twilight years. Across OECD countries, deregulation and mortgage finance innovations have significantly reduced borrowing constraints on households. As prices went up, reducing the affordability of housing, financial innovations were used to loosen the financial constraint of households, especially by lowering initial repayments.

To enhance mobility, Korea may wish to prioritise subsiding individuals and not just houses

In Korea, tenants in social housing are less likely than private tenants to move every year. They may be reluctant to give up below market rents and tenancies which are generally cheaper and more secure. Portable housing allowances may be preferable rather than direct provision of social housing as they do not seem to hinder residential mobility. Therefore, rather than subsidising housing, Korea may wish to subsidise people by strengthening the provision of housing allowances as they do not hinder residential and labour mobility to the same extent as social housing and home ownership. Korea may wish to enhance the housing voucher programme by expanding its subsidy criteria. Indeed, in 2015 the Korean government introduced the housing voucher programme as a rent subsidy for very low-income households without housing ownership or living in rented accommodation. The programme is expected to contribute to improving housing conditions and residential mobility of the lowest income group. The voucher may be re-designed in a way that a larger majority of households can receive rent allowances for any rental dwelling (social or private rental) which makes them more portable and further increases mobility.

The jeonsei and monthly rental tenure schemes are creating pressures on the housing market …

Rental tenure in Korea is more complicated than in other OECD countries because of the existence of jeonsei, and monthly rentals (wolse) with deposits (MRD). For many years, jeonsei - an asset-based lease - was the dominant rental lease in the housing market. Under a jeonsei contract, the tenant makes a large upfront deposit to the landlord at the signing of the lease and does not pay monthly rent during the lease period. The landlord invests the deposit to generate a return equivalent to rents. The deposit is fully refundable at the termination of the lease. Jeonsei emerged during the times of housing shortages, high interest rates, rising housing prices, and inadequate mortgage financing.

As the housing shortage was resolved, housing prices have stabilised and interest rates have fallen to record lows, jeonsei has become economically unviable due to conflicts of interests between landlords and tenants. Today the tenant prefers a jeonsei to an MRD because of the lower costs. The landlord, on the other hand, prefers an MRD because it generates a larger cash flow. This has led to an increase in jeonsei deposits and a shortage of houses available on jeonsei leases. Furthermore, would-be homebuyers tend to wait and see due to the pessimistic outlook of housing price escalation, which leads to an excessive demand in private rental market that drives the rent level higher. As a result, renters in the private market experience a heavy rent burden which requires the government to implement more proactive measures to stabilise the rental housing market.

The jeonsei system works well under the conditions of rising house prices, rising interest rates, the shortage of rental housing units, as well as the scarcity of mobilising financial resources from the market. However, those factors fuelling the jeonsei system have faded out as many housing units began to be provided in large-scale, expectations over housing price escalation turned pessimistic, the prospects of economic recovery became uncertain, and the interest rates decreased. In addition, the rise of the single family increases the demand for monthly rent, rather than jeonsei.

… but modernising and strengthening the private rental market could increase supply and deal with the volatility of housing prices

To provide affordable housing, Korea should not rely exclusively on social housing. Involving the private sector in social housing and developing the private rental sector would lift some of the financial burden of public sector direct assistance. Korea has an extensive private rental market largely operated by individual unregistered landlords. Current legislation recommends a rent increase of less than 5% a year, but this disposition is only applicable to public rental tenants. Moreover, private renters usually face the request of *jeonsei* deposit increase by the end of the two-year contract. If they cannot mobilise the increased amount, then they usually have to move out and find another place within their financial means.

Korea's private rental market requires better regulation to provide a better protection system for private renters. Some measures the Korean government could introduce include: making registration for private landlords mandatory; monitoring the level of *jeonsei* deposit increase; setting the level of taxation according to the landlords' rent income; setting clearer regulations for rent increase in both the *jeonsei* and monthly rental schemes; imposing appropriate tax on the real estate income; introducing the rent increase cap; regulating the increasing rates in consideration of the renters' income level and affordability; and establishing a guaranteed deposit safety by the government for vulnerable groups. The Korean government could provide schemes, together with the private financial sector, to facilitate people accessing affordable rent and at the same time giving the option to buy property such as share ownership schemes.

A well-functioning rental market could help to reduce the volatility of house prices in Korea. When house prices rise relative to rents, an increasing share of households should opt for renting reducing pressures on prices. However, the scarcity of rental housing can prevent households from renting. Thus, if Korea's tax system favours homeownership and adopts tight regulations on the rental market, this may produce a decline in the supply of rental accommodation in quantity and quality. The Korean government may grant fiscal incentives to homeowners to rent their properties at intermediate rent levels. The higher the tax deduction, the higher the tax allowance.

Financing public housing construction requires different alternative sources

As home builders require more funding for construction, and in particular for social housing, Korea needs to offer them different options for accessing credit either in public or private institutions. The availability of cheap land can make a huge difference in the total cost of a housing development project. In this case, to get a building permit private developers need to agree to sell part of the dwellings to social housing providers at a discounted price upon completion of the project. OECD countries have adopted a variety of tax privileges for registered housing organisations, such as: reduced VAT rate, reduction of or exemption from property tax and income/corporate tax. Korean authorities may wish to consider setting some guidelines or principles to ensure the continuous financial health of Korea's public financial institutions and ensure a balance between taxpayer protection, investor returns and consumer costs.

Urban Regeneration

A new context for Korean urban regeneration

Urban regeneration in Korea has historically focused on housing provision to meet the demands of rapid urbanisation. Korea's experience shows that housing policies cannot be separated from a broad urban vision. Indeed, housing demand cannot be addressed by intervening only limited parts of a city, neither through programmes unrelated to overall urban development strategies. However, the Korean government has increasingly recognised the need for a more integrated approach to respond to the more complex challenges of social inclusion, job creation, housing and economic revitalisation. The 2013 Special Act on Urban Regeneration marked a critical shift towards inclusive and integrated urban development approaches. It seeks to strengthen the local capacity, introduce and create new functions, and utilise the local resources. The Act stresses the need for national and local governments to work together in partnership to create a more integrated framework for urban regeneration.

The Urban Regeneration New Deal is a catalyst for balanced local growth, housing and job creation.

The current Moon administration has led to an even greater emphasis on urban regeneration and to an acceleration of efforts to arrest decline in urban areas, reduce disparities and advance an agenda of inclusive growth. The Urban Regeneration New Deal proposes an integrated approach which aligns housing with economic development and neighbourhood renewal projects Currently, 30% of multi-family units in the country are 30 years old or more and require upgrading, retrofitting and renovation. Public rental housing is expected to be more consolidated with urban regeneration in a smaller and more incremental way compared to the previous initiatives such as the "Two Million Housing Drive" (TMHD) implemented in the 1980s. The urban regeneration system has been designed to allow for greater collaboration between levels of government and local stakeholders. National government assumes a supportive role to unlock local growth potential and to build local capacity. 100 projects will be supported by an investment of KRW one trillion from national government. The projects are determined through a national competition.

An enabling framework for urban regeneration has been adopted

The Korean government has created an enabling framework to support the programmes of the Urban Regeneration New Deal through two dedicated bodies. The Urban Regeneration Assistance Organisation (URAO) which supports national and local governments through evidence-based policy and regulation, evaluation, project management, guidelines, consulting and training. The URAO will also support the Urban Regeneration Support Centres (URSC) whose role is to support local governments. The URAO work alongside LH and KRIHS and have benefitted from central government funding to support each of the New Deal Programmes. The URAO currently supports economic development projects to create new spaces for business in Busan, Chungju, Seoul, Daegu, Incheon, Daejeon and Bucheon. A further 29 neighbourhood-based projects are also supported throughout Korea focused on housing renovation and provision, community capacity building, stakeholder engagement etc. This approach will play a critical role in ensuring that all plans and projects associated with the Urban Regeneration New Deal are evidence based, relevant to the local needs, and that capacity is built at the local level to create a sustainable delivery environment.

The Urban Regeneration New Deal is a five-year initiative which benefits from substantial investments by national government. Korean cities such as Seoul also allocate significant budgets for urban regeneration. In 2017, the city invested KRW 231 billion in urban regeneration projects. Urban regeneration, as proposed through the economic and neighbourhood pillars of the Urban Regeneration New Deal, represents significant investment by the public sector which is attracting private sector investment and helping shape new local economies. Each project will benefit from five years of guaranteed funding but it may be prudent to create long-term local investment plans to ensure the sustainability of projects supported under the economic pillar of the New Deal.

The Urban Regeneration New Deal could be reinforced

The Urban Regeneration New Deal marks a change in approach to delivering urban regeneration in Korea. It is too early to assess its full impact but some measures can be taken to strengthen this approach and to ensure that it works in co-ordination with other urban development projects. Korea may wish to consider the following actions:

- To ensure long term outcomes from the Urban Regeneration New Deal, welfare, health, skills, education, employment, transport, investment and business development agendas should become integral aspects of the programme.
- Evaluate projects in the selected areas of the Urban Regeneration New Deal and recalibrate interventions, when necessary to use public funding more effectively.
- Build an effective and rigorous evidence base against which programmes, policies and actions can be developed and monitored.

- Continue fostering housing as a catalyst for urban regeneration.
- Invest in capacity building of local governments to take on leadership, particularly in small cities.
- Make the case for smart urban regeneration. Urban regeneration plans will need to be smart and smart plans will need to demonstrate how they contribute to urban regeneration.

Smart cities

Korea has been a world pioneer of smart cities

Smart cities in Korea utilise cutting-edge ICT infrastructures to advance as the future-driven city that may effectively resolve urban problems such as transport, energy and environment, education, and health. Korea has taken the "U-City" approach since the early 2000s to construct an integrated urban environment that combines ICT with urban infrastructures, as a national initiative for research and development. As a result, Korea is now home to the world's leading smart city pilot cities and testbeds in terms of infrastructure integration.

Government policies to promote open innovation-based smart cities are currently being implemented, such as: civic engagement initiatives and living labs based on open urban innovation, the establishment of a start-up ecosystem, as well as utilisation of open data. Korea's efforts in preparing proactive and anticipatory policies for the rising demands of the smart city indicate the country's nationwide leadership in future-driven smart city development.

In 2008, Korea became the first country to pass specific legislation to enable the smart city. The Act on the Construction of Ubiquitous Cities (U-City Act) focuses on infrastructure, technology and services with the aim of improving competitiveness and quality of life. Korea has since passed the "Ordinance on Smart City Development and Management", which was a renewal of the earlier "Ordinance on Ubiquitous City Construction Projects". U-City projects progressed rapidly with the construction of new cities, such as Songdo and Dongtan.

In 2017 the Korean government launched the Urban Regeneration New Deal and the Smart City New Deal. It is early days for each initiative but the foundations have been soundly laid. Making existing cities work more efficiently is an increasingly important part of addressing urban regeneration and housing challenges, especially with the use of big data. Compelling business cases will need to be made for smart rebuilding, or regeneration, of existing cityscapes, using smart technology and sustainable building materials and constructing denser housing, to revive deprived areas of cities. Urban regeneration plans will need to be smart and smart plans will need to demonstrate how they contribute to urban regeneration.

Along with infra-focus smart city developments, the Ministry of Science, ICT and Future Planning also pioneered the next generation of smart city initiatives by implementing new ICT concepts such as Internet of Things (IoT), big data and cloud computing in new test-bed sites across Busan, Goyang and Daegu. Recently, SK Telecom - the biggest mobile operator in Korea - completed nationwide deployment of Low Power Wide Area Networks (LoRa) for IoT. Korea's new concept of the smart city is "Implementation of Open Infrastructure, Ecosystem and Platform" where anyone can participate through an IoT open platform.

Korea has positioned itself as a leading smart economy through sustained investment

Since 2008, the Korean national government has invested heavily in developing and accelerating smart cities and associated technologies. National government expenditure in smart cities now stands at over KRW 135 billion. Early investment focused on building new cities and accelerating the application of smart infrastructures. This approach has helped Korea position itself as a leading smart economy and enabled a sustainable environment from which to grow the sector mainstream smart systems and platforms throughout Korean cities.

Smart cities as a vehicle for inclusive growth

The Presidential Committee on the Fourth Industrial Revolution of Korea is accelerating the creation of the "smart city" concept to become a broader mechanism to benefit society. MOLIT aims to use digitalisation, clean energy and technologies, as well as innovative transport technologies, to provide options for inhabitants to make more environmentally friendly choices and boost sustainable economic growth and enabling cities to improve their service delivery. For Korea, smart cities are a tool for solving urban problems and improving the quality of life by applying ICTs and new technologies to cities.

A whole of government approach is being led by the President to make smart city thinking a vehicle to promote and reinforce other policy priorities such as inclusive growth and the Urban Regeneration New Deal. In 2017, MOLIT announced a Smart City New Deal project which will be aligned with an Urban Regeneration New Deal project. The chosen city will become a model for other local governments. In addition, the government is planning to integrate existing smart city-related work that has been promoted by the central government, local governments, and the private sector into a platform to enhance smart cities' accomplishments.

Responsible global leadership

Smart city technologies and systems have become valuable global assets. As more cities adopt the smart city concept to foster urban innovation, the smart city market is estimated to grow from USD 312 billion in 2015 to USD 758 billion in 2020. The Asia-Pacific region is forecast to achieve the highest levels of growth during this period and Korea remains one of the most competitive countries in this region. Since 2009, MOLIT has committed to drive U-City industry as a new growth engine and to bolster an entrance in the overseas market.

Korea is also committed to building capacity elsewhere and is supporting smart city developments across the world. In 2016, MOLIT proposed that the concept of a "smart city" be embedded into the New Urban Agenda at Habitat III.

1. The state of housing in Korea

This chapter presents an overview of the state of housing in Korea, looking first at the historical evolution of housing policy stressing both the shift from a quantitative to a qualitative approach and how the housing stock gap has been bridged. It discusses housing tenure distribution emphasising how while homeownership is the main tenure type, the rental market is beginning to change. The chapter also describes housing conditions and subsequent improvements following the introduction of minimal standards. It discusses the housing affordability problem, particularly in urban areas. The chapter also examines housing equity considering issues such as income and housing tenure. Finally, it explores housing from a regional perspective highlighting how socio-economic and demographic factors specific to a region may determine housing conditions.

Ensuring access to decent housing is a top policy priority for Korea. Housing is a critical element of wealth as well as the single biggest expenditure for a majority of households. One of the most important questions facing Korean policy makers is how to provide access to decent housing to citizens in a context of low fertility rates, ageing population, and changes in the household composition. The question is also important as the housing market outcomes can have significant repercussions for the macro-economic performance of the country.

1.1. From housing quantity to housing welfare - housing policy in transition

In Korea, the post-war period in the 1950s made evident the need for the reconstruction of a significant portion of housing in urban and rural areas as well as basic infrastructure for public service delivery. The changed context of ageing population, shrinking households and low fertility rate require shifting the housing policy approach: from central to local, from large-scale development to smaller and incremental production, and from new development to utilising the existing stock and vacant units (Park, 2017). Korea's housing policy depicts a reactive response of government to housing problems as they emerge (Kim & Park, 2016).

1.1.1. The institutional building period – 1960s and 1970s

The 1950s Korean War left a substantial housing and urban infrastructure gap. Over one-third of all dwelling units were destroyed, and urban infrastructure was in great need of substantial repair and expansion. Korea put emphasis on housing construction as a basis for economic growth, and on the investment for industrialisation. Subsequent rapid urbanisation led to a massive migration from rural to urban areas aggravating the housing shortage, especially in large cities. Korea was faced with housing problems both in quantitative and qualitative aspects, in the context of having poor hillside villages and unlawful occupiers.

Consequently, a major housing policy goal in Korea was to first provide a large volume of housing units to tackle the increasing housing demand in cities due to rapid urbanisation caused by industrialisation. In the 1960s, the institutional structure of the housing policy began to emerge. Housing policy became part of economic policy. Bridging the accumulated housing shortage became part of the Five-year Economic Development Plan started in 1962. The Housing Bank Law and the Emergency Measure to Deter Real Estate Speculation were enacted in 1967. The following year the Ministry of Construction [now the Ministry of Land, Infrastructure and Transport, (MOLIT)] was given the task to define and implement housing policy. The Korean National Housing Corporation and the Korea Housing and Commercial Bank began operation in 1968 and 1969 respectively. The Housing Construction Promotion Law (1972), the Korea National Housing Corporation (1973), the Korea Land Development Corporation (1979), and the Land Development Promotion Law (1980) were subsequently incorporated into the institutional framework to tackle the housing shortage.

During the 1960s and 1970s, housing supply failed to meet the increasing demand caused by the growing number of households, rapid economic growth and urbanisation – due to rural-to-urban migration. Housing shortages became serious in large metropolitan areas such as Seoul and Busan. As a response, the government adopted the 10-year plan for housing construction to expand supply and to stabilise prices. In 1972, the government announced the first long-term housing construction plan. Housing investment and construction in the public sector rose to almost 30% of total housing investment in the mid-1970s, much higher than the 13% registered during the 1960s (Lim, 2006). In the late 1970s an over-production problem led government to take a strong anti-speculation measure and scale down all plans to expand low-income housing supply (Lim, 2006).

1.1.2. Controlling housing speculation – 1980s and 1990s

The economic growth of the 1970s and 1980s led to rapidly increasing real estate prices (Park, 2013). The shortage of decent housing deepened over a period of rapid economic growth resulting in a sharp increase of house prices across major cities in the late 1980s (Kim & Park, 2016). In response, the national government announced another long-term housing construction plan to build five million housing units relying on private investments. As the plan was too ambitious in a context of fiscal austerity, the target was reduced several times and eventually abandoned (Lim, 2006). By 1987, housing had become a political priority once again. The Korean government announced the "Two Million Housing Drive" (TMHD) Plan, the aim of which was to build two million housing units between 1988 and 1992 to expand housing supply, stabilise housing prices and support the access of low-income families to housing. This included the development of five new towns in the suburbs of Seoul to secure land for construction. In addition, the government increased the provision of housing loans through the National Housing Fund. By the end of the 1980s, the government had increased the provision of public rental housing.

To control housing speculation, the Korean government adopted anti-speculative measures to stabilise the housing market such as: designating speculative zones, levying heavy taxes, providing transaction limits, imposing sanctions, and monitoring suspicious transactions. As part of the measures, the government developed a housing allocation system based on income class: i) permanent rental housing for the lowest income group; ii) small for-sale housing and rental housing for the mid-income families; and iii) for-sale housing supply for the middle class determined by the market (Park, 2013, p.26). The TMHD was the first attempt to allocate housing units by target income groups. Moreover, mechanisms to steer housing to the target groups such as mandatory savings for housing subscription, an application system for prospective buyers, and housing-related taxation were implemented. It is argued that due to the successful implementation of the TMHD, housing prices remained stable during the 1990s (Kim & Park, 2016, p. 15). The private sector played a significant role in the housing construction as it surpassed its target by 30% (Kim & Park, 2016).

1.1.3. Changes in housing regulation as a response to financial crises

After the 1997 Asian financial crisis, unsold apartments piled up, housing prices fell sharply and many homebuilders went bankrupt. To stimulate demand, the government provided support through the National Housing Fund and temporarily lowered acquisition and registration taxes. The government introduced a national tax on real estate holdings (i.e. the Comprehensive Real Estate Tax); introduced a special levy on unrealised income from redevelopment of old apartments; raised the capital gains tax on owners of two or more homes, and expanded the coverage of the price ceiling on new apartments (Kim & Park, 2016). Measures to prevent excessive lending were also adopted such as debt-income ratio and loan-value ratio. During the first half of the 2000s, housing policy focused on the stabilisation of the housing market and boosting housing welfare. Dilapidated properties were redeveloped but this led to inflated prices of redeveloped apartments (Park, 2013). To control speculation and stabilise the market, measures such as comprehensive real estate taxation, and housing price ceilings on real price registration of housing transactions were introduced. The government established a plan to supply 2.6 million housing units for long-term rental to reinforce the public sector's role in improving housing welfare between 2007 and 2017.

The 2007 global financial crisis led to stable housing prices until they started to decline in real terms in the aftermath of the crisis. Indeed, during the 2000s housing prices rose modestly or declined in Switzerland, Korea, Germany and Japan and residential investment also stagnated (André, 2010). The Korean government, once again, tried to stimulate the market through changes in regulation and easing taxation. Regulation on redevelopments and for remodelling projects was part of the answer to boost the market and ensure a mandatory percentage of redevelopment for small units and rental units. In the inner cities, local authorities designated areas for "new town-in-town" developments, and lifted regulations on redevelopment projects. In the peripheries, a small fraction of greenbelt land was released to build public housing (Kim & Park, 2016). Other measures included the supply of long-term jeonsei housing (see Box 1.1), high-density development of urban regions close to public transit, increased supply of small-sized houses, and assistance to revitalise the regional housing market, among others (Park, 2013).

1.2. The housing market today

1.2.1. The housing stock gap has been bridged

After the Korean war, the government aimed to supply enough dwelling units to match the pace of the increase in the number of households, although housing supply lagged until the 1990s. After the implementation of several housing construction programmes (e.g. the "Two Million Housing Drive", see above), the country resolved its housing shortages (Jeong, 2012). Indeed, the number of housing units passed from 4.36 million units in 1970 to approximately 16 million in 2014 (Kim and Park, 2016). Moreover, the housing supply ratio[1] spiked from 71.2% in 1980 (5.3 million housing units, 7.5 million households) to 103.5% in 2014 (15.9 million housing units, 13.4 million households).[2]

In 2005, the Ministry of Land, Infrastructure and Transport (MOLIT) changed the definition of housing supply rate. In the new definition, single households were included in the number of total households, and the numbers of housing units of multi-dwelling properties were counted based on real dwelling spaces, as opposed to being counted as single dwelling units based on ownership (Kim & Park, 2016). Although the supply ratio decreased with the new definition, it was still 103.5% in 2014 (Figure 1.1).

Figure 1.1. Housing stock, number of households and housing supply in Korea, 1970-2014

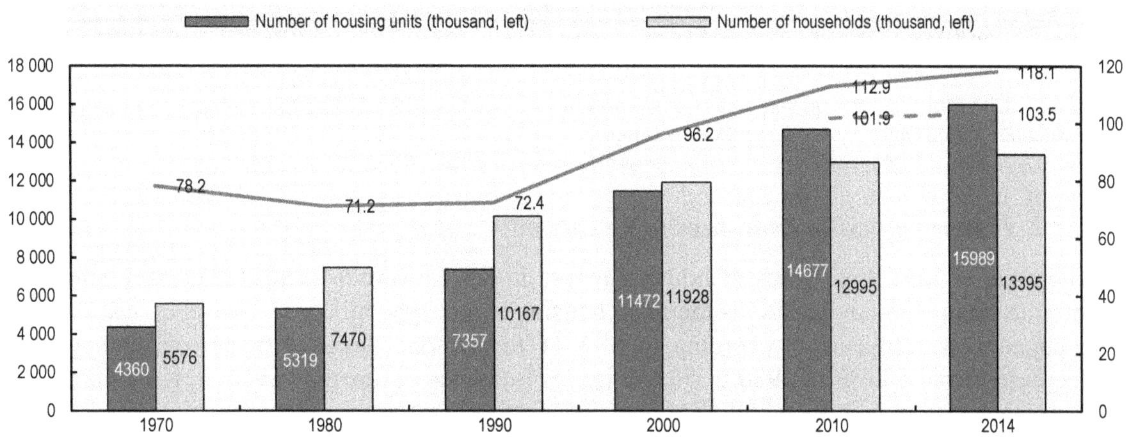

Source: Kim & Park (2016).

Similarly, the number of dwellings[3] per thousand inhabitants increased from 141.2 in 1970 to 383.0 in 2015 (MOLIT, 2016). Since the number of dwellings per thousand inhabitants reflects the relationship between the number of housing units and the number of people, the indicator confirms that the speed of housing provision has been faster than population increase in Korea.

Table 1.1. Dwellings per thousand inhabitants, 1970-2015

	1970	1980	1990	2000	2010	2015
Number of people (thousand)	30 882	37 436	43 411	46 136	48 580	51 069
Number of housing units (thousand)	4 360	5 319	7 357	11 472	17 672	19 559
Number of housing units/thousand	141.2	142.1	169.5	248.7	363.8	383.0

Note: For 2010 and 2015 data, multi-dwelling properties are counted based on real dwelling units, for the other years they are regarded as single dwelling units.
Source: MOLIT's manual of housing policy (2016).

Although Korea has achieved a balance between demand and supply, this does not necessarily mean that the housing stock is sufficiently large nor that all households have easy access to decent housing. Korea's number of dwellings per thousand inhabitants is still significantly lower than in other OECD countries such as France, Japan, the United Kingdom and the United States (Table 1.2). The same phenomenon can be observed at metropolitan level. The number of dwellings per thousand inhabitants is lower in Seoul than in cities such as London, New York, Paris and Tokyo (Table 1.3).

Table 1.2. Dwellings per thousand inhabitants in high income countries

	Korea	Japan	United States	United Kingdom	France
Dwellings per thousand inhabitants	364 (2010)	451 (2008)	421 (2010)	441 (2010)	532 (2010)

Source: Kim & Park (2016).

Table 1.3. Dwellings per thousand inhabitants of metropolitan areas

	Seoul	Tokyo	New York	London	Paris
Dwellings per thousand inhabitants	366.8 (2015)	579.1 (2013)	412.4 (2010)	399.6 (2011)	605.7 (2012)

Source: Kim (2017) and E-national indicator of Korea, http://www.index.go.kr. The value of New York is recalculated from Quick Facts by U.S Census Bureau, https://www.census.gov/quickfacts/fact/table/newyorkcitynewyork/HSG030210#viewtop

1.2.2. Homeownership continues to be the main tenure type

There are at least three types of housing tenure in Korea: owner-occupied, jeonsei, and monthly rent. Homeownership is the main housing tenure type in Korea. However, owner occupancy is decreasing. According to MOLIT the national level of owner occupancy decreased from 58.6% in 1980 to 53.6% in 2014. Owner occupancy levels in Korea are lower than in some advanced OECD countries (Table 1.4).

Box 1.1. Jeonsei rental contract system

Jeonsei is a unique rental contract system in Korea. Instead of paying monthly rent, a tenant deposits a lump-sum of money equivalent to over half of the property price with the homeowner for the rental contract period. Once the contract is over, the landlord is obliged to give the money back to the renter. During times of increasing housing prices and high interest rates, both renters and landlords have favoured jeonsei contracts over monthly rent payments with small deposits. The tenants preferred jeonsei because they did not need to pay the rent on a monthly basis, and they tended to consider the jeonsei deposit as a mandatory saving or seed money to purchase a home in the near future. Landlords also favoured jeonsei because it spared them from the cumbersome rent collection and possible risk of tenants defaulting on the rent payment since the lump-sum deposit acts as a buffer. In addition, landlords can expect financial returns by investing large jeonsei deposits.

Source: Park, M (2015). Changing Landscape of Private Rental Market in Korea. KRIHS Special Report Vol.25. Korea Research Institute for Human Settlements.

Table 1.4. Comparing owner occupancy across OECD countries

	Korea	Japan	USA	UK	Germany	France
Owner occupancy level (%)	53.6	61.7	64	63.3	52.5	65.1

Source: MOLIT, presentation given to the OECD team.

The share of owner-occupied households has remained constant in the mid-50% range in spite of continuous housing supply over the past decades (Figure 1.2). Over the past decades, homeownership has been regarded as an effective means of accumulating wealth for low-income households (Herbert, McCue and Sanchez-Moyano, 2013). Homeownership also has a positive effect on people's self-esteem, and their political and social activities (Dietz and Haurin, 2003). Usually, owner-occupied and jeonsei are regarded as a more stable tenure type for tenants than monthly rent (Kim, 2017).

Figure 1.2. Housing tenure types in Korea, 1980-2015

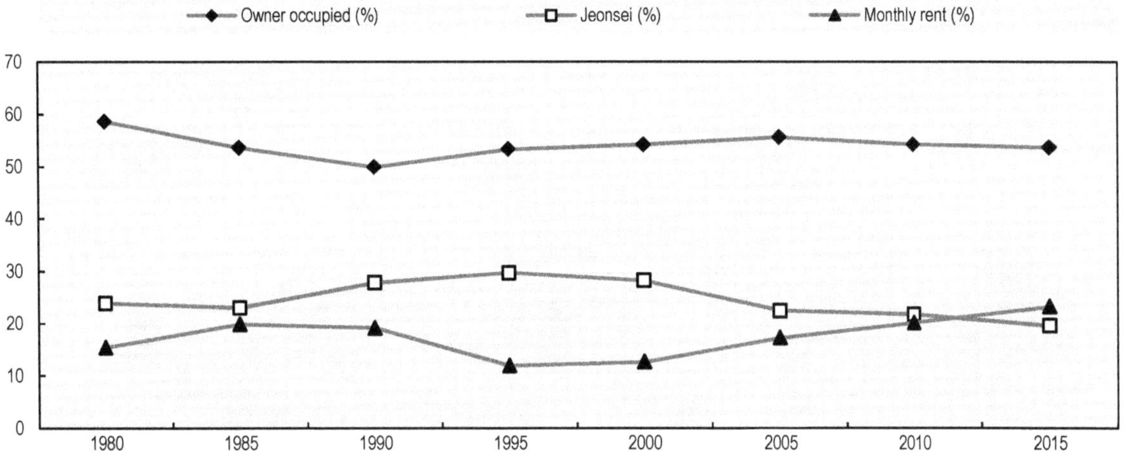

Note: Monthly rent includes monthly rent with deposit, monthly rent without deposit, yearly rent, daily rent.
Source: Statistics Korea, http://kostat.go.kr.

Housing in Korea is roughly equally split between homeownership and renting. 38.4% of Korean households rent in the private market and 14% have a subsidised rent (Figure 1.3). Compared to other OECD countries, Korea's public rental sector is large. For instance, whereas in Chile, Mexico and Spain the public rental sector is virtually non-existent (Salvi del Pero, et.al., 2016), in Australia almost one-third of Australian households were renting: 26% in the private rental sector, 4% in public housing, and 1% in community housing (Martin, Pawson and Van den Nouwelant, 2015, p. 5).

Figure 1.3. Housing tenure distribution, 2014 or latest year available

Share of households in different tenure groups, %

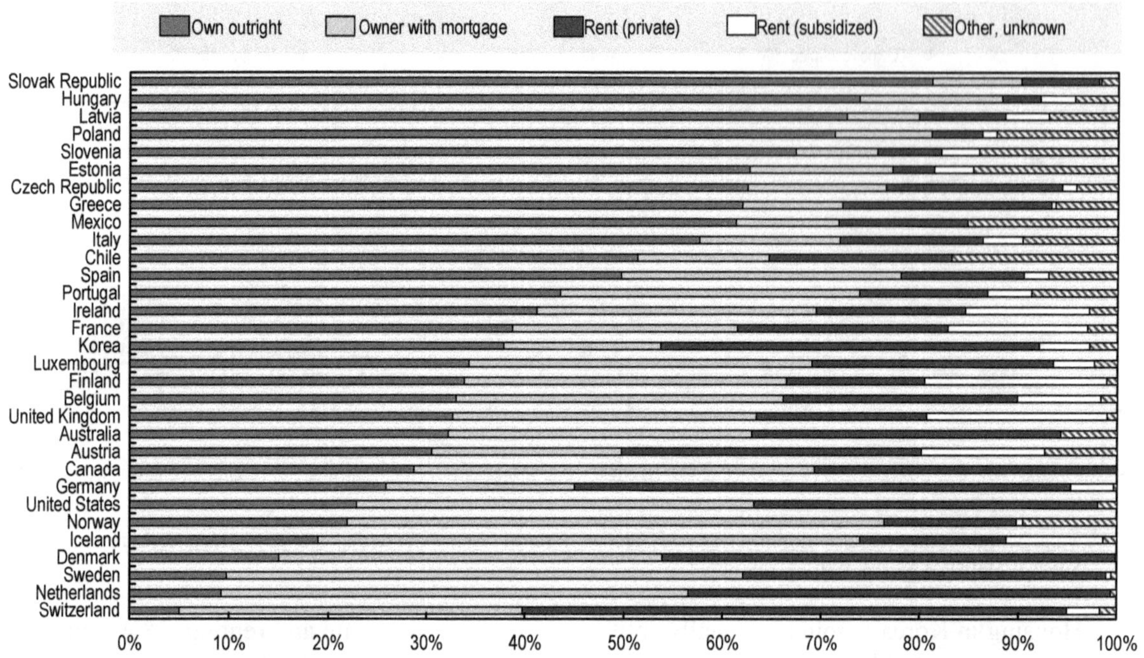

Note: Tenants renting at subsidised rent are lumped together with tenants renting at private rent in Australia, Canada, Chile, Denmark, Mexico, the Netherlands and the United States, and are not capturing the full extent of coverage in Sweden due to data limitations.
Source: New OECD Affordable Housing Database www.oecd.org/social/affordable-housing-database.htm.

1.2.3. The rental market is changing

In the rental housing market, the share of jeonsei, the traditional Korean rental system, has dropped from 23.9% in 1980 to 19.6% in 2014. At the same time, the share of monthly rental increased to 23.9% surpassing jeonsei levels (Figure 1.2 above). This signals a new trend in the rental housing market. Traditionally, the share of jeonsei had been higher than that of monthly rent, but since 2010 the trend began to change. Indeed, the ratio of jeonsei in total rent contract transactions was about 67% in 2011, and it then dropped to 54.8% in 2016. On the other hand, the percentage of monthly rent increased from 33% to 45.2% during the same period.[4]

Song (2016), Hyundai Research Institute (2015) and Park (2015) argue that the jeonsei system seems to have been the preferred option under the conditions of rising house prices and high interest rates. However, those factors fuelling the jeonsei system have faded out as housing supply increased, expectations over housing price escalation turned pessimistic, the prospects of economic recovery became uncertain, and the interest rates decreased.[5] In addition, the rise of single families increases the demand for monthly rent, rather than jeonsei.

1.3. Housing conditions

Korean authorities have placed particular attention on improving the quality of housing over the last decades. Housing is a major element of people's material living standards.

Housing is essential to meet basic needs, such as being sheltered from extreme weather and climate conditions. It should give people a sense of personal security, privacy and personal space, and the possibility of having a family. Measuring housing conditions and their effect on people's well-being is difficult because no international statistical standards are available and the factors shaping people's housing conditions are heterogeneous (OECD, 2011). Consequently, housing conditions in Korea will be analysed considering the elements of the minimum housing standards set by the Korean government.

1.3.1. Housing prices in Korea are comparable to those in other OECD countries

Housing is the largest component of households' net worth, and changes in the conditions and availability of credits or changes in housing prices may have negative effects on households' well-being. Thus, housing price is one of the most important variables of housing policy in Korea. The housing price index has increased since 1986. However, the increase in inflation-adjusted housing prices was moderate, considering that the housing price index increased less than the consumer price index since 1993 (Figure 1.4).

Figure 1.4. Housing price indexes and consumer price index, 1986-2015

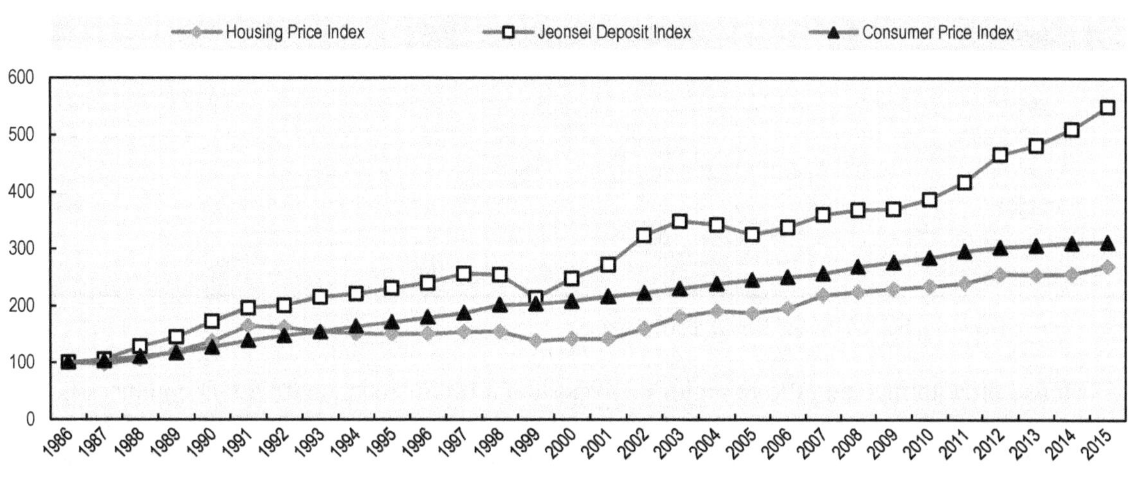

Source: Kim & Park, (2016).

Housing affordability indicators seem to show contradictory information. The house price to income ratio (PIR) and the rent to income ratio (RIR) usually measure housing affordability in Korea. Both ratios have steadily increased since 2006, implying that housing affordability has deteriorated (Table 1.5). On the other hand, Kim and Park (2016) found that the housing affordability index, which measures the debt service burden by the median-income household purchasing a median-priced home using a standard mortgage loan, has been improving over the last years suggesting that for credit financed purchasers housing is not less affordable than before.[6]

Table 1.5. Housing affordability indicators in Korea

	2006	2008	2010	2012	2014
House price-income ratio	4.2	4.3	4.3	5.1	4.7
Rent-income ratio	18.7	17.5	19.2	19.8	20.3
Housing affordability index	66.1	75.3	63.8	59.9	54.3

Source: Kim & Park (2016).

Housing affordability in Korea at both national and metropolitan levels is better than in other OECD countries (Table 1.6) implying that Korean citizens have better access to housing services than citizens in other OECD countries. Although there is a growing concern that housing prices are too high to be affordable for ordinary households in Korea, especially in Seoul metropolitan area where the PIR has constantly stayed high, housing affordability in Korea, in general, is no worse than in other OECD countries.

Table 1.6. Housing affordability by country: major market (over one million inhabitants)

	Affordable (3.0 and under)	Moderately Unaffordable (3.1-4.0)	Seriously Unaffordable (4.1-5.0)	Severely Unaffordable (5.1 and Over)	Median Ratio
United States	14	23	6	9	3.6
Korea	0	2	0	3	3.7
Canada	0	2	2	2	4.3
Ireland	0	0	1	0	4.3
Japan	0	1	1	0	4.4
United Kingdom	0	1	10	6	4.7
Singapore	0	0	1	0	5
Australia	0	0	0	5	6.4
New Zealand	0	0	0	1	8.2
Hong Kong, China	0	0	0	1	17

Source: Demographia (2015) and Kim & Park (2016).

House price to income ratio in major metropolitan areas in Asian and OECD countries is higher than that in Seoul (7.7%). For example, Hong Kong (17%), Beijing (15.6%), Vancouver (10.6%), Sydney (9.8%), San Francisco (9.2%) and London (8.5%) have higher house price to income ratios (Demographia, 2015).

The mortgage burden of Korean households is also among the lowest across OECD countries. Homeowners with a mortgage (or a loan) can face large housing costs across OECD countries that sometimes impose very high burdens on their income. In Korea this does not seem to be the case as homeowners only spend 10% of their income to cover housing costs (mortgage or loans) whereas in other OECD countries such as France (29%), Japan (22%), United Kingdom (17%) and the United States (16%) homeowners pay more of their income to cover mortgages or loans.[7]

1.3.2. Household housing expenditure in Korea has been decreasing

When housing costs make up a large share of the household budget, low-income groups in particular are often constrained by the level of resources left for other essential expenditures, such as food, healthcare and education. Figure 1.5 shows that final housing expenditure in Korea (18.3%) is one of the lowest among OECD countries (OECD average 22%). Korean households dedicate more resources to cover other items (e.g. health and education, clothing).

Figure 1.5. Final household consumption expenditure of households by item, 2013

Share of final household consumption expenditure, three main expenditure items and sum of all others.

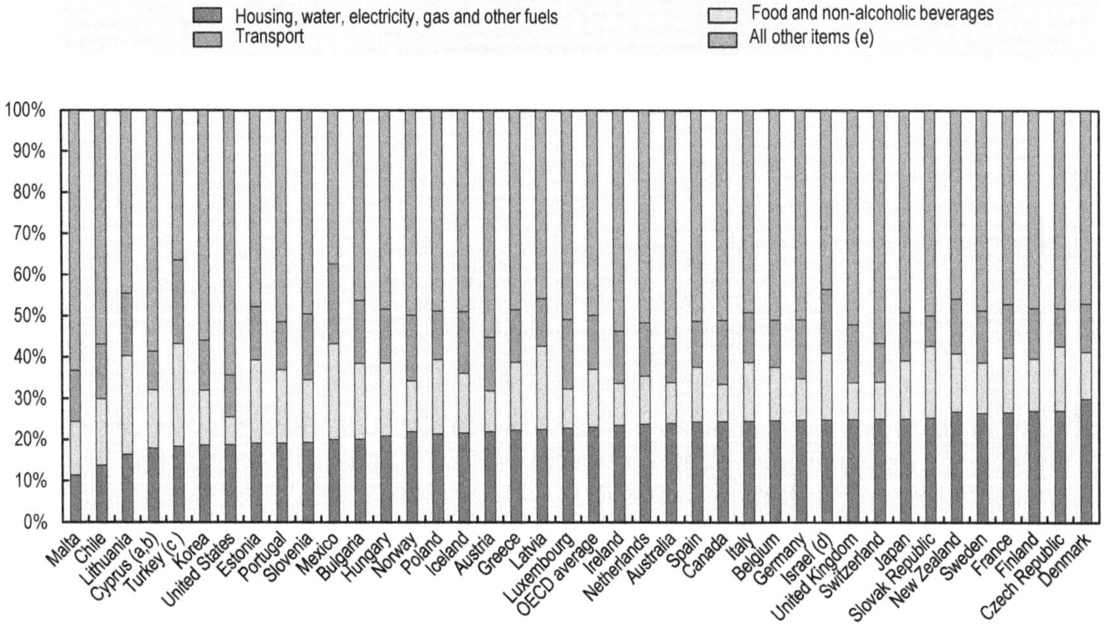

Source: OECD Annual National Accounts Database; Eurostat Annual National Accounts Database.

Moreover, housing expenditure as a share of final consumption expenditure of households has slightly decreased from 20% in 2000 to 18.6% in 2013. Housing expenditure as a share of final consumption expenditure of households in Korea (18.6%) was lower than that of most OECD countries - France (26.7%), Sweden (26.5%), United Kingdom (24.9%), and the US (18.7%) - in 2013. This is important because high housing costs can threaten households' material well-being and economic security (OECD, 2011). They may also generate forms of housing stress that may lead to difficult relations among family members and have a negative effect on society.

OECD measures affordability as the share of household gross adjusted disposable income spent on housing and maintenance of the property. The housing expenditure of Korea in 2012 was 16.1% of household disposable income. This includes actual and imputed rentals for housing, expenditure on maintenance and repair of the dwelling, water supply, electricity, gas and other fuels, as well as expenditure on furniture, furnishings.[8] This is below the OECD average of 20.4% of household disposable income. High income countries show higher levels of housing expenditure, for example in France it was 21.2%, in Japan 22% and in the United Kingdom 22.5% in 2012.

1.3.3. Korea's housing quality has improved significantly but further improvement is needed

Korea should be commended for its efforts to improve housing over the last decades. When the housing shortage was resolved by the large supply of housing units, the government shifted its focus from quantity to quality. Table 1.7 presents a historical comparison of key housing quality indicators. The results show a significant improvement in the access to basic services and floor area per person. Such qualitative improvements were largely attributed to the fact that most of the housing supply came from large-scale construction of apartments. The reason for this is that, in Korea, in most cases apartments are better quality than single houses.

Table 1.7. Korea's housing quality indicators, 1980-2010

	1980	1990	2000	2010
Average number of rooms per household	2.2	2.5	3.4	3.7
Average floor area per person (m^2)	10.1	14.3	20.2	25
Average floor area per household (m^2)	45.8	51	63.1	67.4
Share of dwellings with running water (%)	56.1	74	85	97.9
Share of dwellings with modern toilets (%)	18.4	51.3	86.9	97
Share of dwellings with bathroom (%)	22.1	44.1	89.1	98.4
Share of dwellings with hot water (%)	9.9	34.1	87.4	96.9

Source: Kim & Park (2016).

New minimum housing standards were introduced in 2000. The standards were changed by requiring larger minimum floor area, at the same time, adding a modern kitchen, toilet, and bath/shower. The share of substandard housing has plummeted from 16.6% in 2006 to 5.4% in 2016 (KHS, 2016) implying that the indicator has nearly reached its target of 5%. However, the absolute number of substandard housing at national level has been fluctuating. It had decreased from 1.27 million units in 2012 to 0.99 million in 2014. But it rose again to 1.02 million in 2016.

Table 1.8. Minimum housing standards, 2000 and 2011

Number of Household Members	Household composition	Number of Rooms and Facilities	Floor Area(m^2)	
			2000	2011
1	Single	1 K	12	14
2	Couple	1 D K	20	26
3	Couple + 1 Child	2 D K	29	36
4	Couple + 2 Children	3 D K	37	43
5	Couple + 3 Children	3 D K	41	46
6	Couple + parents of the couple + 2 Children	4 D K	49	55

Note: D = dining room, K = kitchen.
Source: Kim & Park (2016).

Although housing conditions have improved, Korea still has work to do to catch up with the levels of housing welfare observed in other OECD countries (e.g. France, Japan, the United Kingdom and the United States) regarding floor space per person, owner-occupancy rate, and public rental housing as a share of total housing (except the US) (Table 1.9).

Table 1.9. International comparisons of housing welfare indicators

	Korea	Japan	United States	United Kingdom	France
Floor area per person (m^2)	25.0 (2010)	37.3 (2008)	74.3 (2010)	44 (2002)	39.9 (2006)
Owner-occupancy rate (%)	54.2 (2010)	61.1 (2008)	65.1 (2013)	64.6 (2013)	64.3 (2013)
Public rental housing as a share of total housing stock (%)	5.0 (2012)	6.1 (2008)	0.9 (2012)	17.5 (2010)	19 (2007)

Note: Figures in the parentheses represent the year of reference.
Source: Kim & Park (2016) and Jeong (2012).

In general, residential overcrowding, which can be measured by the average number of rooms per household and average floor area per person, has improved (see Table 1.7 above). In particular, the average number of rooms per household was 2.2 in 1980, reaching 3.7 in 2010. The average floor area per person grew from $10.1m^2$ in 1980 to $25m^2$ in 2010 (Kim & Park, 2016). However, in Korea the number of rooms per person is approximately 1.43, and is lower than in Canada (2.52), Australia (2.33), Belgium (2.20), Denmark (1.90), Japan (1.82), and the OECD average (1.7).[9] In Korea, like in many other OECD countries, the share of people living in dwellings without basic sanitary facilities has decreased over the last years but the share is still above the OECD average (Figure 1.6).

Figure 1.6. People living in dwellings without basic sanitary facilities

Percentage of people living in dwellings without an indoor flushing toilet for the sole use of their household

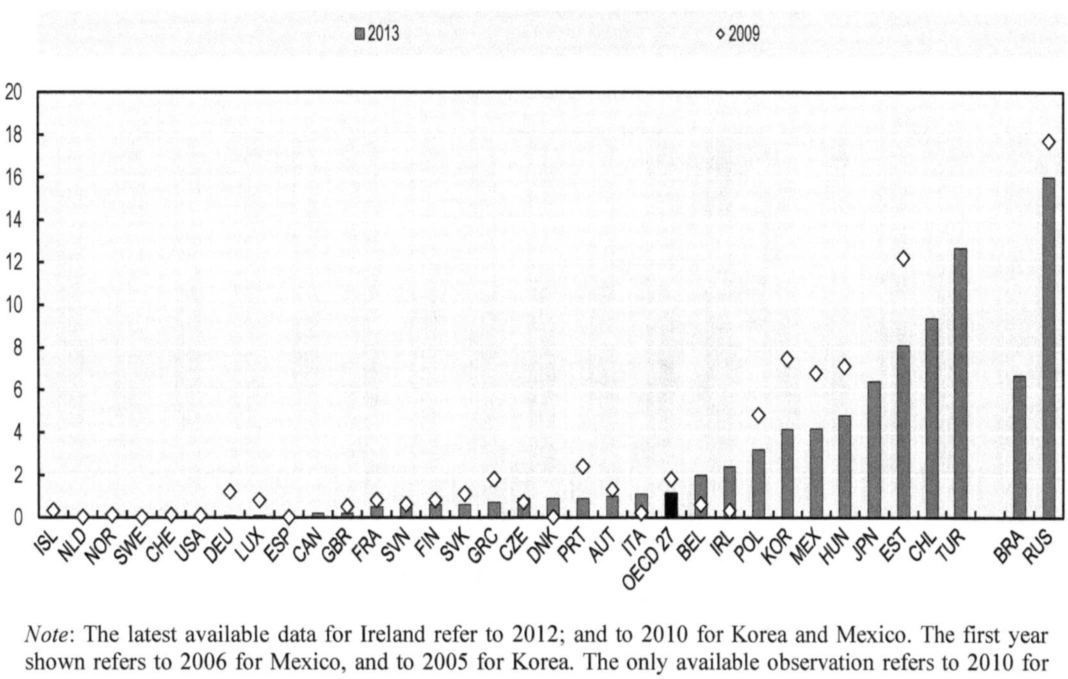

Note: The latest available data for Ireland refer to 2012; and to 2010 for Korea and Mexico. The first year shown refers to 2006 for Mexico, and to 2005 for Korea. The only available observation refers to 2010 for Brazil and Turkey; to 2008 for Japan; to 2001 for Chile; and to 1997 for Canada. The OECD average is population-weighted.
Source: OECD (2015), How's Life? 2015: Measuring Well-being, retrieved from http://dx.doi.org/10.1787/888933259048.

1.3.4. Socio-demographic trends create pressures for housing

Korea faces two main socio-demographic challenges today: an ageing population, and shrinking household size. Korea has one of the lowest fertility rates (220th place out of 224 countries). On average, every woman in the country gives birth to an average of 1.25 children (CIA, 2016). The household size has been shrinking dramatically over the last several decades. In 1980, almost half of the population (49.9%) lived in households with more than five household members while less than 5% lived alone. The latest Census (2015) revealed that single-person households take up the largest share of the whole population (27.2%), followed by two-person households (26.1%). Shrinking households and low fertility rates along with increasing longevity have a significant effect on housing demand and supply; shrinking households may change types and sizes of housing, and low fertility rates can reduce housing demand directly.

1.4. Housing equity

1.4.1. A larger share of low income households live in rental housing

In Korea, like in most OECD countries, low-income households are more likely than middle- and high-income households to live in rented dwellings and less likely to live in owner-occupied dwellings. This separation has further increased over recent decades; low income individuals have moved from owner-occupied/jeonsei to monthly rent, while the high and middle-income level groups have moved from jeonsei to owner-occupied (Kim, 2017) (Figure 1.7).

Figure 1.7. Housing tenure type by income in Korea

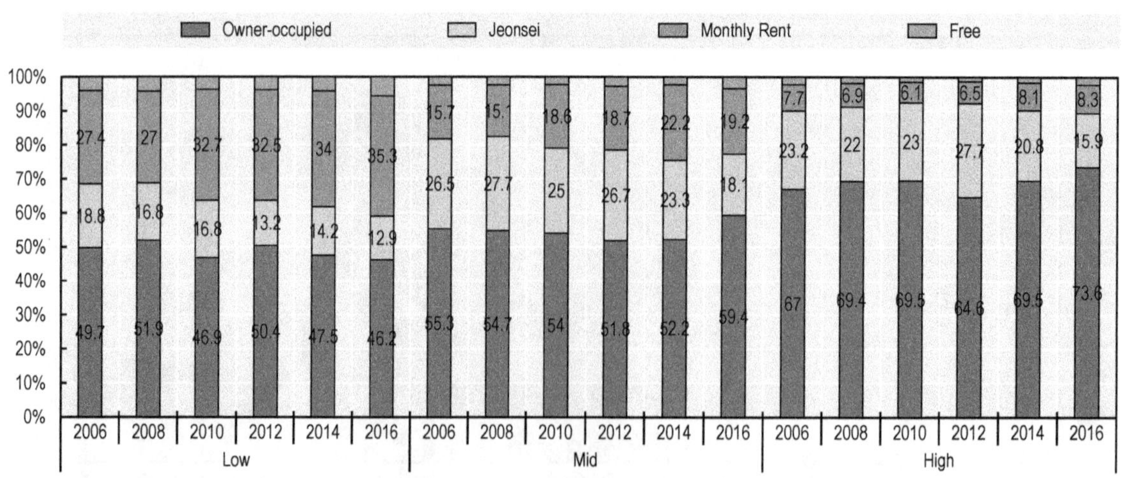

Note: Monthly rent includes monthly rent with deposit, monthly rent without deposit, yearly rent, daily rent.
Source: OECD calculations based on the Korea Housing Survey.

According to the OECD Housing Affordability Survey, in Korea 43% of households in the bottom quintile of the income distribution are owner occupants, 37% live in private rental housing, and 9% live in subsidised rental housing. Owner-occupation tends to be the most common tenure among low-income households in countries where owner-occupation is also the most common tenure among the overall population.

1.4.2. Income is a major driver of inequality in housing conditions and tenure

Individuals in low income households have, on average, larger floor area per person than those in other income groups. However, low income households have, on average, smaller apartments/houses than middle and high-income households. One explanation is the average composition of households. High income families tend to have more members. For example, in 2016, the mean number of household members of low income groups was 1.69 whereas middle (2.90) and high-income households (3.42) have bigger families (KHS, 2016).

Figure 1.8. Average floor area per person by income level (m2)

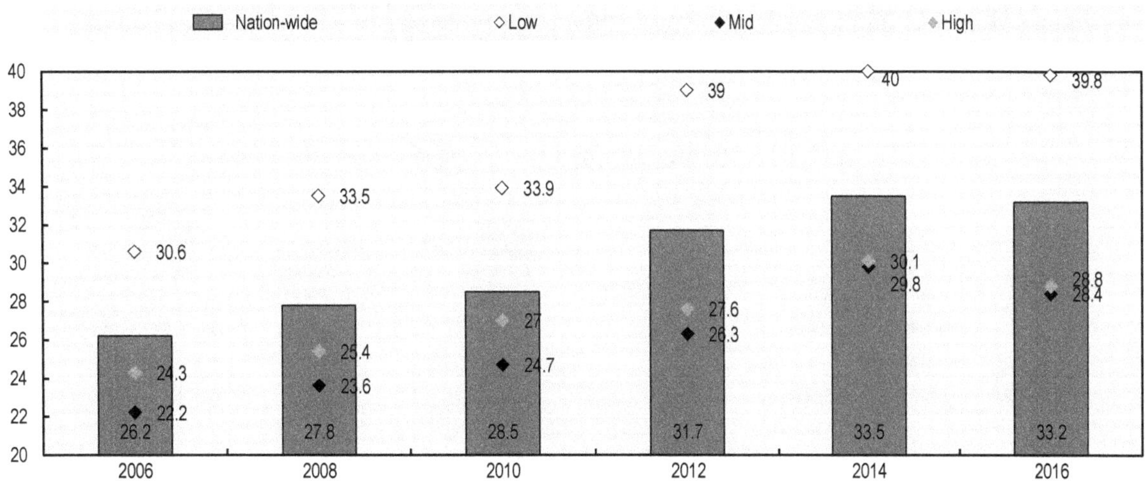

Source: Korea Housing Survey 2016.

From a policy perspective, understanding which groups of the population are more likely to suffer from poor housing conditions and financial burdens is essential for designing effective housing policies. In Korea, low-income households experience more difficulties in meeting their housing needs than other income groups. Indeed, as Table 1.11 shows, the price to yearly income ratio (PIR) has increased for all income groups; however, for low-income households the PIR is almost double the PIR for high-income groups. Not surprisingly, the rent to monthly income ratio (RIR), although with variations over the last decade, is also higher for low-income households.

Table 1.10. PIR and RIR by income level in Korea

	Income level	2006	2008	2010	2012	2014	2016
PIR by income level	Low	6.3	6.4	6.1	7.5	8.3	9.8
	Mid	3.4	4.3	4.2	4.3	5.0	5.6
	High	3.6	4.2	4.0	4.4	4.7	5.0
RIR by income level	Low	27.6	25.0	28.2	21.8	29.0	23.1
	Mid	18.9	17.6	16.6	17.3	17.0	14.9
	High	16.1	17.4	21.1	22.6	21.6	19.0

Note: PIR is calculated as median housing value divided by median yearly income. RIR is calculated as median housing value divided by median yearly income

Source: Korean Housing Survey 2016.

1.5. Housing welfare across regions

1.5.1. Seoul metropolitan area lags behind in housing provision

In Korea, each of the 17 regions has a different level of housing welfare due to differences in socio-economic features, housing stock and built environment. The housing supply ratio by region has improved over the last decade following the national trend. Despite improvements in the housing supply ratio, Seoul metropolitan area (Seoul, Incheon, Gyeonggi) lags behind the rest of the country (Table 1.11). Paradoxically, Seoul metropolitan area has higher levels of construction than any other metropolitan area or province in the country, particularly in Gyeonggi province. The problem is that Seoul metropolitan area accommodates approximately 50% of the country's population, so demand is much higher than in the rest of the country. Moreover, Seoul metropolitan area has higher demand levels than supply, mainly due to job and education opportunities (KB Research Centre, 2016).

Table 1.11. Housing supply ratio by region, 2005-2014

	2005			2010			2014		
	Number of Housing Units	Number of Households	Housing Supply Ratio	Number of Housing	Number of Households	Housing Supply Ratio	Number of Housing Units	Number of Households	Housing Supply Ratio
Nation-wide	15622.6	15887.2	98.3	17672.1	17339.4	101.9	19428.6	18772.5	103.5
Seoul Metropolitan Area	7165.0	7462.1	96.0	8173.2	8254.3	99.0	8886.7	9048.8	98.2
Other Metropolitan Areas	3180.5	3279.1	97.0	3581.3	3534.3	101.3	3940.9	3779.3	104.3
Provinces	5277.1	5146.0	102.5	5917.6	5550.7	106.6	6601.0	5944.1	111.1

Note: Ministry of Land, Infrastructure and Transport in the Republic of Korea (MOLIT) changed the definition of the housing supply ratio in 2005. In the new definition, single households were included in the number of total households, and the numbers of housing units of multi-dwelling properties were counted based on real dwelling spaces, as opposed to being counted as single dwelling units based on ownership (Kim & Park, 2016).

Source: MOLIT Statistics System, http://stat.molit.go.kr.

Box 1.2. Regional classifications in Korea

Korea has seventeen regions: Seoul metropolitan city, six metropolitan areas, eight provinces, one special self-governing city and one special self-governing province. This classification is based on geography, history, economic zone and transport. In provinces, areas with a large population, high rate of fiscal independence, and other beneficial influence to neighbouring areas can be designated as metropolitan areas (MOI, 2016).

The Korea Housing Survey 2016 divides these regions into three groups on the basis of economic characteristics: Seoul metropolitan area, other metropolitan areas, and provinces. According to the Seoul Metropolitan Area Readjustment Planning Act, Seoul, Incheon and Gyeonggi have the largest population and densely located industrial establishments. They are therefore regrouped into Seoul metropolitan area to more clearly understand their economic and socio-demographic dynamics. In addition, metropolitan areas mainly consist of urban areas and have larger populations than the other provinces, which consist of both urban and rural areas and are less densely populated, so they fall into a different category from the provinces.

Administrative regions in Korea

Type	Regions
Seoul metropolitan city (1)	Seoul
Metropolitan areas (6)	Busan, Daegu, Incheon, Gwangju, Daejeon, Ulsan
Provinces (8)	Gyeonggi, Gwangwon, Chungbuk, Chungnam, Jeonbuk, Jeonnam, Gyeongbuk, Gyeongnam
Special self-governing city (1)	Sejong
Special self-governing province (1)	Jeju

Source: MOI (2016).

Regrouping of regions

Group	Regions
Seoul metropolitan area (3)	Seoul, Incheon, Gyeonggi
Other metropolitan areas (5)	Busan, Daegu, Gwangju, Daejeon, Ulsan
Provinces (8)	Gwangwon, Chungbuk, Chungnam, Jeonbuk, Jeonnam, Gyeongbuk, Gyeongnam, Jeju

Source: Korea Housing Survey (2016).

Map showing administrative regions and regrouping

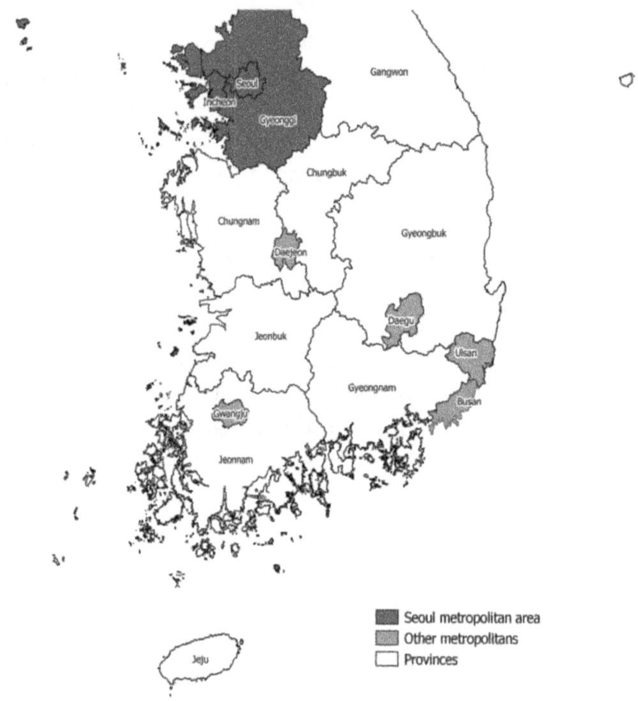

Source: OECD elaboration.

In Seoul, illegal buildings hinder the effectiveness of housing quality improvement programmes. Before the 1990s many buildings and houses were constructed without permits. The city reacted by building *citizens' apartments* to house the residents of illegal settlements. Nonetheless, despite the government's efforts, there are still many illegal settlements located in the central part of the city also characterised by low levels of income.

Since 2006, the average floor area per person, an indicator measuring overcrowding, has increased across the country's regions. People living in the provinces have relatively larger floor space than those living in predominantly urban areas like in Seoul and other metropolitan areas. Figure 1.9 shows that the nation-wide average floor area per person has increased from 26.2 m^2 in 2006 to 33.2m^2 in 2016. Similarly, the nation-wide average floor area per household increased until 2012, and then decreased to 2016. Seoul metropolitan area (30.7 m^2) had the smallest floor area per person in 2016. One possible explanation is that the average number of household members in Seoul metropolitan area is slightly higher (2.58) than in other metropolitan areas (2.51) and provinces (2.42) (KHS, 2016).

Figure 1.9. Average floor area per person by region (m2)

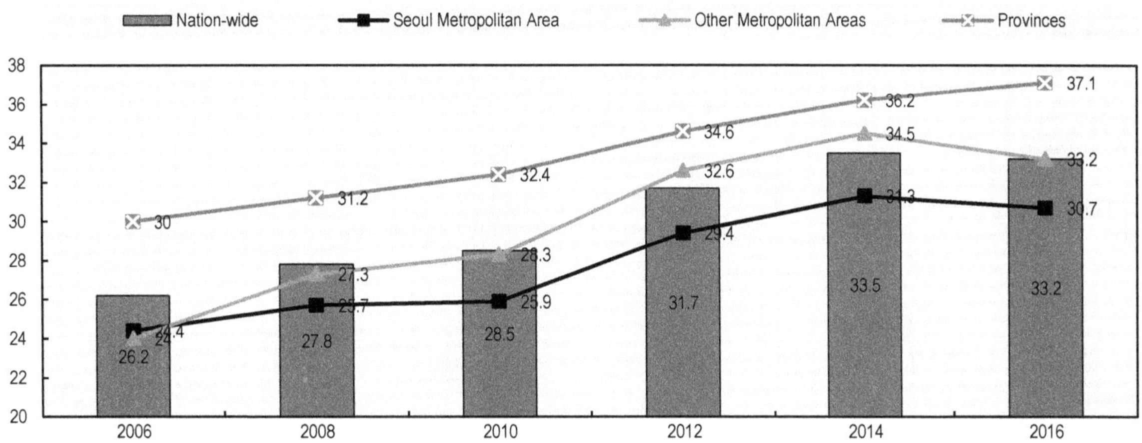

Source: Korea Housing Survey 2016.

The number of substandard housing units in provinces decreased from 0.53 million in 2012 to 0.30 million in 2016 (KHS, 2016). However, the share of substandard housing units in metropolitan areas, including Seoul, shows an upward trend (Figure 1.10). It suggests that governments in urban areas are experiencing more difficulties in meeting the minimum housing standards. The reasons may be the increase of single households and the increasing supply of small-sized housing units in Seoul metropolitan area that do not meet the floor area requirement (KHS, 2016; Kim and Choi, 2013).

Figure 1.10. National stock and relative share of substandard housing by region

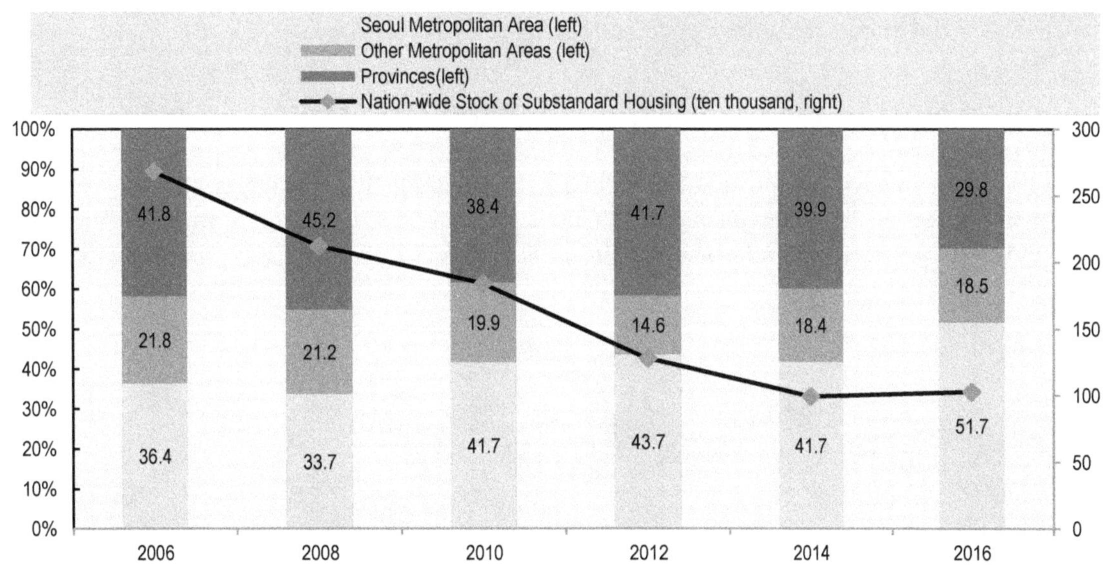

Source: OECD calculations based on the Korea Housing Survey.

Moreover, Seoul, Incheon, and Gyeonggi as well as some metropolitan areas such as Daegu, Daejeon, and Chungbuk provinces have smaller floor areas than the national average (33.2m^2). Seoul, Daegu and Gyeongbuk have the highest share of substandard housing (Table 1.12).

Table 1.12. Housing supply ratio and quality indicators by region

	Housing supply ratio by region		Housing quality indicators by region				
Provinces	Housing supply ratio	Dwellings per thousand inhabitants	Floor Area per Person (m^2)	Floor Area per Household (m^2)	Share of Substandard Housing (%)	Public Rental Housing	Private Rental Housing
Nation-wide	102.3	383	33.2	70.1	5.4	1357701	915661
Seoul	96	366.8	30.8	66.4	6.7	251912	226924
Incheon	101	365.1	30.1	67.6	4.4	62933	41858
Gyeonggi	98.7	346.9	30.8	70.3	5.2	347112	199185
Busan	102.6	397.3	33.4	69.9	5.6	68936	103178
Daegu	101.6	382.6	31	66.2	7.3	62972	14824
Gwangju	103.5	390.4	35	74.7	1.3	60935	32899
Daejeon	102.2	386.9	33	71.7	4.7	47696	25386
Ulsan	106.9	388	35.2	73.3	3	16951	11379
Sejong	123.1	453.7	31.5	68.1	-	11847	7332
Gangwon	106.7	426.1	41.7	78.6	5.1	44578	29835
Chungbuk	111.2	421.2	32.2	65.1	5.4	52540	37305
Chungnam	108.3	409.2	36.9	72.6	4.1	47963	54695
Jeonbuk	107.5	420.3	41	81.4	2.6	65494	24565
Jeonnam	110.4	442.4	39.8	75.1	3.3	85531	33494
Gyeongbuk	112.5	446	34.3	66.1	9.6	50830	30866
Gyeongnam	106.4	401.4	36.1	72.5	4.4	65644	29671
Jeju	100.7	366.4	37.1	75.3	3.1	13827	12265

Source: MOLIT's Housing Policy Manual (2016) and MOLIT Statistics System, http://stat.molit.go.kr. OECD calculations based on the Korea Housing Survey 2016.

1.5.2. Low owner occupancy rates and high housing prices in Seoul metropolitan area

Across Korean regions, the monthly rent ratio increased and the jeonsei ratio decreased between 2006 and 2016 (Figure 1.11). However, the share of owner occupancy increased across the country except in Seoul metropolitan area which has a larger share of renters than the rest of the country's regions. This is probably due to the high prices of housing and high demand for rental housing in Seoul metropolitan area (KB Research Centre, 2017).

Figure 1.11. Trend of housing tenure type by region in Korea

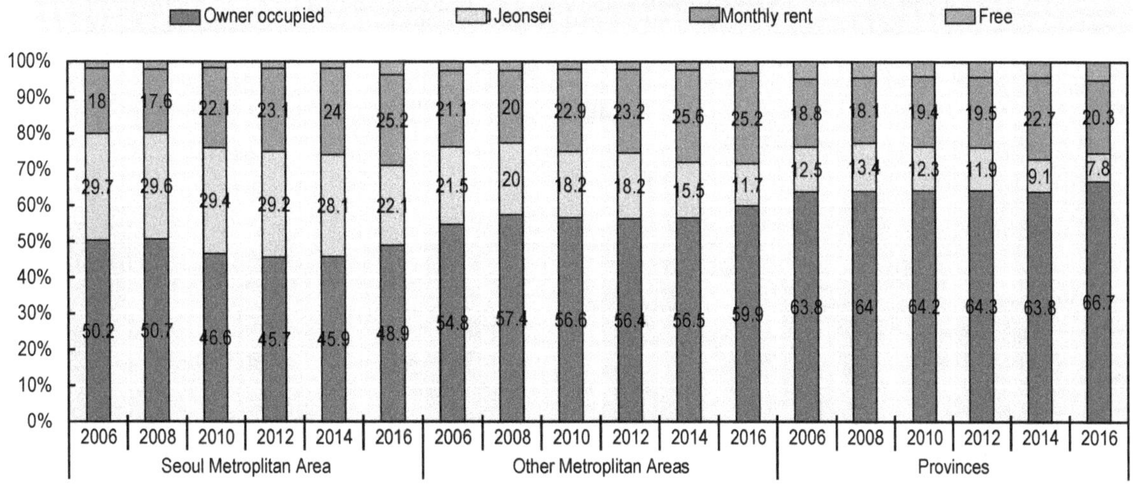

Note: Monthly rent includes monthly rent with deposit, monthly rent without deposit, yearly rent, daily rent.
Source: OECD calculations based on the Korea Housing Survey.

In Korea, there is a growing concern that house prices are too high to be affordable for ordinary households (Park, 2017). The average house price, jeonsei deposit and monthly rent have increased since 2006 (KHS, 2016). Housing prices, on average, increased from KRW 173.2 million in 2006 to KRW 243.5 million in 2016 (Figure 1.12). Similarly, the average jeonsei deposit also increased from KRW 55.5 million to KRW 127.9 million in the same period. Monthly rents and deposits show similar patterns. The housing price index has been rising despite the steady supply of housing units. In terms of housing price, Seoul (KRW 350 million), Gyeonggi (KRW 250 million), Ulsan (KRW 250 million) and Sejong (KRW 210 million) have higher prices than the national median price (KRW 200 million) (KHS, 2016).

Seoul metropolitan area has the highest housing prices in the country, which are even higher than the national average (Figure 1.12). In 2016, the average housing price of Seoul metropolitan area was double the average prices in the provinces. Similarly, jeonsei deposits and monthly rents are higher in Seoul. For example, the average jeonsei deposit in Seoul metropolitan area is KRW 150 million, whereas in other metropolitan areas is KRW 86 million and in the provinces is KRW 71 million in the same year.

High housing prices in Seoul metropolitan area may be a threat to local and national economic growth. They place increasing pressure on existing infrastructure, raise business costs, exacerbate skill shortages, and prevent people from moving to a successful city. High housing prices could also affect the government's quest for equality as first-time buyers in Seoul, generally the younger generations, may find it harder to buy a property, thus affecting their living standards. The specific way in which high housing prices will impact each Korean metropolitan area and their economic performance will depend on the individual context of each city. In Seoul, factors such as skill levels, innovation and business start-ups may be more affected as housing in other areas is cheaper and businesses may struggle to attract talent. At the same time, it is necessary that local and national authorities prevent a sharp drop in prices as this could adversely affect consumer confidence, construction and lead to lower economic growth.

Figure 1.12. Average housing price by region (KRW million)

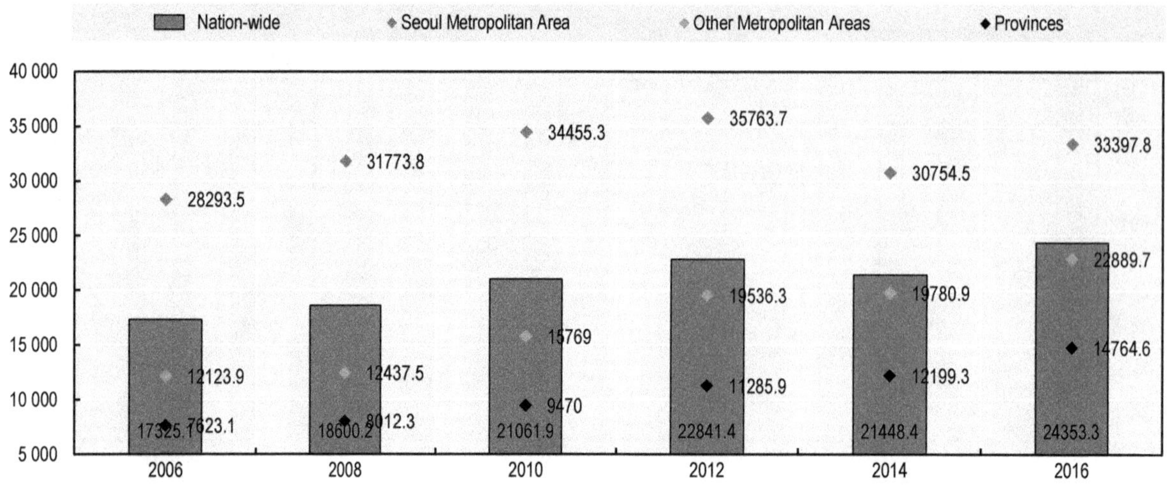

Note: The 2012 price may have been overestimated because households that live in larger than 85m2 were oversampled in 2012 data collection (Korea Housing Survey 2016).
Source: Korea Housing Survey 2016.

Seoul metropolitan area shows the highest level of financial burden of all the regions (Table 1.13). During the past decade, the price to yearly income ratio (PIR) of Seoul metropolitan area has always been higher than those of other metropolitan areas and provinces. In terms of the rent to monthly income ratio (RIR), all regions have shown a decreasing trend since 2014.

Table 1.13. PIR and RIR by region

		2006	2008	2010	2012	2014	2016
PIR by region	Nation-wide	4.2	4.3	4.3	5.1	4.7	5.6
	Seoul Metropolitan Area	5.7	6.9	6.9	6.7	6.9	6.7
	Other metropolitan areas	4.1	3.3	3.5	5.0	4.7	5.3
	Provinces	3.3	3.0	2.9	3.6	4.2	4.0
RIR by region	Nation-wide	18.7	17.5	19.2	19.8	20.3	18.1
	Seoul Metropolitan Area	19.9	22.3	20.9	23.3	21.6	17.9
	Other metropolitan areas	18.5	19.3	16.4	16.8	16.6	15.4
	Provinces	17.8	15.9	14.4	14.5	15.8	14.2

Note: PIR is calculated as median housing value divided by median yearly income. RIR is calculated as median housing value divided by median yearly income
Source: Korea Housing Survey 2016.

1.5.3. Households in urban cores have lower levels of housing conditions

Urban cores in Korea have the lowest share of owner-occupied floor area per household and per person. In contrast, urban cores have the highest share of office and professional jobs, income, college graduates, median price of housing and jeonsei deposit (Table 1.14). This suggests that living conditions in cities, especially for urban cores, are more demanding and therefore accessing housing requires more efforts and investment. For example, the median housing price in the urban core is KRW 220 million, KRW 180 million in the hinterland, and KRW 80 million in rural areas. This implies that housing policies might require specific provisions for urban areas to facilitate access to affordable housing.

Table 1.14. Basic statistics by functional area

		Urban Core	Hinterland	Rural
Socio-economic	Age of householder	56.7	57.6	61.9
	Share of young (<35 years old) householders (%)	8.6	6.2	8.3
	Share of male householders (%)	78.3	79.2	73.1
	Number of household members	2.7	2.8	2.3
	Share of college graduates (%)	37.6	34.9	21.8
	Share of office and professional jobs (%)	64.8	49.7	34.1
	Yearly income ('0000 KRW)	3552	3345	2542.6
Housing welfare	Share of owner-occupied (%)	58.3	69.7	70.3
	Share of apartments (%)	57.7	63.9	41
	Floor area per household (m^2)	73.1	78.5	74.1
	Floor area per person (m^2)	31.9	35	39.2
	Median price of housing (KRW million)	22000	18000	8000
	Median of jeonsei deposit (KRW million)	9500	9000	5750

Note: Definition of young household is borrowed from Lee (2015). Since the Korea Housing Survey does not give weight to functional urban areas, weight is not applied to this calculation. It only allows for the division of the country into three components, that is, urban core, hinterland and rural areas for securing regional representatives when using KHS 2016 dataset.
Source: OECD calculation based on the Korea Housing Survey 2016.

Figure 1.13. Housing welfare conditions by functional area

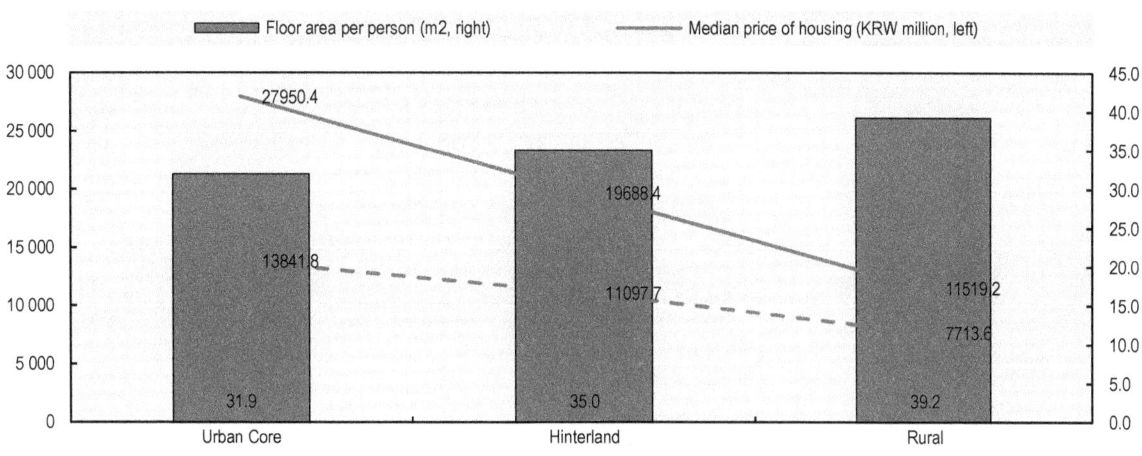

Source: OECD calculation based on the Korea Housing Survey 2016.

Box 1.3. Functional urban areas in Korea

In Korea, regions are usually divided according to physical characteristics, historical backgrounds, and administrative functions. Their jurisdiction is defined by law (MOI, 2016). However, administrative boundaries do not always match up with where people live, work, and spend leisure time. Therefore, OECD and the EU have developed an international methodology for measuring urban areas based on the definition of functional economic units. Using population density and commuting flow, regions can be characterised by densely inhabited "urban core" and "hinterland" whose labour market is highly related to the urban cores, and rural areas which are neither urban core nor hinterland (OECD 2012).

The definition has been applied to 30 OECD countries. 1 197 functional urban areas have been identified. Based on the 2009 data on population density and commuting flow, Korea has 45 functional urban areas. They are divided into four categories: large metropolitan areas with a population above 1.5 million, metropolitan areas with a population between 500 000 and 1.5 million, medium-sized urban areas with a population between 200 000 and 500 000, and small urban areas with a population between 50 000 and 200 000 (OECD 2012). In addition, each functional urban area is divided into urban core and hinterland, resulting in three functional criteria: urban core, hinterland and rural area. By focusing on functional urban areas, Korean policymakers can have a better understanding of the current reality and design better policies for cities, both large and small.

Functional urban areas in Korea

Functional Urban Areas	Name
Large metropolitan (3)	Seoul Incheon, Busan, Daegu
Metropolitan (7)	Gwangju, Daejeon, Ulsan, Changwon, Jeonju, Cheongju, Pohang
Medium-sized (12)	Cheonan, Gumi, Jinju, Jeju, Iksan, Yeosu, Gunsan, Gimhae, Mokpo, Chuncheon, Wonju, Suncheon
Small (23)	Gangneung, Chungju, Gyeongju, Pyeongtaek, Andong, Jecheon, Pyeongtaek Seojeong, Yangsan, Tongyeong, Jinhae, Gongju, Gimcheon, Geoje Gohyeon, Seosan, Yeongju, Jeongeup, Sokcho, Asan, Donghae, Geoje Neungpo, Boryeong, Ulsan Onsan, Gwangyang

Source: OECD (2012), Redefining "Urban": A New Way to Measure Metropolitan Areas.

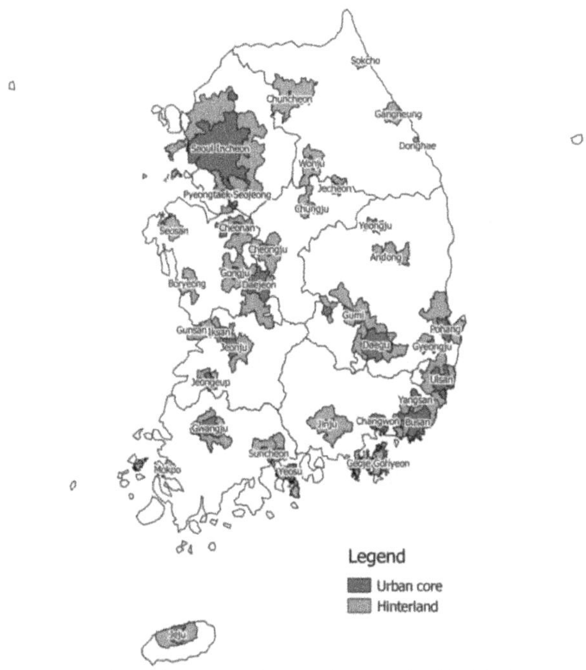

Source: OECD elaboration based on: www.oecd.org/cfe/regional-policy/functionalurbanareasbycountry.htm.

1.6. Housing welfare and regional characteristics

1.6.1. Socio-economic and demographic factors determine, to a certain extent, housing conditions

Socio-economic and demographic characteristics of a household can affect housing welfare (Lim, 2017). In Korea, female householders are more likely to experience substandard housing as they generally earn less and therefore have limited housing options (Lim, Min and Lee, 2009; Lim, 2015). Education level also has an impact on housing options in Korea. A highly educated household is more likely to have higher income, possess better information, and more analytical skills to make informed decisions on housing than a less educated household (Lim et al, 2009; Kim et al, 2010; Kim et al, 2013; Lim, 2014). Disabled householders are more likely to have been excluded from normal education, economic activities and social relations, possibly resulting in inadequate housing. Householders with disabilities are likely to have a higher rate of substandard housing than non-disabled householders in Korea (Lee, 2010; Lim, 2014). Households with higher income are more likely to have accumulated greater capital and are less likely to experience substandard housing (Conley, 2001; Park, Oh and Lee, 2015; Lim, 2015, 2016).

In Korea, a family with a large number of children is more likely to experience substandard housing. This implies higher rents, less floor area per person, and more bank loans (debt) (Chun, 2013; Lim, 2015). Moreover, owners are less likely to live in substandard housing compared to renters as they have incentives to purchase housing that best fits their needs (Kim and Choi, 2013; Rosenbaum, 1996; Park, Oh and Lee, 2015; Lim, 2015, 2016).

1.6.2. Rural areas are more likely to have poor housing conditions

In Korea, quality of housing and housing affordability are remarkably different in urban and rural areas (Latimer and Woldoff, 2010; Park et al, 2015b; Kwon and Choi, 2015; Lim, 2015). Predominantly rural areas with less stable jobs, poor transport infrastructure and less accessible public services do not always have enough housing stock (Gibbs, 2004; as cited in Latimer and Woldoff, 2010).

The provision of public rental housing in a region may increase the share of adequate housing at affordable prices. Lim (2015) argues that in Korean regions with a higher rate of public rental housing there is a lower rate of substandard housing. Similarly, in rural areas of the United Kingdom, homes provided by the Registered Social Landlords (RSL) have helped to sustain mixed communities raising housing satisfaction.[10]

Indeed, an increase in average regional house prices normally leads to the reduction of adequate homes at affordable prices, increasing the risk of homelessness and substandard housing (Fertig and Reingold, 2008). In Korea, higher median house prices increase the risk of living in substandard housing (Lim, 2016).

1.6.3. Regional features determine housing welfare, especially for substandard housing and housing affordability

An increase in public rental housing may be instrumental in solving the housing affordability gap. Regions' specific features are one critical factor that determines housing welfare (Annex 1.A). Their impact can be larger than demographic and socio-economic characteristics (Annex 1.B). For instance, urban areas have on average 7.7m^2 less floor space than homes in rural areas (Figure 1.14). However, a householder's age, education level, size of household, income, and home ownership still have an important impact on the level of housing welfare. Indeed, factors such as lower householder age, education level and income, larger household size and lack of home ownership increase the probability of living in substandard housing (Annex 1.C). Regions must continue providing public rental housing to increase the access to good quality affordable housing for rural area residents.

Figure 1.14. Difference of housing density between urban and rural areas (m2)

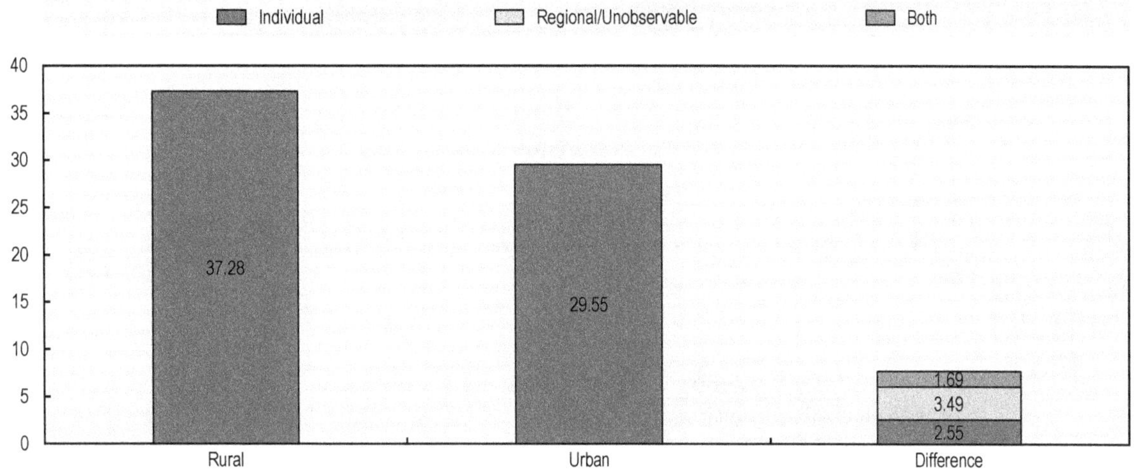

Note: Difference of house prices between urban and rural, and between urban core and hinterland are analysed (see Annex 1.B).
Source: OECD calculation based on data of Korea Housing Survey 2016.

Notes

[1] The housing supply ratio refers to the ratio of the number of housing units to the number of households, www.index.go.kr/potal/main/EachDtlPageDetail.do?idx_cd=1227.

[2] The quantitative housing shortage is measured by the ratio of the number of housing units to the number of households (same as housing supply ratio).

[3] A dwelling can be defined as "a room or suite of rooms and its accessories in a permanent building or structurally separated part for private habitation. It should have a separate access to a street or to a common space such as passage within the building" (UNECE, 2000).

[4] For further information, see Park, M (2017).

[5] For interest rates of a three-year treasury bond, it was 12.94% in 1998 and dropped to 1.44% in 2016.

[6] A smaller value represents greater affordability.

[7] For further information, see OECD Housing Affordability Survey.

[8] This indicator does not include payments for interest and principal on housing mortgages.

[9] For further information see OECD (2015), *How's Life? 2015: Measuring Well-being,* retrieved from http://dx.doi.org/10.1787/888933259048.

[10] For further information see: www.jrf.org.uk/report/social-housing-rural-areas.

Bibliography

Andrews, D., A.C. Sanchez, and A. Johansson (2011), "Housing markets and Structural Policies in OECD Countries", OECD Economics Department Working Papers, No. 836, OECD Publishing, Paris.

Bae, Soonsuk and Mincheol Kim (2013), A Study on Housing Affordability Measures and Standards for Policy Applications, Korea Research Institute for Human Settlements, Gwacheon.

Berger. L. M., T. Heintze, W.B. Naidich and M.K. Meyers (2008), "Subsidized Housing and Household Hardship Among Low-Income Single-Mother Households", *Journal of Marriage and Family*, 70(4). 934-949, https://onlinelibrary.wiley.com/doi/abs/10.1111/j.1741-3737.2008.00537.x (accessed on 12 December 2017).

Chapman, D. and J. Lombard (2006), "Determinants of Neighbourhood Satisfaction in Fee-Based Gated and Non-Gated Communities", *Urban Affairs Review*. 41, Retrieved from http://uar.sagepub.com/content/41/6/769.

Choi, Byungsook and Jeonga Park (2012), "An Effect of Housing Environment on Depression and Self-esteem in Analyzing the 4th Wave of Korea Welfare Panel Study Data in 2009", *Journal of the Korean Housing Association*, Seoul, 23(5): 75−86.

Conley, D. (2001),"A Room with a View or a Room of One's Own? Housing and Social Stratification" Sociological *Forum*, 16(2): 263-280, http://citeseerx.ist.psu.edu/viewdoc/download?doi=10.1.1.600.5906&rep=rep1&type=pdf (accessed December 2017).

Chun, Hyeonsook (2013), "The housing policy as to the trend of low birth rate", *KRIHS Policy Brief*, 423: 1-8, KRIHS, Sejong.

Demographia (2015), 11th International Housing Affordability Survey, New York University, New York.

Dietz, D. and R. Haurin (2003), "The Social and Private micro-level consequences of homeownership", *Journal of Urban Economics*, 54: 401-450.

Downs, A. (1993), "Reducing regulatory barriers to affordable housing erected by local governments in Housing Markets Residential Mobility", edited by Kingsley, G. T. and M. A. Turner, The Urban Institute Press, Washington, DC.

Dwyer, R. E. (2007), "Expanding homes and increasing inequalities: U.S. housing development and the residential segregation of the affluent", *Social Problems,* Tennessee, 54: 23-46.

Elliott, M. and L.J. Krivo (1991), "Structural Determinants of Homelessness in the United States", *Social Problem,* Tennessee, 38(1): 113-128.

Evans, G.W., H. Saltzman and J.L. Cooperman (2001), "Housing Quality and Children's Socioemotional Health" *Environment and Behavior*, Minnesota 33: 389-399.

Evans, G.W., H.N. Ricciuti, S. Hope, I. Schoon, R.H. Bradley, R.F. Corwyn and C. Hazan (2009), "Crowding and Child Cognitive Development-The Mediating Role of Maternal Responsiveness Among 36-Month-Old Children", *Environmental and Behavior*, Minnesota 20(5): 1-14.

Fertig, A.R. and D.A. Reingold (2008), "Homelessness among At-Risk Families with Children in Twenty American Cities", *Social Service Review*, Chicago 62(3): 485-510. https://www.researchgate.net/publication/279609974_Homelessness_among_At-Risk_Families_with_Children_in_Twenty_American_Cities (accessed 23 November 2017).

Gibbs, R. (2004), Rural Education at a Glance, Rural Development Research Report No. RDRR-98, Economic Research Service, U.S. Department of Agriculture, Retrieved 20 March 2010, http//www.ers.usda.gov/publications/rdrrítô.

Haffner, M., J. Hoekstra, M. Oxley and H.V.D. Heijden (2009), "Bridging the gap between social and market rented housing in six European countries?", *Housing and Urban Policy Studies* 33, IOS press, Amsterdam .

Herbert, C., D. McCue and R. Sanchez-Moyano (2013), Homeownership Built to Last: Lessons from the Housing Crisis on Sustaining Homeownership for Low-Income and Minority Families, A National Symposium held on 1 and 2 April 2013 at Harvard Business School, Boston, Massachusetts.

Hong, Sehee (2007), The multilevel model with Hierarchical and longitudinal data, Graduate School of Social Welfare of Yonsei Universty, Seoul.

Hyundai Research Institute (2015), The characteristics and implications of Jeonsei market, Issues and Tasks, 15-32, Hyundai Research Institute, Seoul.

ICESCR, U. (1991), General Comment No. 4: The Right to Adequate Housing (Art. 11 (1) of the Covenant). E/1992/23. 13 December. http://www.refworld.org/docid/47a7079a1.html (accessed 27 July 2016).

Jang Kyoungseok, Younkyoung Hur, Hyungmin Kim, and Sungjin Kim (2009), The Spatial Distribution and Changes of Affordable Housing in Seoul, Journal of the Korea Planning Association 44(1): 87-99, http://www.dbpia.co.kr/Journal/ArticleDetail/NODE01153965 (accessed 21 November 2017).

Jann, B. and E. Zurich, (2008), "The Blinder-Oaxaca decomposition for linear regression models", *The Stata Journal*, 8, No 4: 453-479.

Jeong, O. (2012), Housing Welfare Condition and Policy Direction, Analysis of Housing Market 2012, vol. 1, Korea Development Institute, Seoul.

Jin, H., D. Kang, and S. Lee (2009),"A Study on the Changing Factors of Minimum Housing Standard and Housing Density in Seoul Metropolitan Area, 1995-2005" *Housing Studies Review*, Seoul Vol. 18, No. 1: 41-68.

Jin, Meeyun (2007),"Policy Review of Public Rental Housing Strategies Since 2000", *The Korea Spatial Planning Review*, Seoul 53: 163-186.

Joongang Daily (2011), Owner occupancy rate; increase in province, and decreased in Seoul metropolitan area, http://news.joins.com/article/6204057 (accessed on 7 October 2017).

Joung, Eunhee and Youseok Choi (2014), “A Multidimensional Approach on Poverty of Households with Children: A Typology Using Latent Class Analysis”, *Journal of the Korea contents association*. 14(6): 129-139.

KB Research Center (2017), Housing market trends from Population Census 2015, KB Knowledge Vitamin, 17-07, KB Research Center, Seoul.

KB Research Center (2016), State of housing supply and regional impact analysis, KB Real Estate Market Review, 16-03, KB Research Center, Seoul.

Kang, D., S. Lee and H. Kim (2012), “Does Schwabe’s Hypothesis Hold in Korea: Empirical Evidence from the Characteristics Changes of Homeownership Demand in Seoul Metropolitan Area”, *LHI Journal*,Daejeon, 3(1): 23-32.

Kim, K. and M. Park (2016), “Housing Policy in the Republic of Korea”, ADBI Working Paper Series. No. 5701.

Kim, S. (2017), *The structural change and its response in rental housing market*, Seminar of HUG Housing and Urban Finance Research Institute, Pusan.

Kim, Dongbae, ByungSun You and Sumin Shin (2012), “The effects of Housing Poverty on the Depression of the Elderly: The Mediating Effect of Social Service”, *Journal of Korea Gerontological Society*, 33(1): 105-123.

Kim, Hyunjoong, Dongwoo Kang and Seongwoo Lee (2010), “The Change and Regional Disparity of Elderly Housing Conditions in Rural Areas (1995~2005)”, *Journal of Korean Society of Rural Planning*, Seoul, 16(1): 49-62.

Kim, Seungyun, Serim Kim and Jinsuk Lee (2013), “The effect of Housing on Health”, *Journal of Korea Health and Medical Sociology*, Seoul 34: 109-133.

Kim, Yongchang and Eunyoung Choi (2013), “Spatio-Temporal Changes and Characteristics of Households Failing to Meet the New Minimum Housing Standard in Seoul Metropolitan (1995~2010)”, *Journal of the Korean Geographical Society*, 48(4): 509-532.

Kwak, Insook and Soonmi Kim (1999), “A study on the total housing cost of households living in rental house”, *Journal of the Korean Home Economics Association*,Seoul 37(2): 127-144.

Kwon, Yeonhwa and Yeol Choi (2015), “A Study on Housing Affordability of Elderly Households According to Household Types and Housing Tenure”, *The journal of Korean society of civil engineers* Seoul, 35(4): 977-986.

KRIHS (2013), A Primer on Korean Planning and Policy: Housing Policy, KRIHS GDPC, Gwachen.

Latimer, M. and R. Woldoff (2010), “Good Country Living? Exploring Four Housing Outcomes Among Poor Appalachians”, *Sociological Forum*, 24(2): 315-334.

Lee, H. (2015), "Comparisons of Young Renter Households' Housing Situation by Locations Reflected in the 2012 Korea Housing Survey", *Journal of the Korean Housing Association*, Seoul, Vol. 26, No. 1: 81-90.

Lee, Hogeun (2015), "Housing Assistances Act And the Improvement Of Law & Institutions On The Housing Policy For The Socially Precarious Groups", *The Korean Journal of Social Security*, 31(1): 169-204.

Lee, Jaewoong and Hyelin Yang (2015), "The effect of housing cost burden on the quality of life among tenants living in public rental housing : focused on the moderating effects of social services", *Korean Journal of Social Welfare Studies*, Seoul, 46(3): 153- 177.

Lee, Sungjae (2007), "A study in the Characteristics of Factor in the substandard housing of the Minimum Housing standard - Focused on Jeonju City", *Journal of the Architectural Institute of Korea*, Seoul, 23(12): 269-275.

Lee, Sunwoo (2010), "Comparing Levels of Housing Welfare between Households with Disabled Members and without Disabled Members: Focusing on Minimum Standards of Housing and Housing Affordability", *Journal of Korean social welfare administration*, Seoul, 12(2): 1-21.

Lim, Hyungback, Seonghee Min and Seongwoo Lee (2009), "The disparities of minimum standard of living by household's place of birth in Seoul", *Journal of Korean Association for Local Government Studies*, Seoul 21(1): 55-78.

Lim, Jaehyun (2011), "The Effects of Housing Poverty on Family Life", *Korean Journal of Social Welfare Studies*, Seoul 40(3): 245-265.

Lim, Sehee and Bongjoo Lee (2009), "Effects of Living in Substandard housing conditions on School Achievement", *Korean Journal of Social Welfare Studies*, Seoul 40(3): 245-265.

Lim, Sehee (2010), "The Effects of Housing Poverty on Child Development", Doctoral dissertation of Seoul National University.

Lim, Sehee (2013), "The effect of Public housing on the depression", *Korean Journal of Social Welfare Studies*, Seoul 44(3): 5-30.

Lim, Sehee (2014), "The change of magnitude and characters in households below minimum housing standard (2005-2011)", *The Korean Journal of Social Security*, Seoul 30(3): 215-244.

Lim, Sehee (2015), "The Determinants of Sub-standard Housing: Focusing on the Characters of the Districts", *Social Welfare Policy* Seoul, 42(4): 47-73.

Lim, Sehee (2016), "The Determinants of Housing Affordability", *Korean Journal of Social Welfare*, Seoul, 68(3): 29-50.

Lim, Sehee (2017), "The Effects of Neighborhood Characteristics on Housing Poverty", Unpublished.

Lim, Sehee and Sunsuk Kim (2016), "The effects of housing poverty on adolescent's subjective well-being", *Korean Journal of child Welfare*, Seoul 56: 133-164.

Marks, G. N. and S. Sedgwick (2008), "Is there a housing crisis? The incidence and persistence of housing stress 2001-2006", *Australian Economic Review*, 41(2): 215-221.

Mass. C. and J. Hox. (2004), "The influence of violations of assumptions on multilevel parameter estimates and their standard error", *Computational statistics & Data analysis*, 46: 427-440.

Menard, S. (2009), "The social housing and rental housing markets in an equilibrium rent search model", *Annals of Economics and Statistics*, 95/96: 183-199.

Min, I and P. Choi (2009), STATA: Basic Statistics and Regression Analysis, JIPHIL Seoul.

Min, I and P. Choi (2012), STATA: Introduction and Practical Applications, JIPHIL, Seoul.

MOI (2016), Administrative boundary and population, Ministry of the Interior, Seoul.

MOLIT (2016), The manual of Housing Policy, MOLIT, Sejong.

MOLIT (2016), Korea Housing Survey: MOLIT, Sejong.

Moore, E. and A. Skaburskis (2004), "Canada's increasing housing affordability burdens", *Housing Studies*, 19(3): 395-413.

Mutchler. J.E. and L.J. Krivo (1989), "Availability and Affordability: Household Adaptation to a Housing Squeeze", *Social Forces*, 68(1): 241-261.

O'Donnell, O., E. van Doorslaer, A. Wagstaff and M. Lindelow (2008), Analyzing Health Equity Using Household Survey Data: A Guide to Techniques and Their Implementation, World Bank, Washington, DC.

OECD (2011), How's Life? 2011: Measuring Well-being, OECD Publishing, Paris, http://dx.doi.org/10.1787/9789264121164-en.

OECD (2012), Redefining "Urban": A New Way to Measure Metropolitan Areas, OECD Publishing, Paris, http://dx.doi.org/10.1787/9789264174108-en.

OECD (2015), How's Life? 2015: Measuring Well-being, OECD Publishing, Paris, http://dx.doi.org/10.1787/how_life-2015-en.

Park, Eunchul, Insik Bong, Wonsuk Nam and Keunsang Oh (2013), "The cases and issue about housing benefit", *Urban Information Service*, Seoul, 381: 3-22.

Park, Jungmin, Ukchan Oh and Gunmin Yi (2015), "A Typology of Housing Vulnerability based on Housing Quality and Affordability", *Korean Journal of Social Welfare Studies*, Seoul, 46 (2): 101~123.

Park, Jungmin, Youngchang Heo, Ukchan Oh, and Sookyung Yoon (2015), "Change in Physical and Mental Health as a Function of Substandard Housing Conditions and Unaffordable Housing", *Korean Journal of Social Welfare*, Seoul, 67(2): 137-159.

Park Kyungjun and Seongwoo Lee (2015), "Determinants of Housing Expenditure in Seoul Metropolitan Area, 2006~2014: Application of Multi-level Model", *The Korea Spatial Planning Review*, Seoul, 12: 33-48.

Park, Shinyoung (2012), "Housing Poverty in Korea", *Health and welfare policy forum*, 184: 33-46.

Raudenbush, S.W. (2004), HLM 6: Hierarchical Linear and Nonlinear Modeling, Scientific Software International.

Raudenbush, S and A. Bryk (2002), Hierarchical Linear Models, Advanced Quantitative, Techniques in the Social Science Series.

Rosenbaum, E. (1996), "Racial/Ethnic Differences in Home Ownership and Housing Quality" 1991, *Social Problems*, Tennessee 43(4): 403-426.

Rutherford, A. (2001), Introducing Anova and Ancova: A GLM Approach, SAGE Publications Ltd.

Schachter, J. (2004), Geographical mobility: Population characteristics, U.S. Census Bureau, Washington, DC.

Shim, Young (2002), "An analysis of the economic well-being of Elderly Households based on Housing Ownership and Housing costs", *Journal of Korean association of human ecology* Seoul, 12(1): 1-14.

Snijders, T.A.B. (2012), Multilevel Analysis, http://www.stats.ox.ac.uk/~snijders/mlbook.htm.

Song, I. (2016), "Policy Improvement in Response to Structural Changes in the Housing Rental Market", Korea Development Institute, Sejong.

Squires, G. D. (2002), Urban Sprawl and the Uneven Development of Metropolitan America, pp, 1-22 in Urban Sprawl: Causes, Consequences, and Policy Responses, edited by Gregory D. Squires, Urban Institute Press, Washington DC.

Sullivan, A. (1996), Urban economics, Irwin/McGraw-Hill, Boston.

UNECE (2000), *Bulletin of Housing and Building Statistics for Europe and North America*, Annex II, Definitions and General Terms, page 82. United Nations, Geneva, http://www.unece.org/hlm/prgm/hsstat/Bulletin_00.html.

Voith, R. and S.M. Wachter (2009), "Urban Growth and Housing Affordability: The Conflict", *The Annals of the American Academy of Political and Social Science*, 626: 112-1.

Wooldridge, J. (2012), Introductory Econometrics: A Modern Approach, 5th edition, South-Western.

Yoon, Hyunsik (2015), The Significances and Issues of Framework Act on Housing, *Ilkam real estate law review*, Seoul 11: 53-86.

Annex 1.A. Differences by region: analysis by ANOVA

Analysis of variance (ANOVA) test examines whether one factor has a significant effect on the variance of total observations. In other words, it can examine whether one factor creates different mean values across groups. From a regional perspective, if the average variance between regions is significantly higher than the average variance within regions, it can be argued that regional features make the difference (Min and Choi, 2009). ANOVA can be applied to experimental, quasi-experimental and non-experimental data. It is an ideal statistical technique to assess the average difference of groups in terms of a particular dependent variable (Rutherford, 2001).

The table below indicates the variance of the means of housing welfares by administrative region. All the housing welfare variables such as floor area per person, floor area per household, tenure types, housing price, and jeonsei deposit are different across regions, whereas there are smaller variances of means within a given region.

Analysis of variance by administrative region

Dependent Variables	Source	Sum of Squares	Mean Square	P-value
Floor Area per Person (m^2)	Between regions	212112243.00	13257015.20	0.00
	Within regions	7211300000.00	377.39	
	Total	7423400000.00	388.49	
Floor Area per Household (m^2)	Between regions	295285231.00	18455327.00	0.00
	Within regions	18382000000.00	962.02	
	Total	18678000000.00	977.47	
Tenure Type	Between regions	280962.25	17560.14	0.00
	Within regions	36917660.30	1.93	
	Total	37198622.60	1.95	
Housing Type	Between regions	92466.89	5779.18	0.00
	Within regions	4685097.22	0.25	
	Total	4777564.11	0.25	

Note: Weighted counts and statistical values are presented. Although housing price and jeonsei deposit were analysed, the results were not reported due to space restrictions.
Source: Author's calculation based on data of Korea Housing Survey 2016.

The table below indicates the variance of the means of housing welfares by functional area. The result is similar. The evidence presented thus supports the idea that, regardless of administrative or functional area, regions can have effects on housing welfare.

Analysis of variance by functional area

Dependent Variables	Source	Sum of Squares	Mean Square	P-value
Floor Area per Person (m^2)	Between regions	154902.24	77451.12	0.00
	Within regions	7505073.90	372.98	
	Total	7659976.14	380.64	
Floor Area per Household (m^2)	Between regions	48128.40	24064.20	0.00
	Within regions	18789083.10	933.76	
	Total	18837211.50	936.06	
Tenure Type	Between regions	46.94	23.47	0.00
	Within regions	40394.97	2.01	
	Total	40441.91	2.01	
Housing Type	Between regions	92.39	46.19	0.00
	Within regions	4880.49	0.24	
	Total	4972.88	0.25	

Note: Since the Korea Housing Survey does not give weight to functional urban area, weight is not applied to this calculation. Weighted counts and statistical values are presented. Although housing price and jeonsei deposit were analysed, the results were not reported due to space restrictions.
Source: Author's calculation based on data of Korea Housing Survey 2016.

Annex 1.B. Blinder-Oaxaca decomposition analysis

Blinder-Oaxaca decomposition is one of the counterfactual decomposition techniques, and is widely used for investigating mean outcome differences between groups. In many cases, this technique is often used to study discrimination among groups, for example, wage differences by gender or race (Jann & Zurich, 2008). However, it can also be used in other areas. For urban studies, some prior studies employed this approach to check the relative strength of individual characteristics and regional features on housing density (Jin, Kang, and Lee, 2009).

Blinder-Oaxaca decomposition can reveal the relative strength of regional characteristics/unobservable features and individual socio-economic characteristics on housing welfare. It divides a difference between two groups into two components; one is explained by group difference ($\Delta\chi\beta^{rural}$ in the figure below), and the other is residual part which is unexplained by group difference ($\Delta\beta\chi^{urban}$ in the figure below). Usually the latter is used for a gauge of discrimination. In the case of the labour market, a wage gap by gender can be divided into two parts; one is explained by productivity features of each group, that is education level, experience and so on, and the other is the portion that cannot be explained by the productivity features (Jann & Zurich, 2008). Applying this decomposition to housing welfare, it can be calculated how much individual and socio-economic characteristics such as gender, income and number of household members, and others including regional features, have impact on housing welfare respectively.

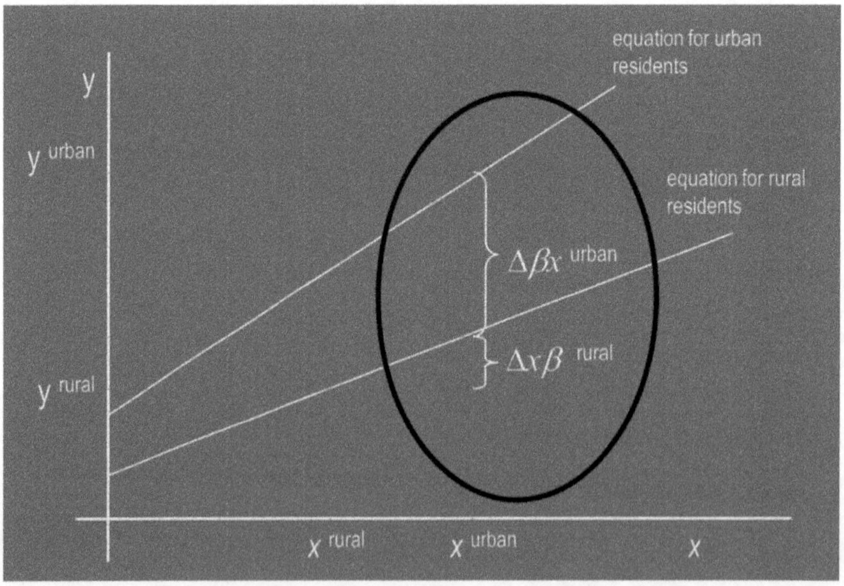

Source: OECD modification based on O'Donnell et al (2008).

For this analysis, the variables which are relevant and available from Korea Housing Survey 2016 are used: housing density (i.e. floor area per person), age, gender, number of household members, education level, income, types of job, housing tenure, housing type, housing prices. In addition, one regional division should be employed for this analysis.

Therefore, regions are divided into either urban vs rural or urban core vs hinterland.[1] To have a more relevant dataset for this study, observations where household income and housing price are extremely high, are removed because they may lead to severe positive skewness. In other words, observations at the 95th percentile or higher are removed from the dataset (Chapman and Lombard, 2006). In addition, income and housing price variables are changed to logarithm form. Finally, only owner-occupied households have house price values, and here the house price value is used, therefore, the observations are constraint to owner occupied households. [2]

First, difference of housing density is checked. For the difference of floor area per person between urban and rural areas, the average difference is about 7.7m^2, which means urban residents have a smaller surface area per person. Decomposition divides the difference into three parts (see table below). The endowment effects reflect the mean decrease in rural residents' density if the rural residents have the same features as the urban residents. In other words, if the rural residents have, on average, the same age, number of household members, income level, housing type and housing price as the urban residents, the average density would decrease by 2.55m^2. The endowment effects explain about 33% of the density difference. The residual effects reflect the mean decrease when applying the urban residents' coefficients to the characteristics of rural residents. This can be attributed to the difference originating from regional features. That is, regional characteristics could explain about 45% of the density difference, which is bigger than the endowment effects. Notably, the residual effects also capture all potential differences from unobserved variables. The interaction measures the effect that both endowment and residual effects give impacts on density simultaneously. In short, the average density difference between urban and rural areas can be attributed to households and housing features by about 33% and regional characteristics and unobservable features by about 45%. It implies that regional characteristics can be a critical factor of individual housing welfare (Jann & Zurich, 2008).

Difference of housing density between urban and rural areas

Average Density (m^2)			Decomposition		
Urban	Rural	Difference	Endowment Effects	Residual Effects	Interaction
29.55	37.28	-7.73	-2.55	-3.49	-1.69

Source: Author's calculation based on data of Korea Housing Survey 2016.

The table below shows the average density difference between the residents of urban cores and hinterlands. Not surprisingly, urban core residents have a smaller surface area per person by 3.1m^2. The endowment effects say if the hinterland residents have, on average, the same characteristics as the urban core residents, the average density would decrease by 0.2m^2. On the other hand, the residual effects explain that regional features are attributed to the difference by 2.47m^2, which is about 80% of the total difference. It implies that regional features have larger influence on housing welfare among urban residents (i.e. urban core and hinterland residents), rather than housing welfare between urban and rural residents.

Difference of housing density between urban cores and hinterlands

Average Density (m2)			Decomposition		
Urban Core	Hinterland	Difference	Endowment Effects	Residual Effects	Interaction
29.07	32.17	-3.1	-0.2	-2.47	-0.43

Source: Author's calculation based on data of Korea Housing Survey 2016.

Second, housing price is investigated. For the difference between urban and rural areas, the average difference is about log 0.7 (unit is KRW 10 000). The endowment effects show that if the rural residents have, on average, the same characteristics as the urban core residents, the average price would increase by 0.2. On the other hand, the residual effects show that regional features are attributed to the difference by 0.4, which is bigger than the endowment effects. Similarly, the difference between urban core and hinterland can be explained more by residual effects, which are influences from regional features and unobserved variables. It also implies that regional features need to be considered as one of the important factors for housing welfare.

Difference of housing price between urban and rural areas

Average Price (KRW ten thousand, log)			Decomposition		
Urban	Rural	Difference	Endowment Effects	Residual Effects	Interaction
9.85	9.14	0.71	0.20	0.40	0.11

Source: Author's calculation based on data of Korea Housing Survey 2016.

Difference of housing price between urban cores and hinterlands

Average Price (KRW ten thousand, log)			Decomposition		
Urban Core	Hinterland	Difference	Endowment Effects	Residual Effects	Interaction
9.87	9.69	0.18	0.06	0.11	0.01

Source: Author's calculation based on data of Korea Housing Survey 2016.

Notes

[1] The latter is limited to only urban areas.

[2] For robustness check, the same analysis is done using jeonsei residents; the implications were the same. For density, urban residents live more densely than rural residents, and urban core residents live more densely than hinterland residents. For jeonsei deposit, the deposit of urban residents, on average, was higher than the deposit of rural residents, and the deposit of urban core residents, on average, was higher than the deposit of hinterland residents. In terms of relative strength between individual/socio-economic characteristics and regional features, the latter is higher than the former; similar to the analysis of data from owner-occupied households.

Annex 1.C. Regional characteristics affecting housing welfare: Analysis by multi-level model

In conducting multivariate analysis, a hierarchical linear model (HLM) is employed because the data has a multi-level structure (that is, a household is nested in a region). HLM accounts for the shared variance in multi-level data in which level 1 data (household data) is nested in level 2 data (regional data). There are arguments in favour of HLM instead of an Ordinary Linear regression (OLS). In particular, it is used with the hierarchical generalised linear model (HGLM) because dependent variables in this study are dichotomous variables (living/not living in substandard housing and facing/not facing unaffordable housing). For the link function, a multi-level logit model with HLM 7.0 is used. For the simplicity of the models, a two-level random intercept model is used but the slopes are estimated using fixed effects (Hong, 2007) with robust standard error (Raudenbush, 2004).

One caveat is that the Korea Housing Survey is conducted at regional level (i.e. SIDO) but the samples are further analysed at area level (i.e. SIGUNGU) in this study, thus it is prone to error of estimation. Future research should collect more representative data samples at area level and examine the effect in more detail.

For the dependent variables, substandard housing and housing affordability are used. To be particular, they are whether a household lives in standard housing or whether a household lives in unaffordable housing. Independent variables are classified into two groups; one is demographic-socioeconomic factor, and the other is regional factor. The former has gender, age, educational level, disability, national basic livelihood act recipients, income, household size and home ownership. The latter has regional housing price, regional monthly rent, urbanisation level, and ratio of public rental housing. Due to data availability, those variables are employed. Analyses begin with an unconditional model to determine if regional characteristics are actually statistically significant. Subsequently, the conditional model is used to examine how the demographic-socioeconomic factors and the regional characteristics can affect substandard housing and unaffordable housing (see Annex 1.D).

Firstly, to gauge the magnitude of variance between areas in housing welfare, it is estimated by the model with no predictors at either level, which is the unconditional model (Raudenbush and Bryk, 2002). The results are shown in the table below[1]. The logit for living in substandard housing is -2.92 and for unaffordable housing is -1.81. The random effect variances (i.e. variability between areas) are 0.603 and 0.461 respectively and both are statistically significant at $p<0.01$. Given this, the regional characteristics should be taken into consideration when analysing the level of housing welfare. Subsequently, the conditional model is conducted to examine the effect of demographic and socio-economic factors (level-1 variable) and the regional characteristics (level-2 variable) on housing welfare.

Unconditional model

	Substandard housing			Unaffordable housing		
Fixed effect	Coefficient	Standard error	Confidence interval (Odds Ratio)	Coefficient	Standard error	Confidence interval (Odds Ratio)
Intercept1	-2.92	0.06***	(0.048, 0.061)	-1.81	0.05***	(0.146, 0.181)
Random effect						
Intercept variance	Variance	Degree of freedom	p-value	variance	Degree of freedom	p-value
	0.063	205	p<.001	0.461	205	P<.001

Note: *** means statistically significant at 99% significance level.
Source: Lim (2017).

The table below illustrates the results of a conditional model[2]. A conditional model is a model with level 1 (household) and level 2 (area) predictors. Among level 1, the demographic-socioeconomic predictors, the age and education level of householder, size of household, income, and home ownership have a statistically significant relationship with the level of housing welfare. In detail, the lower the householder's age, education level, and income and the larger the size of the household, and lack of home ownership increase probability[3] of living in substandard housing. And the lower the householder's age and income and the higher the education level, the larger the size of the households, and lack of home ownership increase probability of living in unaffordable housing. Among level 2 predictors, proportion of public housing, median housing price and median rent of areas affect the probability of housing welfare. As regions provide more public rental housing, the probability of living in substandard housing significantly decreases ($p<0.05$). Also, the median housing price of a given area is positively correlated with the probability of living in unaffordable housing. The association is statistically significant at $p<0.05$. The probability of living in unaffordable housing increases as the median rent of areas goes up ($p<0.01$) (sig=0.58). This result demonstrates that the supply of public housing has a positive effect on the general housing welfare of residents given that the probability of substandard housing decreases for every household regardless of their demographic-socioeconomic characteristics. Also, since the median housing price and rent of areas influence the probability of living in unaffordable housing, it is desirable to maintain a moderate level of the median housing price and rent to achieve housing affordability.

Conditional model

		Substandard housing		Unaffordable Housing	
		Coefficient	SE (robust)	Coefficient	SE (robust)
Intercept1		-3.653	0.218***	-3.218	0.277***
Demographic and socioeconomic factor	Female-headed	0.051	0.09	0.049	0.073
	Age	-0.024	0.003***	-0.022	0.002***
	Educational level	-0.562	0.045***	0.133	0.037***
	Disability	-0.081	0.116	-0.028	0.096
	Size of household	0.487	0.044***	0.064	0.033**
	Income (log)	-0.629	0.063***	-2.677	0.069***
	NBLA recipient	0.133	0.141	-0.108	0.127
	Lack of home ownership	1.315	0.085***	1.041	0.069***

Regional factor	Median house price	-0.021	0.137	0.337	0.132**
	Urbanisation	-0.308	0.247	-0.394	0.313
	Proportion of public housing	-0.023	0.011**	-0.008	0.01
	Median rent	0.002	0.007	0.15	0.008*(p=.058)

Random effect						
Intercept variance	Variance	Df	p-value	variance	df	p-value
	0.603	201	p<.001	0.87	201	p<.001

Note: *** means statistically significant at 99% significance level, and ** means statistically significant at 95%
Source: Lim (2017).

The results suggest that not only household-specific variables, but also regional-level variables affect housing welfare. The householder's age and education level, size of household, income, and home ownership have a statistically significant relationship with housing poverty. Even when household-specific variables are controlled, the high ratio of public rental housing to entire housing lowers the possibility of living in substandard housing significantly and the high level of housing price and monthly rent notably increases the probability of living in unaffordable housing.

Notes

[1] The following results of HGLM are the results by the population-average model. HGLM offers both population-average and unit-specific results. Although they provide very similar results, unit-specific models pay attention to how level 1 variables operate at level 2 units (assuming they live in the same district), but it requires population-averages estimate to know the effect of level 1 coefficient on dependent variables (without assuming they live in the same district). In addition, population-averages are based on fewer assumptions and provide a reliable estimate despite its false assumptions about random effects. However, unit-specific models rely more on assumptions about the distribution of random effects. In other words, even though unit-specific models are richer, the results are more sensitive to model assumptions (Raudenbush and Bryk, 2002, 301-304). Since this study is more interested in the generalisation across the country and the distribution of the random effect model is not strictly assumed, it suggests population-averages model estimates.

[2] All interval ratio variables except dummy variables are transformed to grand-mean centred. If the variable is centred on the grand mean, the intercept is the value of the dependent variable when x is equal to the grand mean, while the group-mean centring gives the intercept is the value of dependent variable when x is equal to the group mean (Raudenbush & Bryk, 2002). This study uses grand-mean centring since it prefers population-average model.

[3] The coefficient of HGLM is log-odds, in other words, logit. When the logit is positive, the probability of housing poverty is greater than 0.5. When the logit is negative, the probability of housing poverty is less than 0.5.

Annex 1.D. Operational definitions of key variables for multi-level analysis

Defining and measuring substandard housing and unaffordable housing

Housing poverty is a state where adequacy of physical condition and the affordability of housing are not satisfied (Lim, 2010; Lim, 2011; Park, 2012). The former is substandard housing and the latter is unaffordable housing. The conditions of physically adequate housing may vary depending on time and location; however, many countries, including Korea, define physically adequate housing as not-too-crowded housing with essential facilities such as separate bathroom, and adequate lighting and heating facilities.

Housing expenses include mortgages, heating, and other maintenance costs. Housing affordability measures if housing-related expenses are within a household income level, and whether these expenses can be sustained for an extended period. Housing affordability can be measured by price to income ratios, residual income assessment model, or even by subjective methods (Bea and Kim, 2013). Price to income ratio is relatively easy to measure and compare across countries, however, it does not accurately show if a household's income after housing expenditure is enough to make a living. By contrast, residential income assessment measures excessiveness of housing expenses based on whether a household can afford living expenses (food, education, medical, etc.) after paying for housing expenses, assuming that a household lives in an adequate home. However, with this approach, households experiencing excessive housing expenses are concentrated among low-income families (Bae and Kim, 2013). It is usually considered that a household that spends more than 30% of their income on housing expense may have a problem of housing affordability (Lee, 2010; Park, 2012; Downs, 1993; Moore and Skabuskis, 2004; Marks and Sedgwick, 2008). This study follows the approach of those prior studies, defining households that spend more than 30% of their income on housing expenses, including mortgages, electricity and maintenance, as households with a problem of housing affordability.

Variables

In measuring and analysing substandard housing, which is one of the dependent variables, the official measurement methods and criteria outlined by the Korean Government are employed. Unaffordable housing, the other dependent variable, is measured on whether a household spends 30% or more of its income on housing expenses. Housing expenses include loan interest (if property is purchased with bank loans or non-financial firm loans) and maintenance costs like heating and lighting. For renters, housing expenses include monthly payments and loan interest (if the deposit is paid with bank loans or non-financial firm loans) as well as maintenance costs like heating and lighting.

The demographic-socioeconomic status of a household is measured as follow: Firstly, value 1 is assigned to female householders and value 0 to male householders. The age of the householder is based on the age of the survey year (i.e. 2016). As for the education level, value 1 is assigned to elementary school graduates or below, 2 to middle school graduates, 3 to high school and 4 to university graduates or higher. Disabled householders are assigned value 1 and non-disabled householders are assigned value 0. National basic livelihood recipients are assigned value 1 and non-recipients value 0. Household income is converted to natural logarithm. The number of family members is based on the number of family members who actually lived together in 2016. Homeowners are assigned value 0 and non-owners were assigned value 1.

Regional characteristics are measured as follow: Firstly, the price of housing in a given area is calculated as a median price of the prices of the current residences. Urban areas are assigned value 1 and rural areas are assigned value 0. Ratio of public rental housing in a given area is calculated by dividing public rental housing registered on MOLIT Statistics System in 2014 by total housing in the area, and then the value is converted to natural logarithm. Public rental houses include permanent rental, 50-year rental, 30-year rental, 10-year rental, 5-year rental, employee rental house, long-term lease and charter rental houses. The median monthly rent of the area is measured by the median rent of the rented houses in the Korean Housing Survey 2016. In order to ensure the representativeness of the sample, this study uses the population weights suggested by KHS 2016. But it is adjusted to avoid the underestimation of standard error which results when population weight is amplified too high so that it surpasses the actual number of the sample.

Descriptive statistics of KHS 2016 data

The table below shows the characteristics of the sample taken from KHS 2016. 24% of householders are female and the average householder age is 52. The average householder has a high school diploma. About 4% of householders are disabled and approximately 4% are national basic livelihood act recipients. The average monthly income of households is about KRW 2 870 000. The average household consists of 2.52 members. 43% of households rent their homes. The median housing price is approximately KRW 248.34 million. The median monthly rent is KRW 279 000. 93% of the respondents live in urban areas and the proportion of public housing to total housing is 7% on average. About 5.4% of total households do not meet the minimum housing standards. Lastly, about 14% of households are classed as unaffordable housing.

Level	Variable	Explanation	Average
Demographic-socioeconomic factor	Householder's gender	Female (1)	24%
	Householder's age	Age (in 2016)	52.4
	Householder's educational level	Elementary school or below (1), middle school (2), high school (3), university or above (4)	3.03
	Householder disability	Disabled (1)	4%
	Basic Livelihood recipients	Recipient (1)	4%
	Household income	Monthly average household income for the past year in 10 000 KRW (unnatural log)	287.2
	Size of household	Actual number of people who live together	2.52
	Home ownership	Lack of home ownership (1)	43%

Regional factor	House price (median)	Area's median house price (2016) in KRW 10 000	24,834
	Urbanisation	Urban (1)	93%
	Ratio of public rental Housing	Number of district's long, short-term public rental houses / total number of houses	7%
	Monthly rent (median)	District's median monthly rent in 10 000 KRW	27.9
Housing welfare	Substandard housing	The measurement of MOLIT (1)	5.40%
	Housing affordability	Housing expense-to-income ratio 30% or above (1)	14%

Source: Author's calculation based on data of Korea Housing Survey 2016.

2. Enhancing Korea's housing welfare policy

This chapter looks at the major elements of housing welfare policy in Korea. It begins with an exploration of housing looking at national welfare policies, their objectives and tools as they focus on the low-income households as their target population. This is followed by an examination of the Korean public housing system and its different schemes to provide low cost housing to a wide variety of social groups such as newlyweds, young people, the elderly, and low-income families. It analyses the programmes intended to facilitate access to private rental housing. A major section focuses on the different policy alternatives that Korea may follow to overcome the challenges and vulnerabilities of the housing welfare system. It covers issues such as regulation, management, the institutional framework and housing finance. Overall, the chapter emphasises the need for a network of housing providers and the consolidation of the housing programmes.

The New Urban Agenda stresses people's right to adequate housing as a component of the right to an adequate standard of living, without discrimination which contributes to fulfil the social function of cities (UN-Habitat, 2016[1]). Sustainable Development Goal 11 on making cities and human settlements inclusive, safe, resilient and sustainable has as a target for 2030 ensuring access for all to adequate, safe and affordable housing and basic services and upgrading slums.[1] Korea's current housing welfare policy seems to be in line with this objective through the strengthening of public rental housing. The country has made significant progress in the quality and quantity of housing units. It has adopted a diversity of types of public rental schemes targeting different groups of the population but giving priority to low-income households and young people.

2.1. Housing policy direction – facing the social and affordable housing challenge

Access to good quality, affordable housing is a fundamental component of quality of life. This is important for promoting a number of social policy objectives such as poverty reduction, equal opportunities, and social inclusion. In the majority of OECD countries 1-8 people in every 1000 lack regular access to housing, 15% of low-income people live in overcrowded dwellings and 14% do not have access to an indoor flushing toilet (Salvi del Pero et al., 2016[2]). During the past decade, in several OECD countries the number of applicants for social housing has increased reflecting declines in housing affordability associated with increases in real house prices (Andrews, Caldera Sánchez and Johansson, 2011[3]). It is therefore one of the most pressing concerns in Korea where, despite progress in housing quality and provision, housing costs are still a burden for many low-income families.

2.1.1. Ensuring access to good quality, affordable housing is a national policy objective

Housing affordability has been a vital policy concern in Korea for the past two decades. Young households, the elderly, and low-income households are particularly affected by soaring house prices, especially in Seoul Metropolitan Area. The country reports a stagnant home ownership rate at around mid-50% on average over the last two decades (Park, 2017). This is in contrast with the large investment in housing construction which accounts for 7% of GDP compared with 3-5% in most OECD countries (Ronald and Jin, 2010, p. 2369[4]). Housing prices have been increasing by 2.2% annually since 2014 (adjusted by inflation) (OECD, 2016, p. 19[5]). Households in the private rental market have faced a heavy housing cost burden and have found it difficult to become homeowners without support from the government (Kim and Park, 2016). Although people in Korea spend on average 16% of their annual gross adjusted disposable household income on housing, which is below the OECD average of 20% (see Chapter 1), increasing access to good quality, affordable housing is an important social policy objective for the country. Housing costs typically take up a sizeable proportion of household budgets. Low and middle-income households are experiencing a heavier housing cost burden due to higher jeonsei (lump sum refundable payment for rental) prices and a shift to wolse (monthly rental scheme). Indeed, rent to income ratio (RIR) has risen from 18.7% in 2006 to 20.3% in 2014. The share of wolse in the total volume of jeonsei and wolse passed from 34% in 2012 to 44% in 2015 (see Chapter 1). In Korea, there is the perception that housing prices are too high relative to income compared to other countries. However, based on the house price-income ratio, researchers concluded that housing in Korea is not less affordable than in most other countries, nor is Seoul among the most expensive metropolitan cities in the world (Kim and Park, 2016, p. 9[6]).

To ensure that low-income households have access to good quality, affordable housing, the Korean government is focusing on strengthening the social rental market. As Figure 2.1 shows, the national government has a leading role in the provision of social rental housing with limited participation of the regional and municipal authorities and the private sector. Non-profit organisations have no role in the provision of social rental housing in Korea. Across OECD countries, in comparison, the social housing stock is predominantly public-owned, directly by local governments or through municipal housing companies. In some countries non-profit organisations own a significant proportion of social dwellings (e.g. the Netherlands, Austria, Denmark, the United Kingdom, Ireland and the United States), while private owners are frequent in the United States, France, and Spain (Andrews, Caldera Sánchez and Johansson, 2011[3]).

Figure 2.1. Providers of social rental housing

Share of total social rental housing stock by type of providers, 2015 or latest year available.

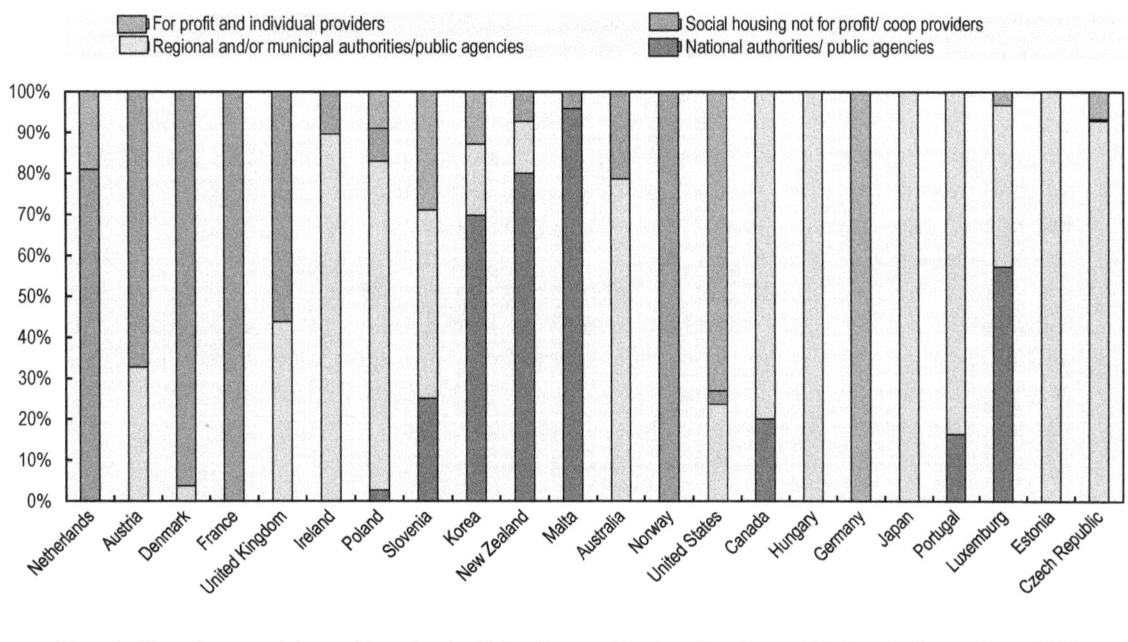

Note: 1. There is no social rental housing in Chile, Greece, Mexico, Sweden and Turkey.2. Data refer to 2011 for Canada, Hungary, Ireland, Luxemburg and Malta; 2012 for Germany; 2013 for Denmark, Estonia, Japan and Poland; 2014 for Australia, Austria, France, Norway and the United Kingdom.
Source: OECD, Questionnaire on Affordable Social Housing 2016 www.oecd.org/social/affordable-housing-database.htm.

Korea, like other OECD countries such as Chile, the Czech Republic, Finland, France, Japan, Luxembourg, Mexico and the Netherlands, has a centralised housing system. However, national programmes are usually implemented in close co-operation with local authorities, for example housing allowances and social rental housing. In other countries such as Austria and Germany, responsibility for housing policy measures is almost entirely devolved to the regions/states. In the United Kingdom, housing policy measures are the responsibility of devolved administrations. In Switzerland most housing policy measures are organised differently in the different cantons.

2.1.2. Strong demand, geographical constraints and extensive land use regulations may be leading to high house prices in urban areas

One of the key issues in Korean housing policy discussion is why, despite the considerable increase in the housing stock, housing prices are not affordable to many citizens. It is clear that for the Korean government, speculation is partly the cause of rising house prices. The government has therefore adopted a number of measures to fight speculation such as the 2017 Housing Market Stability Measures (known as the "8.2 measures") which aim to stabilise the housing market by designating some districts in Seoul and Sejong as speculation restriction zones (apartment prices have risen 3.13% in Seoul in 2017[2]). The aim of these measures is to keep demand within supply by imposing higher capital gains taxes on multiple homeowners as well as restricting mortgages.

In Korea, the national government has almost full control over the housing supply, as it is the only supplier of land for residential use and has the highest share of the supply of housing credit (Park and Xiao, 2009[7]). The scarcity of developable land for residential purposes is more acute in urban areas such as Seoul. However, it is worth noting that Seoul Metropolitan Area (SMA) has the highest share of housing construction (see Chapter 1). The problem is that the green belt in the city of Seoul takes up to 50% of its developable land. Controlling the growth of the SMA, which represents 11% of Korea's territory and accommodates almost 50% of the national population, remains a top priority for the government. Thus, rigid supply due to the large number of land use regulations and concentrated demand is giving room for speculation (Park and Xiao, 2009[7]). A similar situation has been experienced in London where strong demand in conjunction with geographical constraints and a rigid planning system are seen as the origin of high house prices (Hilber and Vermeulen, 2016[8]). In Korea, this context gave origin to the jeonsei rental contract which is an interest-free loan from the tenant to the landlord in exchange for the use of the landlord's property (see below). Park and Xiao (2009) suggest that the large number of renters implies substantial numbers of multiple homeowners as some owners use the jeonsei deposit to invest in additional homes.

The "8.2 measures" to control speculation may lead owners of multiple homes to consider whether they should sell their assets to avoid heavier taxes, and those who plan to buy a home may take a wait-and-see approach. People who recently bought a property may also be concerned about the possibility of falling house prices. It is worth noting that the measures do not include any land use reform to allow an orderly and planned supply of housing. Moreover, limited financing options and negative perception towards public rental housing complexes accommodating low-income people are making it difficult to meet housing welfare demand with the supply of public rental housing alone.

2.1.3. Korea disposes of a wide set of housing policy tools

Ensuring affordable housing requires a wide set of policy tools. Korea has a wide set of instruments to implement its housing policy that covers different dimensions: planning, financial, land supply, legal, institutional etc. (Table 2.1). Land use policies and planning are critical to understanding constraints to access to affordable housing. The 2015 Comprehensive Housing Plan for Residential Stabilisation (CHP) is the central policy document on housing as it sets the targets for housing construction for a 10-year period but is revised every 5 years. It also guides the Annual Action Housing Plan, contains estimates of the demand and supply of housing, and sets the vision for the housing sector.

Table 2.1. Major components of Korea's housing policy

Policy tools	Components
Plan	Comprehensive housing plan
	Housing welfare roadmap
	Public rental housing provision plan
	Minimum housing standards
Financial	National Housing Fund
	Budget, loan, subsidy
Legal	Housing Benefit Act
	Public Housing Promotion Production Act
	Housing Act
Land supply	Service land with affordable price infrastructure
	Social mix
Regulation	Price ceiling
	Minimum occupation period
	Anti-speculation measures
Institutional	Land and Housing Corporation
	Local Housing Corporation
	Housing Guarantee Corporation

Source: Park, Miseon (2017), *Evolution of Housing Policy in Korea*, KRIHS, Colloquium on Housing, Urban Regeneration and Smart City Policies for Inclusive Growth. Presentation given to the OECD.

In 2015 the CHP aimed to complete the construction of 343 000 homes, of which 88 000 were public homes. That same year the CHP planned to provide a total of 120 000 public rental homes, of which 70 000 were newly constructed, 15 000 rental homes (12 000 existing homes and 3 000 reconstructed) and 35 000 jeonsei rental homes. The number of public rental homes has fluctuated since 2005 with a record low in 2012 (only 56 000 public rental homes) and a record high in 2015 (Figure 2.2). In addition, 205 000 households received low interest-rate deposit on rentals and purchasing funds. The current CHP aims to support up to 1.26 million households through public rental housing (120 000), financial support – housing fund – (205 000), housing vouchers (970 000).

Figure 2.2. Public rental housing in Korea, 2005-2015

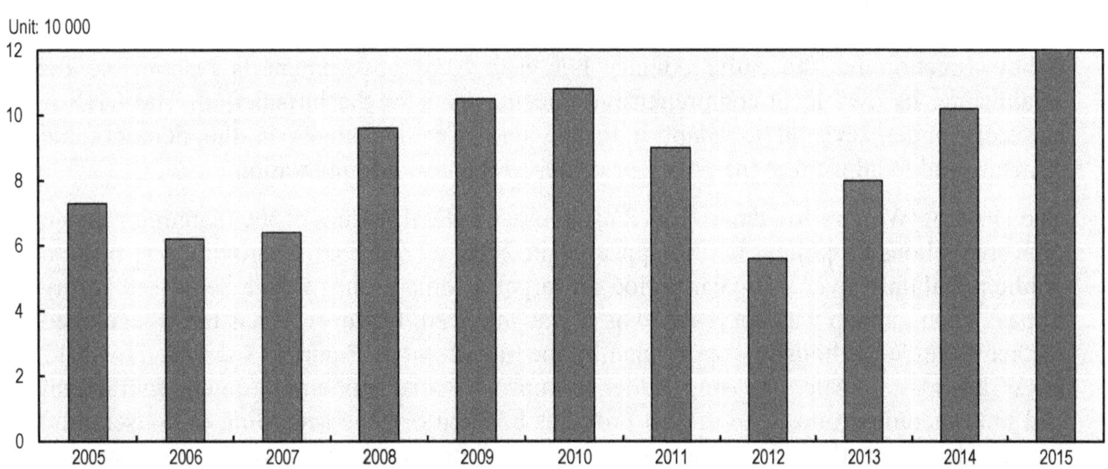

Source: Based on: www.korea.net/koreanet/print.

The CHP also includes measures to improve residential environments and maintenance management. For example, there is work on the enactment of the public housing management act to settle disputes related to public housing and better manage public housing support; distribute public housing diagnosis manuals and make maintenance activities including external audit transparent; and establish standards for public housing exhaust installation to reduce housing energy consumption (construction of zero-energy housing complexes, etc.), and implement the certification system for longevity housing. The CHP also includes provisions for the improvement of old housing environments through the renovation of old public housing, and the improvement of the public management system.

2.1.4. The comprehensive housing plan and the housing welfare roadmap provide long-term policy direction

The Comprehensive Housing Plan (CHP) and the Housing Welfare Roadmap are Korea's main housing policy documents. Based on section 7 of the Housing Law, the government has to establish long-term housing plans every ten years in consideration of the housing market conditions as well as the economic situation.

The second Comprehensive Housing Plan 2013-2022 sets the goal of housing policy, and dictates the sectoral strategies to achieve the objectives.[3] It has five dimensions to respond to the changes of the housing market situation, socio-economic conditions, demographic shift, urban land use pattern, and housing preferences. The dimensions are: i) seamless housing safety net as a welfare policy focusing on vulnerable households; ii) community and residents-focused living environment; iii) maintenance of existing housing stock and enhancing housing quality; iv) needs-based provision of housing units in urban areas rather than a large production on the outskirts of cities; and v) increased risk management for the housing market and financial system. The CHP allocates public rental units across the country based on the estimated demand. According to the CHP, central government should provide serviced residential land to build dwelling units by public and private homebuilders. Moreover, the CHP provides the housing outlook for the target year. For example, it is projected that long-term rental units will increase from 930 000 in 2012 to 1.9 million units in 2022, housing units per thousand inhabitants will rise from 364 units in 2010 to 422 in 2022, and the percentage of households residing within substandard units will drop from 10.6% in 2010 to 5% in 2022 (MOLIT, 2013[9]). The CHP provides policy direction for the entire country but each local government is responsible for establishing its own local comprehensive housing plan for the jurisdiction. The CHP is currently under revision to adapt it to the unexpected changes in the demographic structure and to adjust it to the policy priorities of the new administration.

The Housing Welfare Roadmap (HWR) is another critical feature of the planning scheme of Korea's housing policy. It first appeared in 2003 with a plan to provide one million public rental units over a 10-year period for target income groups with a decreased ability to pay. The roadmap was not realised as it was intended; however, it has been developed further to guide the housing supply plan by income group as Figure 2.3 shows. The 2017 HRW intends to create a housing ladder to improve social mix among inter-generational and inter-income groups (Box 2.1). It provides housing options according to households' income levels, and divides the target groups into would-be owners, renters, and vulnerable groups. Small-size and heavily subsidised public rental units are allocated for the poorest tenants considering their ability to pay.

Figure 2.3. Korea's housing supply plan by income group (2009-2018)

<table>
<tr><th>Target</th><th colspan="3">Establishing housing safety net</th><th colspan="3">Promote home ownership</th><th colspan="4">Stablise housing prices</th></tr>
<tr><td>Income percentile</td><td>10%</td><td>20%</td><td>30%</td><td>40%</td><td>50%</td><td>60%</td><td>70%</td><td>80%</td><td>90%</td><td>100%</td></tr>
<tr><td>Needs</td><td colspan="2">Cannot afford rent</td><td colspan="2">Cannot afford purchase</td><td colspan="2">Can afford purchase with government aid</td><td colspan="4">Can afford purchase and has replacement demand</td></tr>
<tr><td rowspan="3">Housing supply for sale</td><td rowspan="3"></td><td rowspan="3"></td><td rowspan="2"></td><td colspan="3">Multi-family and detached housing (1 million)</td><td colspan="4">Private mid-largesale (2 million) (improved regulations)</td></tr>
<tr><td></td><td colspan="2">Private mid-small sale (400 000). Land and fund support, etc)</td><td rowspan="2"></td><td rowspan="2"></td><td rowspan="2"></td><td rowspan="2"></td></tr>
<tr><td colspan="3">Public sale (700 000)</td><td></td></tr>
<tr><td rowspan="3">Rental housing</td><td></td><td></td><td colspan="3">Public rental housing (300 000) (shared ownership, Jeonsei)</td><td>Private rental housing (100 000)</td><td rowspan="3"></td><td rowspan="3"></td><td rowspan="3"></td><td rowspan="3"></td></tr>
<tr><td></td><td colspan="3">National Rental Housing (40 000)</td><td rowspan="2"></td><td rowspan="2"></td></tr>
<tr><td>Permanent Rental Housing (100 000)</td><td></td><td></td><td></td></tr>
<tr><td>Supplier</td><td colspan="3">Mainly public sector</td><td colspan="3">Public + Private</td><td colspan="4">Mainly private</td></tr>
<tr><td>Public support</td><td colspan="3">Budget, housing fund, land</td><td colspan="3">Housing fund, land</td><td colspan="4">Improved regulation</td></tr>
<tr><td>Size</td><td colspan="3">Up to 60m2</td><td colspan="3">60 - 85m2</td><td colspan="4">More than 85m2</td></tr>
</table>

Source: (KDI School, 2012[10]).

Box 2.1. Korea's Housing Welfare Roadmap

The 2017 Housing Welfare Roadmap (HWR) acknowledges the problems citizens face in becoming homeowners, the lack of regulations in the private housing market, and the insufficient housing supply for young people, newlyweds and the elderly, as well as the weak governance arrangements across levels of government and between the public and private sectors.

The HWR aims to create a "housing ladder" to improve social cohesion and to facilitate the transition from low to middle-income groups and for newlyweds to start a family. For that purpose, the public sector is expected to adopt a package of housing benefits such as public rental housing supply, financial support and other welfare services. The HWR intends to supply housing welfare solutions based on the life-cycle and income level of the target groups.

- For young people, the government will provide 300 000 rooms within five years. Young people under 29 years old and with a yearly income of less than KRW 30 million will be able to open a housing subscription deposit account benefiting from high interest rates and tax cuts. The age for obtaining a jeonsei deposit loan has been lowered from 25 to 19 years of age.
- For newlyweds, over the next five years the government will provide 200 000 public rental housing units including "Happy Housing". Newlyweds will be able to benefit from a customised financial support programme, lower interest rates (up to 0.35% lower than usual), and a low interest jeonsei deposit loan.
- For the elderly, 50 000 customised public rental housing units will be provided over five years. A rental housing pension scheme is introduced by which the Korea Land and Housing Corporation (LH) buys homes owned by the elderly making them eligible to live in public rental housing receiving monthly instalments over the course of 10 or 20 years which correspond to the price of the property.
- For the low-income group, the government intends to build 410 000 public rental units over the next five years.

Source: (MOLIT, 2017[11]).

2.1.5. Housing welfare policy focuses on the supply of rental housing

For those who cannot afford their own homes, public rental housing has played a significant role in providing decent units with affordable rent, particularly for the extremely low to low-income households. More recently, the major concern of housing policy is placed on housing welfare for the underprivileged and the emerging target groups such as the younger generation, single-person households, and newlyweds. Thus, the Korean government has strong initiatives to provide a significant amount of housing units as well as diverse types of public rental units to meet the needs of the specific target groups.

Korea's housing welfare policy focus has shifted from a quantitative expansion of public rental housing to ensuring a sustainable supply of rental housing. This involves the diversification of support measures such as private rental and expanding housing benefits. During the previous administration there was an annual supply of 110 000 units for public rental housing; efforts focused on the acceleration of private rental supply (deregulation and land/fund/tax assistance), and there was greater support for young adults and newlyweds ("Happy Housing", jeonsei rental housing, and special housing supply for newlyweds). In terms of financial support, the previous administration introduced housing benefits for low-income households (810 000 households, KRW 115 000) and low-rate loans to finance jeonse, wolse and house purchase (200 000 households per year). As Figure 2.4 suggests, public spending on supporting social rental housing in Korea has an upwards trend. Among OECD countries Korea has the highest level of public spending on social rental housing as a percentage of GDP. Low levels of support do not necessarily mean that the social rental sector is small. This can be the result of reliance on other forms of support such as housing allowances.

Figure 2.4. Recent trends in public spending on supporting social rental housing in selected OECD countries

Public spending on supporting social rental housing in selected OECD countries, % of GDP (2013, 2015)

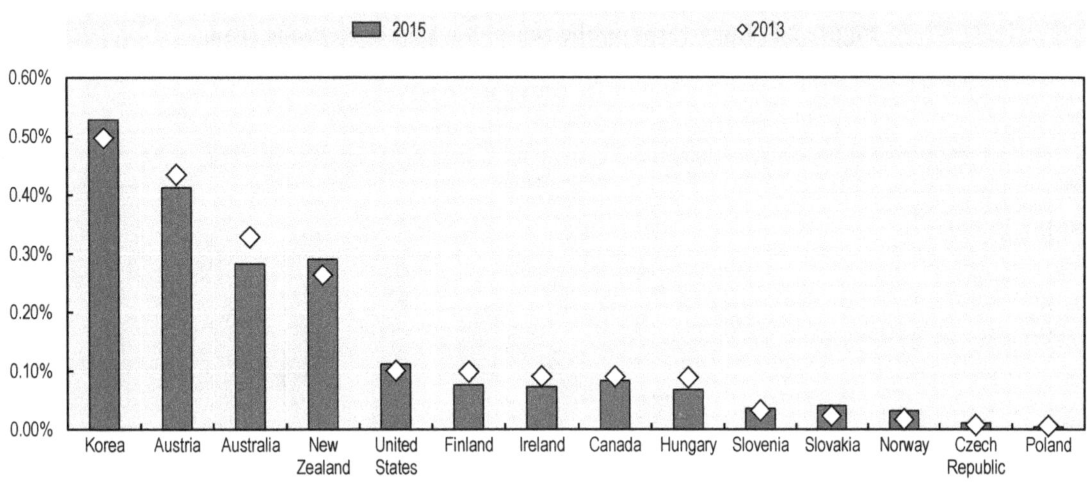

Note: Figures refer to central government spending only, with the exception of Australia, Austria and Korea where funding at regional level is included.
Source: OECD Questionnaire on Affordable Social Housing (2014, 2016) www.oecd.org/social/affordable-housing-database.htm.

Public housing in Korea is defined as that constructed with the support of public housing funds and with government subsidy; rentals are below market rates and target low-income households (Table 2.2). Public housing has two tenure types: public for-sale and public rental. Although public rental is regarded as the most appropriate tenure type for low-income people, its provision has been limited. Only "permanent rental housing" and "national rental housing" can be classified as social housing in Korea (Lim, 2006[12]).

Table 2.2. Definition of public housing in Korea

Finance	Government subsidy	+	Loan supported by HUF (Housing and Urban Fund)
Rent regulation	Below-market rent		
Eligibility rule	Low-income households		

Note: The loan supported by HUF is for buying a property.
Source: Presentation given by the Korea Land and Housing Institute to the OECD.

According to MOLIT the long-term rental housing inventory has been steadily rising over the last decade as Figure 2.5 shows. However, the share of long-term public rental housing represented only 6.3% of total housing in 2016, below the OECD average (8%) (MOLIT, 2017, p. 1[11]). Through the HWR, Korea aims to increase the share of public rental housing to 9% by 2022. Interestingly, in recent years, an increasing number of households have chosen to rent private homes although they are capable of purchasing one (Kim & Park, 2016).

Figure 2.5. Long-term public rental housing in Korea is rising

10 000 units

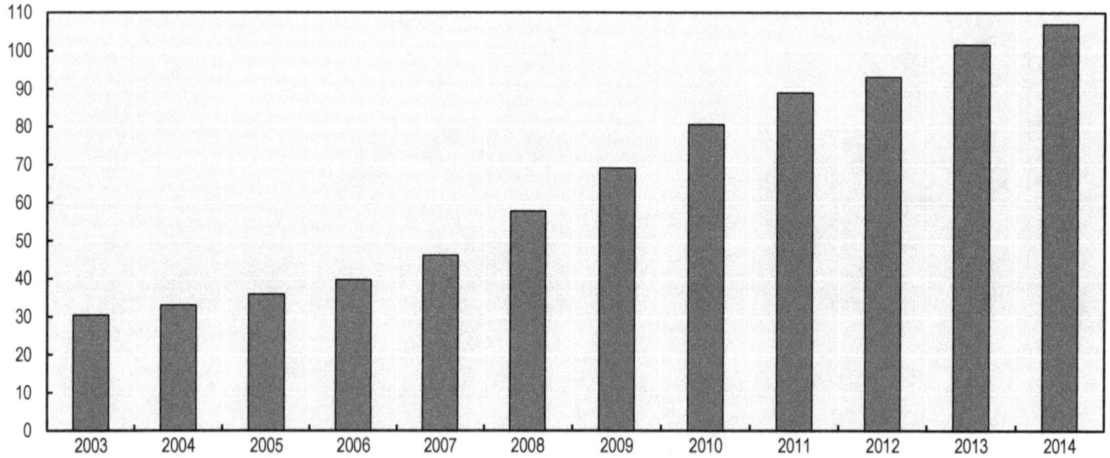

Source: Information provided by the Korean Ministry of Land, Infrastructure and Transport.

2.1.6. Housing welfare targets rental housing for low-income households

The Korean government seems to be committed to a housing welfare policy oriented towards directly addressing the needs of low-income people. This is in contrast with past approaches when government tried to enable the market to provide low-cost housing. The reason is that despite past efforts to improve the housing conditions of low-income households, they still suffer from housing poverty in terms of housing stability, affordability and quality. Korea's social housing system can be described as a targeted system as it operates separately from the private rental market and only households for which the market is deemed unable to deliver housing will benefit from it. In this system, housing is allocated to eligible tenants based on income thresholds via a waiting list system with consideration given to the priority rating of tenants; in some countries greater emphasis is placed on the needs of the most vulnerable (Andrews, Caldera Sánchez and Johansson, 2011[3]).

For many years, Korean housing policy focused exclusively on the general objective of building as many units of good quality housing as allocated funds would permit (Lim, 2006, p. 25[12]). A similar approach was followed in Mexico during the 2000s but did not address the housing shortage and created additional urban problems (OECD, 2015[13]). Housing programmes in Korea have been evolving over the last decades (Table 1.3). In general, those programmes have been providing direct financial assistance to tenants from low and middle-income households and home buyers. Korean authorities have typically utilised three types of subsidies for different income groups to provide homes and/or to relieve rent burdens by: i) providing public housing for renting and owner occupation as a conventional and direct method, ii) providing housing benefits as demand-side assistance, and iii) providing low-interest loans for jeonsei support. The lowest income group is eligible for at least one of the subsidies. Of the lowest income group, almost 20% live in public rental housing, 33% borrow a jeonsei deposit loan, and over 50% receive the housing benefit (Kim & Park, 2016).

Table 2.3. Evolution of housing programmes by target group in Korea

Income bracket	1988 – 1992 (Two million project)		2003 - 2007 (Housing welfare roadmap)		2005 - 2012		2013 to present	
1 Extremely low	Permanent PRH		National PRH (small size)	Housing benefit	Permanent PRH	Housing benefit	Permanent PRH	Housing benefit (new)
2 Low	Long-term PRH		National PRH	Loans for jeonsei deposit	National PRH		National PRH jeonsei rental Purchase Lease	
3 Middle low		Small- size for sale units				For-sale (public) units		Loan for jeonsei / MRD deposit
4								
5 Middle		Middle- size for sale units	Small- size for sale units			PRH	PRH (Happy Housing)	Private rental (New stay)
6						Private rental		
7 High					Private market, mortgage programmes			

Note: MRD: monthly rental deposit, PRH: subsidised public rental housing.
Source: Based on (Kim and Park, 2016, p. 19[6]).

2.1.7. There is a large discrepancy between homeownership and owner-occupancy

Despite the government's focus on home purchase and the extensive home building projects conducted over decades, the level of homeownership is just above 60% which is comparable with other countries such as France, Japan, the United Kingdom and the United States (Kim and Park, 2016[6]). However, the owner occupancy level is significantly lower at 53% according to MOLIT (see Chapter 1). The reason for this discrepancy is the separation of residence and ownership in Korea. At least until 2010, 40% of the housing stock was occupied by owners, but 61% of households owned at least one home. Over 20% of renters owned homes somewhere else. Since the public rental sector accommodates only 7.8% of households, about 38% of households live in the extra homes owned by other individuals (Kim & Park, 2016, pp. 10-11). The problem is that not all renters can be classified as those who require attention since a substantial part of them chose to rent although they could afford to buy homes if they wished. They could also increase the amount of the deposit on the units they lease out to finance the increase in the deposits on the units in which they reside. This sometimes creates pressures on the jeonsei deposit (Kim & Park, 2016). It is not uncommon in Korea to own a property but actually live in a rented one, sometimes for economic reasons or for the convenience of being closer to the workplace.

Although government policy has focused on promoting home ownership, the characteristics of the system have actually slowed this process. Previous housing policies have assumed that increases in the housing stock would resolve the access to housing. However, in the case of Korea, increases in the housing stock have not been matched by growth in owner-occupied rates. The housing system has become imbalanced by the rapid growth of multiple property ownership among wealthier homeowners, as well as volatile house prices (Ronald and Jin, 2010, p. 2368[4]). Underdevelopment of housing finance and mortgage provision, the government's anti-speculation measures, a tax system that does not adequately target low and middle-income households, and the structure of the public and private rental markets are factors that have constrained home ownership. Banks are not providing adequate loans and until recently long-term fixed-rate interests were not provided. Ronald and Jin (2010[4]) suggest that the failure to advance home ownership among broader classes of income groups may well be the reason why demands for increases in housing welfare have been particularly intense in Korea. Taxation has not incentivised home ownership either. Buying, selling or owning a home requires paying numerous taxes (e.g. acquisition tax, registration tax, property tax, comprehensive real estate tax, and capital gains tax) which are disincentives for home ownership.

2.1.8. Housing policy measures are indirectly linked to demographic trends

According to MOLIT, there is currently greater demand for housing welfare due to a low birth rate and ageing population. The composition of households has also changed as the share of one person households rose from 4.8% in 1980 to 24% in 2010, and the share of 5 or more person households fell from 50% to 8.1% in the same period.[4] Indeed, in Korea like in most OECD countries, the size of households has generally been diminishing over time, because of a reduction in the number of children per family, increasing numbers of lone-parent families, and an ageing population accompanied by improved autonomy of elderly people. As a result, the number of households has tended to increase faster than the population, contributing to the increase in housing demand (André, 2010, p. 23[14]). Affordability is also affected by the size of households.

In the coming years, the housing agenda aims to alleviate the housing cost burden for young people, newlyweds, and multi-child families by: i) supplying and providing maintenance of public rental housing (200 000 units for public rental housing annually), ii) enhancing the coverage of housing allowance, iii) improving the regulation of the private rental market; and iv) increasing loans for both rental housing and housing for purchase (Presidential Office, 2017). Homes will be customised for newlyweds (tailored housing design and proximity to childcare centres). In addition, the government will promote home rental for newlyweds with a greater supply of homes in city centres. Families with multiple children will have priority access to larger homes through the National Rental Housing scheme (five or ten-year rental).

The government has developed financial instruments directed to support newlyweds such as higher loan limits, and better interest rates when borrowing money for the jeonsei or wolse. In addition, Korea plans to ease housing cost burdens on young adults by: i) supplying 200 000 units – public and private rental – in mass transit areas and near universities or industrial complexes; ii) providing 50 000 shared-housing units for young adults (sharing spaces such as kitchens) through the reconstruction or remodelling of old buildings; iii) expanding university dormitory capacity by 50 000 units; and iv) conducting the pilot construction of SOHO clusters (public rental housing model with the combination of start-up facilities and services) in university neighbourhoods.[5]

2.2. The Korean public housing system

Providing public rental housing for low to middle-income households has been an integral element of Korea's housing policy since the "Two Million Housing Drive" (TMHD). The TMHD, a milestone of the country's housing policy, was developed as a housing supply plan dictated by income group. In executing the housing supply plan, the government created permanent rental housing for those in the lowest income bracket by utilising the government budget along with the NHUF.

2.2.1. Korea has a unique and complex public rental system

In Korea, public rental housing refers to the rental housing units that are built, purchased, or leased with funding from the government, the NHUF, or the assistance of public land acquisition. The focus of Korean housing policy has shifted over time from owner-occupied to renter-occupied housing and from the production of private-sector housing to public rental housing. To facilitate the production of public rental housing, the government prepared a legal basis with new legislations, established a public agency to supply housing, set up public funds, and established a planning system to specify the policy target. Legislation efforts started in 1984 with the passing of the Public Rental Housing Construction Promotion Act.

Private rental housing is built by private companies without public assistance and requires a leasing term of at least five years. There is no limit to the size of properties and the eligibility criteria is set by the lessor. Public rental housing units are built with funding from the central or municipal government, the NHUF or public land acquisition assistance, and the housing built by the private sector if financial support is provided from the government or the NHUF. Public rental is a complex modality as it has different types of housing each with different eligibility criteria, varying levels of government subsidies and financial support, and different lease periods (see Table 2.4). The reason for the diversity of schemes is to effectively tackle the housing needs of socially vulnerable groups of different income levels (mainly disabled, low-income households, and welfare-dependent families). Each type of public housing has a different policy target group with a different income level.

Table 2.4. Korea's public housing system

		Young-gu (Permanent)	Kookmin (National Rental)	5-year rental	10-year rental		Buy to lease (Existing rental)	Rent to lease (Existing rental)
					Below 85m²	Over 85m²		
Target		Low-income (1-2 decile)	Low-income (under 4 decile)	Under 8 decile Support home ownership	Under 8 decile Support home ownership	8-9 decile Support home ownership	Low income (1-2 decile)	Low income (1-2 decile)
Provider		LH, Local Authority	LH, Local Authority	LH, Local Authority, Private company	LH, Local Authority, Private company	LH, Local Authority, Private company	LH, Local Authority	LH, Local Authority
Rental period		50 years	30 years	5 years	10 years	10 years	20 years (1)	20 years (1)
Housing size		Below 40m²	Below 60m²	Below 85m²	Below 85m²	Below 149m²	Below 85m²	Below 85m²
Applicants		People who receive basic living security	Below 70% of average monthly income	People who have a subscription deposit	People who have a subscription deposit	People who have a subscription deposit	People who receive basic living security	People who receive basic living security
		Men of national merit					Single parent family	Single parent family
Rental condition		30% of market price	60-80% of market price	90% of market price	90% of market price	Below market price	30-40% of market price	5% of deposit (jeonsei)
Sales		Not permitted	Not permitted	After 5 years Sale to resident	After 10 years Sale to resident	After 10 years Sale to resident	Not permitted	Impossible (private rental)
Finance	Government subsidy	85%	30%				45%	
	HUG		40% (IR3%)	~60m² 55M Won (IR 3%) 60-85m² 75M Won (IR 4%)	~60m2 55M Won (IR 3%) 60-85m² 75M Won (IR 4%)		50% (IR1%)	95% (IR 1-2%) SMR areas 80M Won, other 50-60M Won
	LH	12.50%	20%			100%		
	Residence	2.50%	10%				5%	5%

Note: (1) Most rental housing period is based on the type of building. IR: interest rate.
Source: Ministry of Land, Infrastructure and Transport of Korea.

There are more than 20 types of public rental housing in Korea. Depending on the type of securement, they are construction, acquisition and jeonsei-based rental. The different schemes include:

- *Permanent rental housing (Young-gu)*: This was introduced to alleviate the housing conditions of the urban poor and control housing instability. In the late 1980s, as part of the TMHD, the government announced a construction plan for permanent rental housing units for the lowest income group. Out of 2 million units, 0.9 million were allocated to low-income households. Of the 0.9 million units, 250 000 units were set aside as permanent rental housing for households in the lowest income bracket who depend on the national living allowance. To ensure affordability for the tenants of permanent rental housing, more than 85% of the construction funds came from the government budget and the rest from the residents. Rental prices are usually a quarter of market prices. The unit size was set relatively small, ranging from 23-39m². This type of rental housing has not been built since the 1990s due to heavy financial burdens for the government.

- *50-year rental housing*: This was introduced to complement permanent rental housing with the purpose of relieving the financial burden on central government. A combined 100 007 units were built from 1992 to 1997. Half of the budget came from central government, 20% from the National Housing Fund (NHF), 10% from the construction agency, and 20% from the tenants. Eligible tenants were people with housing subscription savings, veterans, or residents evicted from demolished homes that were classified as special provision cases. The average size of a housing unit ranged from $23m^2$ to $49.5m^2$. The leasing contract could be renewed every two years, but purchase of the home was not allowed. The number of public rental housing units with 50-year leases decreased when the state financial support stopped in 1994 and from then onwards, 70% of the budget came from the funds and the rest from tenants.

- *National rental housing (kookmin)*: This was introduced in 1998 when the Korean economy and real estate market were in the middle of the country's worst recession under the supervision of the International Monetary Fund (IMF). The aim was to alleviate mass unemployment and housing shortage for the low-income population with a 10-year lease national public rental housing. The Kim Dae-Jung administration (1998-2003) aimed to build 500 000 rental housing units. But the economic crisis led the government to reduce the target to 50 000 units. However, due to high demand for affordable rental housing for low-income groups, the government built public rental housing units with 10 and 20-year leases. National public rental housing encompassed not only the newly built units but also the purchased rental units in the private housing market, as well as the newly built units purchased from the unsold apartments. The programme had a 30-year mandatory period to serve those whose income levels fell to the second to fourth deciles and who were unable to purchase their own homes without support.

- *10-year and 5-year rental housing*: This type of public rental housing was introduced to attract private participation in the market. The target population was households who could not afford to purchase homes immediately but could save the money to do so over several years. The plan raised expectations of increased home ownership and enhanced collaboration with the private sector. The Five-year Public Rental Housing Programme, which started after the enactment of the Act on Promotion of Rental Housing Construction, was continued mainly by private builders who used government loans for their projects. Such units required a leasing period of at least five years and could be sold to the tenants after that period. Eligible tenants had to be non-homeowners who had housing subscription savings. The NHF provided loans depending on the unit size. The goal was to stabilise the housing situation of low-income residents. However, only a few low-income households could afford to live there for a long period since the units were converted into for-sale after the mandatory lease period of ten or five years. Nowadays, this rental type is no longer regarded as long-term public rental units in Korea because they are eventually sold to the tenants. However, it is a system that provides an attractive way to become owner-occupiers for low to middle-income households.
- *Employee rental*: In this scheme, industrial companies buy properties at subsidised prices and then rent them to their employees. In 1990, a state-initiated system for such housing was implemented to stabilise the living environment of

workers. Initially, those who worked for companies in manufacturing, transportation or cleaning with more than ten employees and whose families did not own homes could apply for this type of rental housing. Eventually, the qualification standards were gradually eased to accommodate more residents. The programme was implemented by the LH, local public corporations, private builders and employers. The mandatory rental period is five years.

- *Purchased rental housing*: For a purchased rental unit, ownership was acquired through a deal with the rental management operator or public agency. Purchased rental housing was categorised into three types according to the rental period (10, 20 or 30 years), with differing tenant qualifications by type. The size of buildings was kept below 85m^2, the rental deposit was set at 5% of the purchase price, and monthly rent was 30% of the market value.

- *Jeonsei rental housing*: This is leased by a public agency that mediates the lease contract from the original homeowner as a renter, and then acts as the landlord to low-income tenants. This rental type was introduced based on the general preference of Korean households for jeonsei contracts over monthly rent payments. In addition, for the lowest-income and vulnerable groups, public funds are available as jeonsei deposits with low interest rates. These groups include victims of violence, teenage households without parents, and households in the lowest income bracket.

- *"Happy Housing"*: This was initiated in 2013 and aims to enhance housing welfare for the young adult generation who are less likely to be public tenants. These include college students, college graduates, job seekers, newly-employed workers, and newlyweds. These groups tend to be excluded from public assistance because they are young, do not have dependent family members to support, and are capable of engaging in economic activities and providing for themselves. However, high housing prices and rental burdens in urban areas make it difficult for them to get married and move up to the next life stage, which makes society less sustainable in a context of low fertility and ageing population. With the opportunity to reside in public rental housing with low rental costs, they can have the chance to accumulate assets to move upward to a better housing situation.

Rental tenure in Korea is more complicated than in other OECD countries because of the existence of jeonsei (or chonsei), and monthly rentals (wolse) with deposits. For many years, jeonsei - an asset-based lease - was the dominant rental lease in the housing market (see Chapter 1). Under a jeonsei contract, the tenant makes a large upfront deposit to the landlord at the signing of the lease and does not pay monthly rent during the lease period. The landlord invests the deposit to generate a return equivalent to rents. The deposit is fully refundable at the termination of the lease. Jeonsei emerged during times of housing shortages, high interest rates, rising house prices, and inadequate mortgage financing (Kim & Park, 2016). Increasing house prices were a major source of investment return for the landlord which kept the deposit smaller than the price of the property. Some landlords even used jeonsei to finance the purchase of another home when mortgage loans were difficult to get. It represents an informal loan to a landlord extended by the tenant in return for the right to reside in the rented housing for the lease period. For the tenants, jeonsei is a step towards home ownership as the deposit could be used later as seed money for a property purchase. Public rental housing, excluding five-year rental that cannot be regarded as social housing, currently accounts for only 2.5% of total housing stock (Lim, 2006, p. 12). Jeonsei can have various forms and can be combined with monthly rentals, for example semi-jeonsei would mean a lower jeonsei deposit but a monthly rent would have to be paid, albeit lower than a full monthly rental. It is worth noting that the Korean government does not consider jeonsei as a private rental business as the scheme had its origin in the particular Korean context.

Eligible for public for-sale housing are household heads who have resided in the same administrative area as the place where the new housing is provided. They should have been statutory homeless for one or more years at the time of the first advertisement of the sale of new houses. Those who have saved with the Housing Subscription Savings have priority. According to MOLIT, the average period of residence for owner-occupied housing units is 11.2 years while that for rented units in both jeonsei and wolse schemes is 3.5 years on average. This suggests a relative instability in the rental private housing market.

2.2.2. The National Housing Urban Fund is central in providing low-cost and stable financing for households and builders

Low-cost and stable financing support for homebuyers and renters is provided by the National Housing Urban Fund (NHUF) and also diverse government funds run by different ministries. The NHUF has a housing account that provides funds to private consumers who wish to purchase or lease housing and to housing providers for the construction of low-income rental housing and affordable pre-sale housing by raising capital through national housing bonds, subscription savings of prospective homebuyers, and loan collection. Consumers of low to middle-income households can obtain low-interest loans from the fund when they purchase a home or mobilise a deposit for jeonsei under the various schemes run by the NHUF (Cho, 2013). The NHUF also has an urban account that raises funds from borrowings of housing accounts to pay for infrastructure installation, and urban renewal projects. Support for homebuilders had been prevalent compared to support for consumers until the early 2000s. Increasing house prices and rent burdens require provision of loans to consumers to help them purchase property or pay for a jeonsei deposit.

Table 2.5. Functioning of the National Housing Urban Fund

	Resources	Use	
Housing account	National housing bonds Housing subscriptions savings account Self-financing (return on investment, loans, asset securitisation, interest revenue on loans, etc.) Money transferred from general account – national lottery fund deposit	Rental housing construction fund Housing sale construction fund Home purchase funds Housing jeonsei loan funds Housing upgrade fund Investment on rental housing – current subsidies, etc.	Total assets in 2016: KRW 148.8 trillion Debt: KRW 132.4 trillion Net assets: KRW 16.4 trillion

Urban account	Housing account pre-deposit / borrowings Self-financing (recover finances, investment-loans, asset securitisation, interest revenue on loans Regional development special accounts All deposits / debts	Urban regeneration business fund Economy base type (create economic strongholds through rehabilitation / development of industrial complex, ports, station areas, etc.) Community regeneration type (redevelop run-down commercial areas and residential areas)

Source: HUG (2017) Role of HUG in Guarantee and NHUF. Presentation given to the OECD Secretariat on 18 September 2017 and www.khug.or.kr/hug/web/en/02/en02000008.jsp.

The National Housing Fund was transformed into the National Housing Urban Fund (NHUF) to support rental housing and urban renewal projects. This reform is expected to diversify methods to supply rental housing, improve the housing environment for small-size housing residents through the rehabilitation of run-down private housing and financial assistance for small-size rental housing construction, improve the landscape of commercial facilities and vitalisation of community groups formed by residents, and revitalise economic activities (Figure 2.7).

Figure 2.6. Evolution of the National Housing Urban Fund

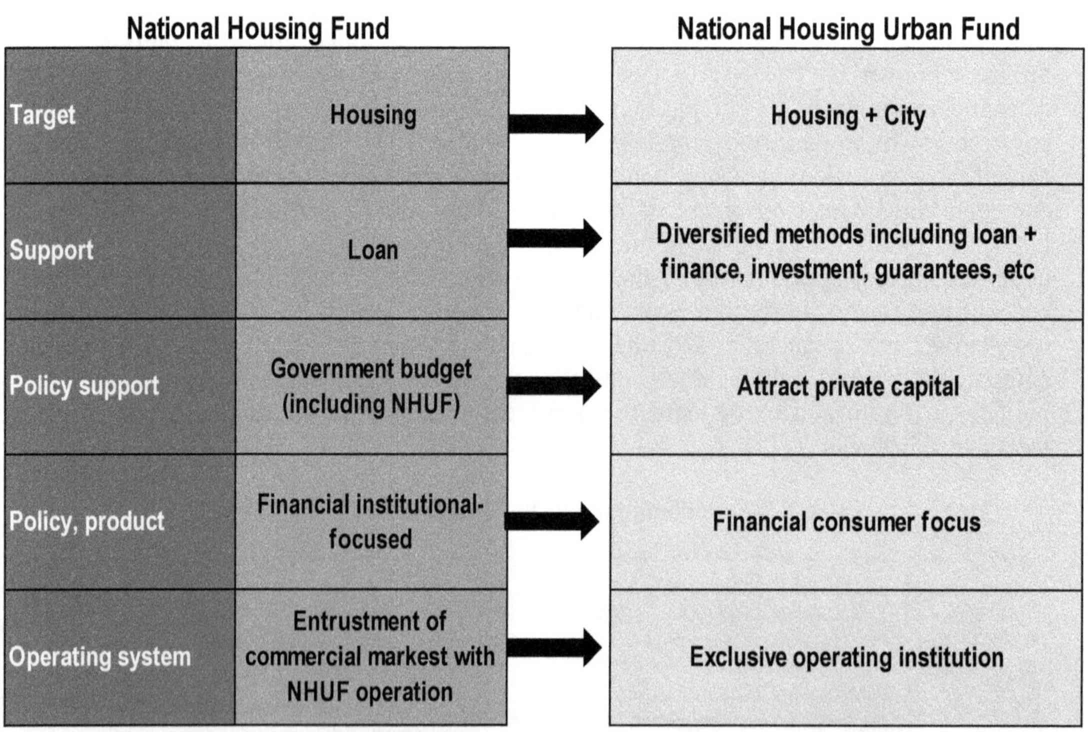

Source: Korea Housing and Urban Guarantee Corporation (HUG) www.khug.or.kr/hug/web/en/02/en02000008.jsp.

2.2.3. The jeonsei and monthly rental tenure schemes are creating pressures on the housing market

The jeonsei scheme has had implications for the state of the housing market. Housing prices have appreciated at a moderate pace. The rental market remains tight for jeonsei, but the rent for monthly rentals (MRDs) has been falling. The current state of the housing market reflects the close linkages among the owner-occupied housing market, jeonsei market, and MRD market in the context of the structural changes taking place in the country. As the housing shortage was resolved, housing prices have stabilised and interest rates have fallen to record lows. Thus, jeonsei has become economically unviable due to conflicts of interests between landlords and tenants. Today the tenant prefers a jeonsei to an MRD because of the lower user costs. The interest rate that is used to convert a deposit into monthly rent is much higher than the interest rates banks charge on loans for jeonsei deposits. The landlord, on the other hand, prefers an MRD because it generates a larger cash flow (Kim and Park, 2016, p. 13[6]). Moreover, when the housing market is weak, people tend to prefer jeonsei rental rather than buying a home leading to an intense competition to secure a jeonsei rental. Since the interest rate is usually low during a down-cycle, landlords want to raise the jeonsei deposit which represents a heavier burden to tenants who struggle to secure a jeonsei contract. Furthermore, would-be homebuyers tend to wait and see due to the pessimistic outlook of housing price escalation, which leads to an excessive demand in the private rental market that drives the rent level higher. As a result, renters in the private market experience a heavy rent burden which requires the government to implement more proactive measures to stabilise the rental housing market.

The results of this tension between jeonsei and MRD have been an increase in jeonsei deposits and a shortage of homes available on jeonsei leases. Korean authorities have set as a policy objective the stabilisation of jeonsei, as this has been the most popular rental tenure for the middle classes. This will only be achieved if demand decreases or supply increases. As a result, the government has been trying to promote home ownership by providing tax incentives and favourable mortgage terms to homebuyers. It has also encouraged the supply of rental housing from investors who own two or more homes by removing disincentives for rental housing, such as a high rate of taxation on capital gains for these owners. The government is also increasing the supply of rental housing as part of this strategy by introducing a package of incentives to promote large-scale private rental business. It has also introduced tax deductions on rental payments and housing benefits to alleviate the increasing burden of housing costs on moderate and low-income households.

Other measures that the national government has introduced to stabilise the housing market and enhance housing welfare have been the deregulation and modification of tax laws to encourage new housing supply and to facilitate home purchases. It has also introduced a new brand of public housing called *Haengbok Jutaik* ("Happy Housing") that targets the younger generations, and has passed a law to promote the private rental-housing sector (Kim and Park, 2016[6]). The 2017 Housing Market Stability Measures (known as the "8.2 measures") include initiatives to provide more public rental housing and increase taxes for those individuals who own more than one home, and restrict the financial support benefits for those who want to buy a second or third home.

2.3. Financing public housing in Korea

2.3.1. Financial institutions and private developers seem to dominate the housing sector

The formulation and implementation of housing policy is a complex process influenced by the interplay of numerous actors. The Ministry of Land, Infrastructure and Transport (MOLIT) is responsible for leading the making and implementation of housing policy. Its mission is to achieve a balanced territorial development and environmentally friendly territorial management and ensure residential stability for low-income people through universal residential welfare. However, Kim and Park (2016) argue that the relationship among key players in social housing is changing. The Ministry of Finance and Strategy, the Bank of Korea and the Financial Supervisory Committee are playing bigger roles than MOLIT. The reason is that taxation and finance are becoming more important policy tools compared to land-use control and development regulations. This gives the Korea Housing Finance Corporation (HF) and the Korea Housing and Urban Guarantee Corporation (HUG) a leading role in the steering of the housing policy as they design and manage the different mechanisms to finance housing in the country (Box 2.2).

Another critical actor in the housing sector is the Korea Land and Housing Corporation (LH) as it is a public housing provider. LH was established to spearhead the improvement of the quality of life and development of the national economy through the realisation of stable housing and the efficient use of national land. Among its major duties, LH is responsible for: i) constructing and supplying good quality, affordable housing units to the vulnerable groups of the population and improving their residential environment, as well as implementing tailored residential welfare programmes; ii) developing housing land, new towns, Multi-functional Administrative Cities and Innovation Cities, as well as executing projects aimed at regenerating cities in a bid to create comfortable residential spaces and urban environments; iii) developing industrial and logistic complexes to boost national competitiveness and create jobs; and iv) managing land reserve, rental housing and land and housing informatisation.[6] LH builds housing but is not directly involved in financial services. Until 2015, LH had built 1.2 million long-term public rental housing units (5.9% of total housing stock). LH is the largest provider of long-term public rental housing units with a 74.4% share, whereas local governments and the private sector contribute only 19.3% and 6.3% respectively.

Box 2.2. Key financial actors in the Korean housing sector

In Korea, there are two financial actors that contribute to the implementation of central government's housing policy:

- The Korea Housing Finance Corporation (HF), created in 2004, is a state-run enterprise that facilitates the long-term, stable supply of housing funds. It provides housing finance services for low and middle-income families. It offers mortgage loans, housing guarantees for individuals and builders, and a government guaranteed reverse mortgage programme for elderly Koreans. HF is also involved in the issuance of mortgage-backed securities, mortgage-backed bonds, and student loan guarantee.
- The Korea Housing and Urban Guarantee Corporation (HUG) aims to improve housing well-being and revitalise urban renewal projects to contribute to a better quality of life for the public by offering various types of housing guarantees and implementing government policies such as the National Housing Fund Act. HUG's main areas are: i) guarantee business for housing (guarantee for housing completion, guarantee for rental deposits, guarantee for co-operative housing completion, etc); ii) guarantee business in support of national policies (guarantee for refund of jeonsei deposits, guarantee for mortgages, etc.); and iii) business entrusted by national or local governments (the entrustment of profit (loss) sharing mortgage programmes, among others). The government owns 67.8% of HUG's shares, the rest are owned by home builders, financial institutions, treasury stock and others. By 2015, HUG had provided guarantees for a value of USD 136 billion.

Source: Korea Housing Finance Corporation (HF): https://hf.go.kr/ehf/index.do; Korea Housing and Urban Guarantee Corporation (HUG): www.khug.or.kr/hug/web/en/01/en01000002.jsp.

Until the mid-1970s the construction of public housing was very limited. The government tried to make up for the shortage of public investment in housing by promoting public housing development by private firms. Therefore, Lim (2006, p. 15[12]) argues that the Korean public housing system was designed to be based on private investment and speculative housing development, but driven by administrative control rather than by economic principles. The government requested private developers to provide low-cost housing in order to facilitate low-income households' access to housing (Box 2.3). Price control and regulation of housing size were the means by which the government pressed developers to build low-cost housing. After the economic crisis of 1997, when the housing market nearly collapsed, all regulation on the private housing market was either relaxed or abolished. Instead, direct financial assistance to home buyers and tenants as well as developers was expanded (Lim, 2006).

Box 2.3. Understanding the control of the housing market in Korea

Price control. In the late 1970s, housing and land prices rose rapidly and developers were under increasing public criticism. Housing developers were blamed for appropriating excessive profits from the people while they benefited from various favours including exemption or reduction of VAT, corporate tax and transfer tax. The Seoul Metropolitan Government announced a plan to control such profiteering through administrative guidance and to consider setting a price ceiling in accordance with the Price Stabilisation and Fair Trade Act. Consequently, any housing development plan that proposed building more than 50 homes at a time on one site had to be approved and supervised by the Ministry of Construction or Heads of Municipalities. The plans for housing sales and sale prices also had to be approved.

In 1981, when the government had to promote housing development as a way of stimulating the economy, as well as supporting the Five Million Housing Construction Plan, the Seoul Metropolitan Government suspended price control for housing over 85m^2. The selling prices of new apartments began to rise immediately. This attracted fresh criticism towards private developers for their excessive profiteering leading the government to set a price ceiling. The price control was criticised for encouraging housing speculation. There was always excess demand for homes under price control because the selling prices of new homes were, in many cases, well above market prices. Thus, government had to also regulate the sale of new homes. New homes built with resources from National Housing Fund (NHF) loans are to be sold preferably to housing subscription depositors. Those acquiring NHF dwellings are not allowed to sell their homes before a stipulated period of time (normally two years).

Housing size. Controlling the size of housing has been an attempt to facilitate low-income households' access to new housing. The government regulated the size of housing built with resources of the NHF which were provided for apartments of less than 85m^2. Public development agencies have played a major role in the provision of small-sized for-sale apartments and rental housing. Private developers had to comply with a number of requisites such as capital stock, number of licensed engineers and annual housing construction to be nominated as Designated Developers. Along with this registration, private developers obtained incentives such as the right to issue company bonds redeemable in housing. They also received housing loans and were able to purchase land from public agencies. In return they had to build small-sized apartments for rental housing.

Private developers are normally reluctant to build small units because they are less marketable and profitable. The government issues guidelines on the size of new homes. By 1997, at least 75% of a housing project had to be built in smaller units (85m^2 or less). The guidelines and other regulations were relaxed or abolished after the 1997 economic crisis.

Source: Lim (2006$_{[12]}$).

2.3.2. The government's housing financing strategy focuses on direct financial assistance provision

After the 1997 economic crisis, Korea's government expanded direct financial assistance to individuals and developers for purchasing or building housing. For this purpose, Korea adopted a number of housing financing instruments managed by the national government and in some cases the municipal authorities. Some of the existing instruments are subsidies mortgages and mortgage guarantees for home buyers, tax relief for access to home ownership, housing allowances provided by municipalities with funding from the national level, subsidies for the development of affordable rental housing, and social rental housing provided by both national and municipal governments. Instruments such as grants to homeowners, mortgage relief for over-indebted homeowners and subsidies for the development of affordable home ownership are not available in Korea. Across OECD countries housing allowances are the most widespread type of housing policy measure, followed by social rental housing (Salvi del Pero et al., 2016[2]).

To enhance the residential stability of low income households, alleviate the burden of deposits for monthly rents, and safeguard against bankruptcy of constructors, Korea has designed a system of presale and guarantee for housing completion. Developers can choose either "build-then-sell" or "sell-then-build" schemes. The latter is the most common option for projects but it is only allowed when developers secure the ownership of the project land and obtain a guarantee certificate for housing completion issued by HUG. Indeed, HUG issues guarantees for housing completion in a structured housing pre-sale system. Some of its main products are: i) guarantee for home purchase; ii) guarantee for a refund of jeonsei deposit; iii) guarantee for payment of rent; and iv) redevelopment business loan guarantee (Table 2.6).

Table 2.6. HUG's guarantee records in 2015

Unit: USD 100 million

	Housing completion	Housing purchase	Project finance	Rental deposit	Housing redevelopment	Co-operative housing	Others (defect repair etc.)	TOTAL
Guarantee in 2015	813.8	354.9	39.6	62.2	40.8	22.8	33.7	**1 367.8**
Ratio	59.5	25.9	2.9	4.5	3.0	1.7	2.5	**100**

Source: HUG (2017) Role of HUG in Guarantee and NHUF. Presentation given to the OECD Secretariat on 18 September 2017.

HF also provides guarantees for individuals who seek to obtain loans from financial institutions to rent or buy a property or pay instalments for newly built apartments, and for home builders who seek to obtain loans to build homes to let out or lease. One of the distinctive services HF provides is the reverse mortgage (*JooTaekYeonKeum*), a government programme for elderly Koreans who own property but do not have adequate cash flow for their retirement years so that they can receive reverse mortgage payments by collateralising their home. HF also provides two kinds of mortgages, the didimdol loan (70% of collateralised value of a property of 85m^2 or less whose value is less than KRW 500 million) and the bogeumjari loan (70% of the collateralised value of a property whose value is no more than KRW 600 million). The Comprehensive Housing Plan (CHP) intends to support 85 000 households through housing funds including didimdol mortgages (low-interest mortgages for low-income households or those who do not own property), and revenue sharing mortgages. The didimdol mortgage is to be improved by lowering the interest rates by 0.3%. Households who do not own property will also be supported to purchase a home through trial revenue-sharing mortgages from commercial banks, didimdol mortgages (housing funds) mortgage guarantees, and the limited responsibility mortgage system (housing fund mortgage).

In Korea, the provision of guarantees by the state or local authorities on loans taken on the private market is another increasingly used form of public support. This is also the case in the Netherlands, Finland and Germany. Given the fact that social housing providers increasingly have to resort to private borrowing to finance their activities, public guarantees are expected to be in increased demand as a way to make sure providers can access better conditions on the market (CECODHAS, 2013[15]).

In 2015, the Korean government introduced the housing voucher programme as a rent subsidy for very low-income households who are not homeowners or who are living in rented accommodation. The housing voucher programme is expected to contribute to improve housing conditions and residential mobility of the lowest income group. In 2015, a total of 970 000 households were expected to receive the housing voucher. The target population are those who receive 33% of the median income (700 000 households). This was just recently expanded to 43% (970 000 households). An average monthly voucher payment per household was KRW 40 000 in 2014 and KRW 110 000 in 2015.

2.3.3. "Housing benefits" and "jeonsei deposit loan" programmes intend to facilitate access to private rental housing

An important element in supporting access to public housing is the availability of individual housing benefits and allowances for tenants. Benefits are not considered as subsidies specific to the social housing sector but they guarantee the financial stability and sustainability of social housing. The general trend over the past decades has been a shift from supply-side subsidies to demand-side subsidies (CECODHAS, 2013[15]). Korean authorities have adopted two housing programmes to allow residents to select locations, housing types, and housing size depending on their preferences and needs for rental housing in the private market: i) the housing benefit programme for the lowest-income households; and ii) the deposit loan programme for the general renters in the private market.

The housing benefit was introduced in 1999 as a component of the general welfare grant for the lowest-income households. It originally targeted individuals who lacked family support and did not have the ability to work. The government provided them with the minimum living expenses based on the National Basic Livelihood Security (NBLS) system. Welfare beneficiaries under the NBLS system received a fixed subsidy based on their income and the number of people in the household. However, this system did not consider the housing rent burden of the region in which beneficiaries reside. Moreover, the NBLS system had an all-or-nothing structure. That meant that when the household's income exceeded a certain level (minimum living cost), they became ineligible for welfare benefits.

In 2015, the Korean government passed the new Housing Benefit Act to relieve the rent burden and to ensure the minimum housing standard for vulnerable households. The new housing benefit system comprises a revised legal basis, rent standards, and public inspection (Figure 2.7). According to the Housing Benefit Act, a monthly cash subsidy is provided based on household income, rent level, family size, and location. Localities are divided into four categories: Seoul, Seoul Metropolitan Area, other metropolitan areas, and small cities and rural areas. Basic rent standards are calculated by locality and family size in consideration of the differences in local rent level to ensure minimum housing standards. Local rent level data are available from the lease transaction data of the whole country as the Korean government mandates the reporting of real estate transaction to the local public office. Thus, the rent level is calculated to reflect the recent changes.

Figure 2.7. Features of Korea's new housing benefit system

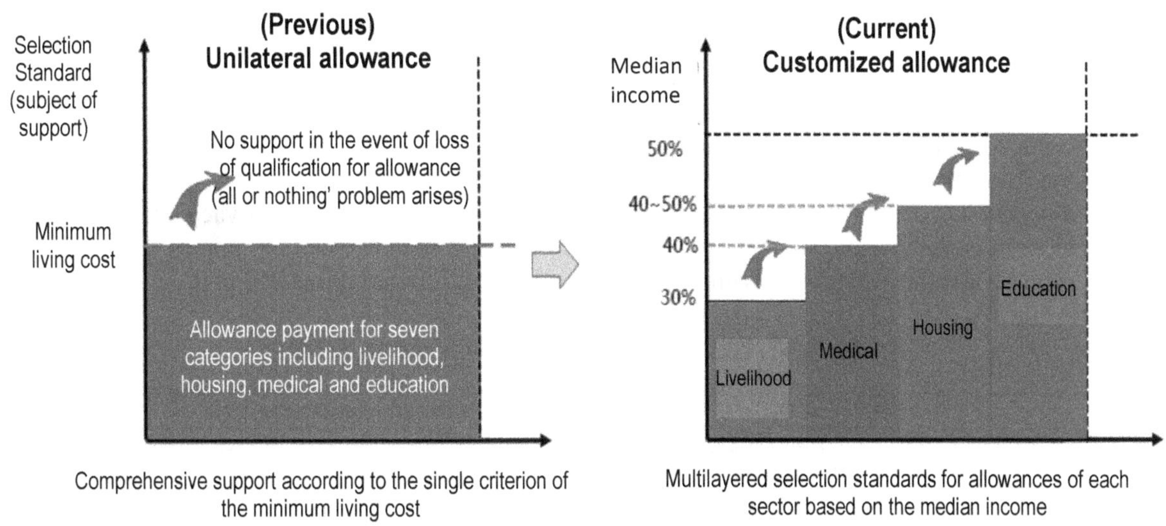

Source: (Park, 2017[16]).

There are almost one million households receiving housing benefit and most of the recipients are in the first decile of income level (Park, 2017[16]). The housing benefit system serves as the most crucial element for underprivileged renters. Due to the new housing benefit scheme, the beneficiaries increased from 700 000 to 970 000 households and the average monthly subsidy per household also rose 20% compared to the previous system (Park, 2017[16]).

The jeonsei deposit loan programme was introduced in 1990 for the extremely low-income households who find it difficult to mobilise the jeonsei deposit money in the private sector. The increasing demand for rental housing in the private market has raised the price of jeonsei, resulting in a higher housing cost burden. As a response, the government decided to provide a portion of jeonsei deposit at a below-market rate through the NHUF. There are several conditions to take a jeonsei deposit loan. The amount of money should not exceed a certain proportion (70% of the jeonsei deposit) or the cap imposed by the government. The level of cap depends on the household's residence location. The loan amount is higher in the Seoul Metropolitan Area considering the higher jeonsei price. If the borrowers belong to the low-income or special needs group, then they can receive a discount in the interest rate. Moreover, if the household's income level falls between USD 20 000 to USD 40 000 a year and they borrow less than USD 50 000 for the deposit loan, then the interest rate is set at 2.5% a year. Newlywed couples are entitled to receive a discount of 0.7%, setting the interest rate at 1.8%. By 2016 more than 600 000 households utilised the jeonsei deposit loan programme. More than 100 000 households have borrowed the deposit loan each year, accumulating more than a million beneficiaries during the last decade (Park, 2017[16]).

2.3.4. The rent level of public rental housing depends on households' income levels

The Public Housing Act establishes the rent level of public rental housing in consideration of the target groups and their income levels. However, the rent level should also consider all relevant construction costs such as land price, financial assistance from the NHUF, repair and maintenance expenses, insurance, loan interest, taxes and public utilities charges. In this way, for example, "permanent public rental housing" is intended to serve the lowest income group, so the rent level is set at 30% of the market rate. Table 2.7 provides some examples of rent levels for each type of rental housing. Similarly, in order to balance cost and revenues, countries such as Austria and France have rents that are basically cost-based. They are calculated taking into account loan interests and amortisations, maintenance, management costs, taxes, and provisions for vacancies. Rents have to comply with limits set by the specific funding scheme used to support a specific project, and the obligations with regards to the level of rent are unlimited in time.

Table 2.7. Rent levels of public rental housing in Korea

Type of public housing	Rent level in relation to market prices
Permanent rental housing	Less than 30%
National rental housing	50%-80%
10-year / 5-year rental	Up to 90%
Happy Housing	60%-80%

Source: (Kim et al., 2015[17]).

A tenant of a public rental housing unit must pay a deposit and monthly rent. The amount of deposit for rental housing differs by the type of public rental unit. In the case of permanent and 50-year rental housing, the deposit is set at 20% of the housing price. Occupying national rental units requires a deposit equivalent to 20% of the housing price or more considering the unit size and locality; the bigger the size, the higher the deposit required. 5-year and 10-year rental units need higher deposits because the income level of the target population is higher than that for other types of rental housing.

2.3.5. The government aims to streamline regulations for housing construction

The Korean government aims to make the regulations for housing construction adopted during overheated market periods more efficient. For this purpose, the government intends to simplify redevelopment reconstruction procedures; and reorganise the housing supply system by eliminating one of the qualifications of a subscription that requires being without any housing ownership, and simplifying the process of selecting residents. Moreover, the housing supply plan has been switched from the licensing system with less predictability to a manageable construction completion system. In 2015, MOLIT expected to construct a total of 434 000 homes, similar to the figure of 2014 (431 000), of which 88 000 are public homes (70 000 rentals and 18 000 for sale). Moreover, central government is establishing the parameters of rent conversion into monthly rent in accordance with the Housing Lease Protection Act.[7] The government also intends to strengthen support for deposit repayment by reducing guarantee fees by 25% and improve housing statistics, including rental housing, aiming for detailed monthly rental statistics and developing a composite jeonsei monthly rental index.

2.3.6. Financing public housing construction requires significant government contributions

Providing public rental housing requires government contributions that range from direct subsidies in the form of budget allocation to indirect subsidies such as low-interest loans through the NHUF. For instance, in the case of permanent rental housing units, the government provided up to 85% of financing (and tenants covered the remaining 15%) because of the belief that permanent rental units should go to the most underprivileged households in society (Table 2.8). The financing structure of national rental housing construction for non-homeowners differs by unit size based on the tenants' ability to pay. Funding for 5-year or 10-year rental housing and rental units for employees came from subsidies from the NHUF at discounted interest rates based on the housing unit size.

National rental housing has three types based on the size of the units. The smaller the unit, the larger the support from the government budget. For example, Type I national rental housing is built under 40m^2 and is expected to house lower-income tenants, so the government provides a higher proportion of financial resources and there is less contribution from the tenants. However, at least 10% of the construction cost is to be delivered by a public agency such as the LH.

Table 2.8. Financial structure for the construction of public rental housing in Korea

Category		Funding Distribution per construction cost required			
		Government budget	National Housing Fund loan	Tenants	Agent
Permanent rental housing		85%	0%	15%	0%
50-year rental housing	1992-93	50%	20%	30%	0%
	After 1994	0%	70%	30%	0%
National rental housing	Type I (below 40 m^2)	50%	37%	3%	10%
	Type II (40-50m^2)	32%	39%	19%	10%
	Type III (below 60m^2)	20%	42%	28%	10%
	Average	30%	40%	20%	10%
5-year & 10-year rental housing	Below 60m^2	-	USD 70 000 per unit (Max)	-	-
	60-85m^2	-	USD 90 000 per unit (Max)	-	-
Purchased national rental housing		45%	50%	5%	0
Happy Housing		30%	40%		30%

Source: (MOLIT, 2016[18]).

Contrary to long-term public rental housing, 5-year or 10-year rental housing receives a different financial support from the NHUF. These types eventually convert into ownership units. Based on the unit size, a fixed loan is provided regardless of the construction cost. Recently developed "Happy Housing" is built with 30% government budget and 40% low-interest loan from the NHUF.

2.4. Addressing the challenges and vulnerabilities of the housing welfare policy

2.4.1. Housing policy should have a holistic view that leads to a more inclusive society and sustainable economic growth

Korea's central government has been a key actor in the provision of public rental housing. The results have been a substantial improvement in the quality and quantity of housing and the increasing living standards of Korean citizens. Today, Korea's public opinion and policy-makers are of the view that it is better to have more public housing. Linking housing policy to urban policy is a positive development as it will facilitate creating synergies across different urban policy sectors, and develop a more sustainable approach to urban development. Despite its success, Korea's public housing system needs to evolve to be able to respond to the country's housing needs in the context of an ageing population, shrinking households and low fertility rates. Korea needs a bigger and more co-ordinated approach to housing that takes a holistic view of issues such as urban policies, land use, land value, taxes and sustainability strategies that will help build a stronger urban structure (housing, transport, public centres etc.).

Table 2.9. Enabling Korea's housing market to work better

Policy recommendations in brief.

	Korea may wish to:	Korea may wish to avoid:
Organising the building industry	Encourage community sector participation Encourage small firm entry Set limited-profit housing organisations	Instituting regulations inhibiting participation of small firms, NGOs and voluntary sector Relying mostly on LH for housing construction (financial burden)
Developing a policy and institutional framework	Conduct a gradual decentralisation of housing policy Redefine the roles of central and subnational governments Develop enabling strategies for subnational governments' active participation	Overlapping roles of government in housing policy design and implementation Neglecting local governments' role in housing
Management of rental housing	Consolidate the types of public rental housing Revise the rent setting rules based on tenants' income level Involve the private sector in social housing Encourage the development of the private rental sector Monitor the level of jeonsei deposit increase	Maintaining disconnected social housing programmes Setting renting rules that hinder upward mobility Allowing private renters to freely increase monthly rent or jeonsei deposit without government oversight Using rent control as a subsidy
Regulating land and housing development	Reduce regulatory complexity (land use) Make registration of private landlords compulsory	Imposing unaffordable housing standards A rigid planning system and complex land use regulations Designing projects without link to urban development plans
Rationalising housing sector instruments	Target subsidies to low-income households and people with special needs Design specific programmes for 2nd quantile income groups Subsidise people, not houses Subject housing sector instruments to periodical review	Neglecting middle-income groups Preventing low-income households from home ownership
Developing mortgage finance and alternatives for financing construction	Innovate in mortgage markets (switch the loan repayment structure from interest-only bullet loans to monthly amortisation loans) Ensure healthy balance between access to credit and sustainability of house prices Ensure prudential regulation Introduce better loan instruments for builders	Imposing borrowing constraints on households Allowing interest-rate subsidies Neglecting resource mobilisation

The experience of OECD countries suggests that housing policy has a double edge as it can contribute to meeting social and economic goals. But the key part is to integrate that in the vision of the housing policy. Korea has already adopted key housing policy instruments such as the Korea Comprehensive Housing Plan that sets the targets to be achieved. However, Korean authorities may consider revising it to state how those objectives will contribute to other social and economic goals and how they are going to be achieved in a simple manner. This revision may draw from Canada's experience in designing its National Housing Strategy that includes not only the number of homes to be built or rebuilt but also the principles that lead the strategy.

Table 2.10. Canada: Principles of the National Housing Strategy

Vision: Canadians have housing that meets their needs and that they can afford. Affordable housing is a cornerstone of sustainable, inclusive communities and a Canadian economy where everyone can prosper and thrive.		
Housing is more than just a roof over our heads		
People	Communities	Partnerships
Every Canadian deserves a safe and affordable home. Housing investments must prioritise those most in need, including women and children fleeing family violence; seniors; Indigenous peoples; people with disabilities; those dealing with mental health and addiction issues; veterans; and young adults. Housing policy should be grounded in the principles of inclusion, participation, accountability, and non-discrimination.	Housing programmes should align with public investments in job creation, skills training, transit, early learning, healthcare, and cultural and recreational infrastructure. Housing investments should support Canada's climate change agenda and commitment to accessible communities. Communities should be empowered to develop and implement local solutions to housing challenges.	First Nations, Inuit and Métis Nation housing strategies must be co-developed and founded in the values of self-determination, reconciliation, respect, and co-operation. Good housing policy requires transparent and accountable partnership between the federal government, provinces, territories, municipalities, the social and private sectors, and people with lived experience of housing need. The community housing sector must be prioritised, protected and grown.

Source: Adapted from Government of Canada (2017, p. 5[19])

One element that Korea could add to the Comprehensive Housing Plan, which is not included in other countries' strategies such as Canada, is the issue of sustainability. OECD's work in Southeast Asian countries has revealed that the demand for housing investment in light of rapid urbanisation and income growth generates high potential for urban green growth. Insufficient quantity or quality of housing supply can be a major obstacle to urban green growth (OECD, 2016[20]). Similarly, housing policies are opening up opportunities for Korean cities to increase the quality of in-house environment and welfare for residents, and promote resource and energy efficiency, given the increasing energy and material consumption and GHG emissions in buildings. Moreover, if Korean housing policies focus more on sustainable housing they will also be contributing more to the economy. For example, retrofitting existing buildings stock for improved energy efficiency can create jobs, new services and innovation. For that, it is important to develop a more comprehensive regulatory framework which considers water efficiency, indoor air quality and use of environmentally friendly materials. Although green building should have a special focus on new buildings as they have the greatest potential to achieve high efficiency, retrofitting of old buildings in urban centres should also be part of the strategy.

2.4.2. Korea needs to expand its network of public housing providers

To improve the functioning of the public rental market, Korea could continue its efforts to revamp the idea of community initiative, part of the self-help philosophy. The rationale is that the problems of housing poverty are very much local and socio-economic specific, which need to be dealt with at community level and not only through universal programmes like those adopted in the past. Urban regeneration efforts led by community groups in Seoul seem to be going in this direction (see Chapter 3). Incentivising the participation of the community sector in public housing provision would contribute to a stable provision of public rental housing and alleviate the financial burden of LH. Indeed, LH has been increasing its share in the public rental housing market (50%), but it is faced with a heavy financial burden. As the largest public company, LH is responsible for the construction and long-term management of public rental housing, especially for units with the mandatory leasing period of more than 10 years. LH had a financial loss because it could not sell the units due to the mandatory leasing term and could not raise rent level due to the rent setting rules for low-income tenants. Moreover, LH lacks the administrative flexibility to adapt to the rapidly changing housing needs. Small public corporations, private homebuilders, and the community sector would be better suited for this situation.

Korea's central government may need to devise innovative tools and incentives to encourage the participation of diverse players in supplying public rental housing with different types of leasing terms, and different target groups. For instance, in the United Kingdom there are three types of developers in the country: private enterprise, local authorities and housing associations. Housing associations are non-profit organisations, usually with a mission to provide affordable housing for lower income and vulnerable households (Williams and Whitehead, 2015, p. 14[21]). The proportion of homes built for the social housing sector by local authorities has declined considerably over the last decades. For instance, in England and Wales 87% of social housing was built by local authorities in 1951, but by 2016 the proportion was just 1% (Wilson, Barton and Smith, 2017[22]). Building by housing associations, on the other hand, increased and now makes up slightly less than a quarter of all housing building. The overall proportion of building by the social sector increased relative to the private sector in the years following the financial crisis, although the actual number of completions reduced.

In the Netherlands, about one third of the total housing market (33.2% or 76% of the total rented stock) is owned by social housing organisations or "housing corporations" (CECODHAS, 2013[15]). They are accountable for six types of activities: housing the target group, quality of dwellings, involving inhabitants, financial continuity, liveability, housing and care. They act independently but according to output and performance agreements with local and provincial governments. There are approximately 389 registered social housing organisations in the country (CECODHAS, 2013[15]). They are private rental associations but operate in a heavily controlled market. As registered organisations, their capital cannot be employed for any other purpose than housing. Social housing providers also conduct commercial activities (rent and sale). But this only represents 2% of their activities on average. All profits must be reinvested in the housing sector (revolving system) but they have to keep separate accounts for social and other activities.

Korea may explore the possibility of setting limited-profit housing organisations that operate at local level. For instance, in Austria, limited-profit housing organisations manage 56% of social housing. Unlike for-profit providers, limited-profit housing companies cannot carry out activities other than provision and management of rental and owner-occupied housing at limited rents and prices. For-profit providers manage 11% of social housing (CECODHAS, 2013[15]). In France, social housing is provided by the HLM organisations (*organismes d'habitations à loyer modéré – organisations providing housing at moderated rents*). They are specific actors entrusted by the state to fulfil a mission of general interest. They include publicly and privately-owned companies acting on a non-profit basis and under the control of the Ministry of Housing and Finance. To a lesser extent, semi-public enterprises and some non-profit associations are also involved in social housing provision.

2.4.3. Subnational levels of government should be gradually granted a more active role in public housing provision

A more effective and tailored provision of public rental housing requires the active role of local governments. So far, centralised initiatives and policy management have been effective in the case of Korea; however, regions, cities, and villages have particular housing needs that require a flexible and localised response (see Chapter 1). Therefore, the national housing policy needs to be much more flexible and cities need to be given much more freedom to respond to their particular circumstances if they are to make the most of housing's potential to deliver economic growth and meet people's social needs. Local housing funds should be set up by local governments to provide tailored programmes for local needs. The role of central government could be shifted from controlling every detail to managing and supervising high-level matters, while providing block grants to give more discretion to local governments. At the same time, local governments should be expected to be more responsible for tackling their local needs and be more proactive in mobilising local resources such as housing inventories, funds, and local activists. Local governments can provide public or social rental housing at below market rents to low-income and particularly vulnerable households through, for example, local housing associations.

Local governments, with the support of national government, could integrate housing policy objectives within their urban planning responsibilities to support sustainable urban development. The reason is that local governments influence public and private housing markets through their planning and development control decisions, have strong connections to the local community, and are well positioned to facilitate a whole of government approach to housing outcomes. Korean local authorities could formulate "local housing strategies" incorporating an analysis of local housing supply, expected demand, socio-demographic and market trends as well as recommendations for planning processes, land use plans and development regulations. Local housing funds should be set up by local governments to provide tailored programmes for local needs.

Korean authorities may wish to analyse the case of Austria where municipalities manage approximately 33% of the social housing stock but have withdrawn from new construction. Since 1989, it is up to the provinces to define the financial framework for housing subsidy. However, until 2008 the federal state granted earmarked means for housing promotion to the provinces. From 2009, the system was changed and the provinces also have complete financial responsibility. A contribution from employers and employees (0.5% of wages) is collected at state level and then passed onto the federal provinces so they can add it to their budget dedicated to supporting social housing promotion. In some provinces, annuity grants are paid to social housing providers in order to lower rents.

In Italy, some changes in housing policies can be tracked at the regional and local level after the decentralisation process that transferred housing sector-related competencies to regions and municipalities. Most of the interesting developments of housing policy in Italy are taking place at regional and municipal level. For example, the inclusion of different measures targeting the demands of diverse groups: young people, the elderly, temporary residents, immigrants, etc. Rental policies are now becoming central to housing policies as rented housing has never been central to housing policies in Italy before (Governa and Saccomani, 2009[23]).

The experience of Germany shows how giving a more predominant role to subnational governments could result in more tailored solutions to housing needs. Indeed, in

Germany, since 2006, the responsibility for social housing including financing has been fully transferred to the federal states (Länder). The federal government has withdrawn to provide a framework-legislation only. With this reform, the funds dedicated to social housing were transferred from the federal budget to the Länder. Korean authorities may note that the Länder were obliged to use these funds for social housing although only for a limited period. This could provide Korea with some examples on how to proceed with a decentralisation of housing policy. Currently, social housing funding arrangements vary significantly across the different Länder. Some of them have continued spending on new social housing, others have changed to acquiring individual dwellings in market developments as contracted social housing. Social housing is implemented in different ways across the country. For example, North-Rhine Westphalia and Hamburg employ direct subsidies and Hamburg also practices a specific allocation strategy aimed at increasing social mix (CECODHAS, 2013, p. 21[15]).

In other OECD countries such as Australia, Canada and Switzerland regional governments have the main responsibility for funding and managing social rental housing. In the cases of Canada and Switzerland local governments also have responsibility for housing allowances.

2.4.4. Use strategic land use planning as an instrument to influence house prices, not just financial instruments

Local governments play an essential role in ensuring equitable access to an adequate supply of affordable and good quality housing for their entire population. They can implement measures that reduce house prices and rents in the private housing market. Local governments can influence house prices and rents through land use regulations and the building approval process. If land use regulations prevent housing supply from adjusting to growing demand, house prices will rise. Local governments can require from developers that a share of newly built housing is made available to low-income residents at below market rents. Decisions on where to locate public and social housing can also contribute to inclusion by promoting mixed-income neighbourhoods and preventing the risks linked with spatial segregation by income.

In cities and regions with fast-growing populations, such as Seoul and Sejong, land use regulations need to permit sufficient housing construction to meet growing demand for housing while preventing the negative externalities of urban sprawl, for example by encouraging the densification of the existing housing stock. This would be in complement to the anti-speculation measures adopted by the government. Like in Germany, Korea may use a planning policy that includes strategic 'spreading' into rural areas while balancing competing land use interests. Korea would need to provide detailed environmental targets and greater differentiation between different types of urban sprawl, as used in the German planning system.[8]

Local governments, with the support of national government, should integrate housing policy objectives within their urban planning responsibilities to support sustainable urban development. The reason is that local governments influence public and private housing markets through their planning and development control decisions, have strong connections to the local community, and are well positioned to facilitate a whole of government approach to housing outcomes. Korean local authorities could formulate "local housing strategies" incorporating an analysis of local housing supply, expected demand, socio-demographic and market trends as well as recommendations for planning processes, land use plans and development regulations. Local housing funds should be set up by local governments to provide tailored programmes for local needs.

2.4.5. Consolidation of the types of public rental housing and waiting lists is essential to improve public housing management provision

Korea requires innovation on the types of public rental housing, rent setting rules, and waiting lists. The problem is that there are more than 20 types of public rental housing according to lease term, building methods, purchasing types, subsidy types, and providers. Moreover, new administrations tend to introduce new types of public rental units to differentiate themselves from previous governments, which makes the situation more complex. Instead of formulating brand new types of public rental, Korea could consolidate and simplify the types of public rental housing and rearrange them by recipients' income. In addition, it would be important to prepare a consistent waiting list for public rental housing across different providers. Currently, the frequency of the opening and management of waiting lists differs by type of public rental housing and by local municipality. It is crucial to reform the waiting list system to enable a systematic operation and make it user-friendly and easily accessible for all public rental housing types and regions.

Moreover, the rent setting rule may be reconstructed based on the tenants' income level in a way that encourages upward mobility. Since living in public housing contributes to enhancing residential satisfaction, relieving rent burden, and tenure stability, turnover rates stay relatively low (4-8%) in permanent rental and national rental housing (Jin & Lee, 2013). Even though the tenant's income is a critical element for selection in the initial phase, once they start residing, it is difficult to increase the rent level or enforce eviction based on improvements in their income level. On the other hand, while the lowest income group is eligible for permanent rental housing, the insufficient housing stock and low turnover rates lead them to national rental housing that requires higher rent than permanent rental units. Similarly, those who are eligible for national rental housing (middle-income renters) have the possibility to reside in permanent rental units paying extremely affordable rent compared to their income level. Public rental housing reform should include the rearranging of public rental types and the rent setting rule not only based on the construction cost, but also in consideration of the tenants' income, and be able to increase rent levels according to a rise in income. This will reduce financial losses for providers and increase the responsibility of tenants (Park, 2017$_{[16]}$).

In Austria, for instance, income limits exist to determine who can have access to subsidised housing. The limits are defined by the federal provinces, and are only applicable for new leases during the subsidisation period. Income limits (corresponding to the household's net yearly income after social security contributions and income tax) depend on the number of members in the household, plus a "bonus" for young families, children with disabilities and in some cases also for single parents. Income ceilings virtually allow about 80% of households to access social housing. The logic behind this comparatively high level of income is that the proportion of subsidised housing is also comparatively high (60-80% of total new construction). Non-profit housing companies can directly nominate tenants for part of the stock. Furthermore, social mix is an important goal for Austrian housing policies. The problem is that new build homes are comparatively expensive compared to existing stock, making social mix sometimes difficult from the point of view of financial equilibrium (CECODHAS, 2013$_{[15]}$). In Japan, affordable housing, including public rental, is provided via two schemes: i) Publicly-operated housing that provides rental housing for low-income households. For this, national and municipal governments purchase, build or rent housing to offer as public housing. Municipal governments decide the low-income thresholds for general households and for those whose residential stability needs to be promoted, such as the elderly, disabled people and households with children. The rent is based on the tenants' income, location and housing conditions. ii) The Good Quality Regional Rental Housing programme provides housing for households who require special assistance and is managed by municipal governments and private providers. The eligibility criteria is based on the type of household and tenants' income.

2.4.6. A periodical assessment of the effectiveness of the housing sector programmes and instruments (benefits, tax reliefs and subsidies) is necessary to improve the system

One critical lesson from the experience of OECD countries is that it is important to assess periodically the effectiveness of housing programmes and instruments at national and local levels so as to detect any negative impacts, and make the necessary adjustments. This evaluation should show how effective national policies and local strategies have been in addressing defined housing needs and meeting objectives. For this, it is important that local governments produce the necessary data and define measurable objectives and indicators for performance monitoring, as the national government does. The evaluation should be in relation to the defined housing needs and objectives and should try to identify legislative, institutional and even political constraints that may exist in each local government, as well as factors that have contributed to success.

Furthermore, Korea may also wish to assess whether the taxes, tax reliefs and subsidies in the housing sector are achieving their social objectives or whether they are destabilising the housing market and the wider economy (André, $2010_{[14]}$). It is essential that while diversifying the mechanisms for facilitating access to housing, Korean authorities consider the perverse effects some of them may have on the wider economy, as it has happened in other OECD countries. For instance, to encourage home ownership governments introduce non-taxable imputed rents, mortgage interest deductible from personal income tax, and exemptions from taxes on capital gains (André, $2010_{[14]}$). However, other mechanisms that affect the structure and functioning of the housing market are property taxes which are generally rather unrelated to the evolution of house prices. In Denmark, for example, until 2002 the property tax rate used to be revised annually contributing to macroeconomic stabilisation. Taxes on transactions (stamp duties, cadastral taxes, VAT) vary widely across OECD countries and account for a large share of acquisition costs. Higher transaction costs reduce the mobility of households but they also limit speculative transactions. In Ireland, stamp duties have been used to restrain housing demand but with mixed results.

2.4.7. Broaden the target group to promote social mix and mobility

One key question for Korea is how the target group of the public housing policy could be broadened to encourage social mobility. Too much attention is dedicated to the lowest income group, but households in the 2nd and 3rd deciles do not have the same benefits. In 2018, Korea expects to implement the housing benefit reform which aims to broaden the group of recipients covered by the regulation. The new housing benefit is expected to cover an additional 30% of current beneficiaries. This is a positive step; however, the 2nd lowest decile group will still receive relatively less benefit compared to the bottom group such as the opportunity to reside in public rental housing and receive housing benefit.

Housing policy could place more emphasis on how to address the needs of the income groups in the bottom 2nd and 3rd deciles who do not qualify for the same benefits as the lowest income households (Park, 2017[16]). Korean authorities may wish to consider that, according to the experience of OECD countries, social housing systems which are directed towards the most in need seem to be able to achieve their goals at a lower cost than less targeted systems, but they need to be carefully designed to avoid any negative implication for social mix, mobility and associated labour outcomes (OECD, 2011[24]). Canada's National Housing Strategy prioritises the most vulnerable, for example women and children fleeing from family violence, Indigenous peoples, seniors, people with disabilities, those dealing with mental health and addiction issues, veterans and young adults (Government of Canada, 2017[19]). Japan provides special assistance in securing housing for low-income households, the elderly, disabled and households with children.

A particular group that needs more attention is the younger generation. Young people are less likely to receive public housing subsidy even though they face difficulty due to rent burdens and end up living in substandard units. Nowadays, there is a growing concern over the housing needs of the younger generations (i.e. "Happy Housing"). However, Korea could introduce a scheme to provide housing benefit to young people at least for a temporary period, since these young people are in a transitionary phase of their lives and are expected to move upwards, start a family, and purchase their own home. To facilitate their climb up the housing ladder, temporary housing benefit for young people would be helpful, which would contribute to creating a sustainable society in an era of increased longevity and low fertility rates. In addition, housing literacy education should be provided for those entering the private rental market for the first time, to enhance their awareness of legal requirements on lease contracts, obligations and responsibility, and the rights of tenants and landlords so that they can be prepared for unexpected situations (Park, 2017[16]).

Korea may wish to analyse the case of France where housing benefits are available for tenants in the social and private sectors. In 2009, 6.3 million households received rent allowances. Nearly half of the tenants in the social housing sector receive housing allowances. In the social rented sector, the average monthly amount of benefit paid is EUR 215 (out of a total rent of EUR 335 or EUR 500 including charges and energy bills) (CECODHAS, 2013[15]).

2.4.8. The private rental market needs regulation and modernisation

To provide affordable housing, Korea should not rely exclusively on social housing. Involving the private sector in social housing and developing the private rental sector would lift some of the financial burden of public sector direct assistance. Korea has an extensive private rental market with a unique rental scheme – jeonsei – that, until recently, has been the preferred option for renting in the country. However, the private rental market is currently being largely operated by individual unregistered landlords. Thus, finding a rental place in the private market is mostly an individual, independent task, and residential stability is provided only for two years based on the tenant protection law. Current legislation recommends a rent increase of less than 5% a year, but this disposition is only applicable to public rental tenants. Moreover, private renters usually face the request of a jeonsei deposit increase by the end of the two-year contract. If they cannot mobilise the increased amount, then they usually have to move out and find another place within their financial means. Moreover, due to the unique form of lease contract through jeonsei, private renters might risk losing their deposit in extreme cases.

Legal protection is guaranteed; however, it is limited to a certain amount capped by the region, but the ever-increasing jeonsei deposit is outpacing the protection ceiling.

In many OECD countries, government involvement in the private rental market includes taxation, building and rental regulations, and rent allowances (Andrews, Caldera Sánchez and Johansson, 2011, p. 43[3]). Korea's private rental market requires better regulation to provide a better protection system for private renters. The measures announced in December 2017 to facilitate the registration of private rental housing constitute a positive step towards the modernisation of the private rental sector. They present a package of incentives for landlords to register their rental housing (e.g. reduction in property tax) and limit the increases in rent to 5% per year. Some other measures the Korean government could introduce include:

- making registration for private landlords mandatory (it is currently voluntary);
- providing registered landlords with better protection of their rights and property, as well as training on how to manage a property for rental;
- monitoring the level of jeonsei deposit increase;
- setting the level of taxation according to the landlords' rent income;
- setting clearer regulations for rent increase in both the jeonsei and monthly rental schemes;
- imposing appropriate tax on the real estate income;
- introducing the rent increase cap;
- regulating the increasing rates in consideration of the renters' income level and affordability; and
- establishing a guaranteed deposit safety by the government for vulnerable groups (Park, 2017[16]).

Box 2.4 presents the experience of Wales in the United Kingdom in registering landlords through Rent Smart Wales. The interesting aspect of this scheme for Korea is that landlords could even be assessed on their knowledge of housing rental procedures, and they should receive training. In 2017, Japan introduced a registration system for rental housing specialising in households who require special assistance in securing housing. Under this system, managed by national and municipal governments, rental housing owners apply for registration of their rental housing for which they have to meet certain conditions concerning criteria such as housing quality.

Box 2.4. Landlord registration – the case of the Rent Smart Wales programme

In November 2015, Wales (UK) introduced the registration and licensing scheme for landlords. The aim is to monitor private landlords and agents and ensure that they are suitable people to let out property. Since then, all private landlords of "domestic tenancies" in Wales must be registered with the Rent Smart Scheme. To be registered, a landlord must provide accurate and up-to-date information about themselves and all their properties that they operate in Wales. They are also required to pay a fee. If they do not register they can face penalties (a fixed penalty notice, a rent stopping order, or a rent repayment order).

The scheme requires any person who lets or manages a "domestic tenancy" in the country to have a licence from Rent Smart Wales. To obtain a licence, a landlord must pass a "fit and proper person test" and provide evidence that they have been on training about their rights and responsibilities as a landlord. The test is designed to weed any bad landlords or agents out of the system and to improve the standards in the private sector generally, helping to protect tenants. People can check if their landlord is registered through the public register online. If a tenant has a shorthold tenancy and the landlord is not registered or licenced, then any eviction cannot take place.

Source: Shelter Cymru accessed at: https://sheltercymru.org.uk/get-advice/finding-a-place-to-live/renting-privately/landlord-registration-and-licensing/.

As part of the modernisation of the private rental market, the Korean government could provide schemes, together with the private financial sector, to facilitate access to affordable rent and at the same time giving the option to buy property. Shared ownership schemes could be of interest to people who cannot afford a 100% mortgage, but could obtain a share. In this sense, Korea may analyse the possibility of replicating the schemes adopted in the United Kingdom. The UK government also introduced a scheme called Shared Ownership aimed at those individuals who cannot afford the mortgage on 100% of a home. Through this scheme people have the chance to buy a share of their home (between 25% and 75% of the home's value) and pay the rent on the remaining share.[9] Eligibility is based on income; applicants should earn less than GBP 80 000 (less than GBP 90 000 in London) a year. People can buy a newly built home or an existing one through resale programmes from housing associations. This scheme is particularly helpful for people with long-term disabilities. People aged over 55 can buy up to 75% of their home and then they do not have to pay rent for the remaining share. Shared Ownership properties are always leasehold.

To ease the transition of renting to buy a home, the UK government introduced the Rent to Buy scheme by which it provides a subsidised rent. The scheme provides homes for rent that will be sold on in the medium term with sitting tenants getting first refusal. Beneficiaries of this scheme may rent a newly built home at approximately 20% below the market rate for up to five years (exact time period varies by property). During that time period, tenants have the option to buy the property or to buy part of the property under the Shared Ownership scheme. The expectation (although no obligation) is that this shorthold period of paying less rent gives tenants the opportunity to save a cash deposit so they can apply to buy a share of the home later. If tenants do not wish to buy then they must leave.

The existence of well-functioning rental markets could help to reduce the volatility of house prices (André, 2010, p. 33[14]). Indeed, when house prices rise relative to rents, an increasing share of households should opt for renting, reducing pressures on prices. However, the scarcity of rental housing can prevent households from renting. André (2010) notes that countries such as Ireland and Spain with very thin rental markets experienced large housing booms, whereas Germany and Switzerland, which have large rental markets, did not participate in the latest house price boom. The experience of OECD countries suggests that if Korea's tax system favours home ownership and adopts tight regulations on the rental market, this may produce a decline in the supply of rental accommodation in terms of both quantity and quality. More neutral tax systems should allow a better balance between tenures producing more stable housing markets (André, 2010[14]). One example for Korea on incentivising the private rental market is the French programme to provide incentives to homeowners to rent. Indeed, the French government grants fiscal incentives to homeowners to rent their properties at intermediate rent levels through the "more affordable rent" (*louer abordable*) programme. The higher the tax deduction, the higher the tax allowance. Fiscal deductions are between 15-70% for a property in a classic lease and up to 85% for a rented flat through the social housing agency or an approved association (rental intermediation) (CECODHAS, 2013[15]). Some other OECD countries provide subsidies to increase the profitability of construction for rent or to offset high development costs. For instance, in the United States the Low Income Tax Credit Program provides tax breaks to developers in exchange for setting aside units for rent to lower-income households (Andrews, Caldera Sánchez and Johansson, 2011, pp. 43-44[3]).

2.4.9. Promote safe and sustainable mortgages (credit models) that target creditworthy low and middle-income households

Inadequate access to housing loans has been a stumbling block preventing low and middle-income people from owning a home. The paradox is that the Korean authorities are pursuing policies aimed at reducing the Loan to Value Ratio (LVT) and the Debt Income Ratio (DTI) which banks use to set the limits individuals can get in order to minimise the harmful consequences of over indebted households and speculation. This is very understandable as mortgage debts may affect households' financial stability. Rather than restricting or tightening credit access, Korea may wish to adopt safe and sustainable mortgage options for low and middle-income borrowers of different age groups (seniors and younger generations). These measures should be accompanied by carefully designed regulatory oversight and prudent banking regulations. Financial liberalisation and mortgage innovations have increased access to credit and lowered the cost of housing finance (OECD, 2011[24]). For example, one option for Korean authorities and financial institutions may be to switch the loan repayment structure from interest-only bullet loans to monthly amortisation loans, and support the adoption of long-term fixed-rate mortgages provided by commercial banks. Since household income in Korea tends to significantly decrease after retirement, the government needs to induce households not to defer their debt burden until their retirement years (Kim, 2016[25]). Delaying the repayment period exposes households to financial risks if interest rates increase. It is likely that not all households fully understand the risks involved in taking variable rate or interest-only loans, as is the case in Korea. Many borrowers tend to choose mortgages with the lowest repayments, at the expense of higher risks. Korea could explore the creation of community development financial institutions (CDFI), like in the United States, which are mission-driven entities specialised in helping non-traditional borrowers and others underserved by the mainstream mortgage market. The CDFIs provide mortgages that often come with low interest rates and down payment requirements, offer homebuyer education and counselling to prepare households for home ownership, and flexible underwriting criteria based on individual borrowers' circumstances.[10]

Korea could also explore the introduction of the Location Efficient Mortgage (LEM), particularly for urban areas, as in the United States. This mortgage takes into account where consumers are buying homes, and how much it costs for residents to travel around the city from their homes. For residents living in high-density, transit-rich areas that require little to no automobile dependency, extra savings are factored in and the total debt-to-income ratio to qualify for a loan becomes more forgiving.[11] The LEM could be an interesting option for place such as Seoul as it encompasses and encourages a more holistic lifestyle. Moreover, local programmes that provide property tax relief or assist with maintenance costs, along with financing options, may help older and low-income homeowners with mortgage debt. Across OECD countries, deregulation and mortgage finance innovations have significantly reduced borrowing constraints on households. As prices went up, reducing the affordability of housing, financial innovations were used to loosen the financial constraint of households, especially by lowering initial repayments (André, 2010[14]). However, by boosting demand through easy access to credit the price of houses can increase. Therefore, Korea needs to ensure a healthy balance between facilitating access to credit and regulation to ensure the sustainability of house prices.

Korea may wish to keep in mind that, according to the experience of other OECD countries, tax advantages increase demand for housing and the level of house prices, offsetting part of the tax advantage. In countries where supply is rigid, a great part of the tax subsidy is likely to be capitalised into house prices, thus the improvement in affordability is limited. André (2010) argues that housing-related tax advantages are usually regressive in terms of redistribution and costly for the government budget. They may also increase price volatility. According to Van der Noord (2005[26]), a tax system that subsidises home ownership tends to increase house price volatility. Finland, Ireland, the Netherlands and Spain have the highest subsidies for home ownership and also the most volatile house prices.

2.4.10. To enhance mobility, Korea may wish to prioritise subsiding individuals and not just houses

In Korea, like in other OECD countries, tenants in social housing are on average 6% less likely than private tenants to move every year. This is perhaps because they are reluctant to give up below market rents and tenancies which are generally more secure. Moreover, OECD analysis shows that homeowners tend to be less mobile than private renters (OECD, 2011[24]). Therefore, rather than subsidising housing, Korea may wish to subsidise people by providing housing allowances as they do not hinder residential and labour mobility to the same extent as social housing and home ownership. Korea may wish to enhance the housing voucher programme by expanding its subsidy criteria. The voucher can be redesigned in a way that a larger majority of households can receive rent allowances for any rental dwelling (social or private rental) which makes them more portable and further increases mobility.

2.4.11. Financing public housing construction requires different alternative sources

As home builders require more funding for construction, and in particular for social housing, Korea needs to offer them different options for accessing credit either in public or private institutions. The experience of the US suggests that in order to address housing shortages there need to be conversations around stronger financial incentives and sources of credit, along with more systematic solutions to attract developers to build more affordable urban housing. Indeed, a number of housing development projects fail due to strict requirements set by local municipalities, the cost and value of land, and the inconsistencies with policies in a given region.[12] The lack of flexibility for developers and inconsistencies in policies prevents them from building for the community. As mentioned above, in Korea the provision of guarantees by public institutions such as LH and HUG on loans taken in the private market is common practice. However, Korea may explore other options of support. For example, in some OECD countries like Austria, Finland and the UK local authorities provide land at discounted rates. The availability of cheap land can make a huge difference to the total cost of a housing development project. In the UK (England), Ireland, and the Belgian region of Flanders local authorities make use of the planning system to involve private developers. In this case, to get a building permit private developers need to agree to sell part of the dwellings to social housing providers at a discounted price upon completion of the project. OECD countries have adopted a variety of tax privileges for registered housing organisations, such as: reduced VAT rate, reduction or exemption from property tax and income/corporate tax.

Access to private funding – either through borrowing from banks or directly from the capital markets – is gaining importance in the financing of social housing across OECD countries. Thus, social housing providers are getting rated by international rating agencies (UK and the Netherlands), as is the same in Korea. However, Korea may analyse the convenience of adopting a similar system of security, as in the Netherlands, for financing the social housing sector. The three-level security structure of the Dutch social housing sector is considered a system that guarantees the solidarity and financial health of the sector, allowing housing associations to get more beneficial interest rates on the market (Box 2.5). It is worth noting that overall, in the Netherlands, housing associations do not recover through rents 30% on construction of new dwellings. But they have the possibility of selling existing dwellings to raise money. In 2012 they sold 17 000 dwellings overall (CECODHAS, 2013[15]). There are no limits on the size of dwellings. Limits on costs have been removed after the state decided to fix rent for dwellings with state aid (EUR 681.02 in 2013). With this rent limit, social housing organisations have to restrain the costs of housing production. In France, most of the funding for new construction comes from finance loans, where the main lender is the *Caisse des Dépôts et Consignations* (CDC) which provides funds from "Livret A" accounts. This is a savings fund with a regulated interest rate and not subject to income tax. Every French household has the right to open a tax free Livret A savings account at their local bank. 65% of these regulated savings are pooled by the CDC, which pays a fee to the banks for collecting the funds and a defined interest rate (CECODHAS, 2013[15]).

Box 2.5. Guarantees of the Dutch social housing sector

Since 1993 the Dutch social housing sector is basically financially independent from public funding. Apart from a backup guarantee system, there is hardly any public financial support to the sector. Financing new projects mainly consists of borrowing from banks (70-80% of the project) and the housing association's own equity. Social housing associations have access to a three-layer security scheme to guarantee their loans which include:

1. The Central Fund for Social Housing (CFV), a special independent public body that ensures financial supervision of the organisations, notably through two yearly reports, that classifies organisations depending on their solvency and liquidity. The CFV reports to the Ministry of Housing that expects social housing organisations to comply with the conclusions of the report. The CFV is financed through charges levied on all social housing organisations. When an organisation is in financial difficulties, the CFV can rescue and sanction it or give specific project support in order to enable it to get through its activities.
2. The Guarantee for Social Housing (WSW), a private organisation set up by the organisations themselves. Its security reserve was established through the guarantee fees organisations have to pay when contracting a loan with the WSW guarantee. These guarantees enable housing associations to borrow from banks on favourable terms. WSW has a solid security structure, and the guarantees it provides are very highly regarded. It can also act as a second guarantee in case of financial difficulties of a social housing organisation if the CFV runs out of capacity.
3. The Dutch state and municipalities come as a last resort guarantor with interest-free loans in case the sector can no longer overcome its financial problems and the WSW is nearly exhausted.

Source: (CECODHAS, 2013[15]).

In Korea, LH and HUG, as government sponsored enterprises, bear most of the burden of financing. Although they seem to be in good financial health (HUG has an AAA credit rating), the Korean authorities may wish to consider setting some guidelines or principles to ensure their continuous financial health and ensure a balance between taxpayer protection, investor returns and consumer costs and access to credit is ensured.

Box 2.6. Unites States: Core Principles of the GSE Reform

In the aftermath of the financial crisis, public discourse in the US reflected a growing consensus that policy preferences of numerous administrations had encouraged a level of home ownership and real estate investment that was out of proportion with the capacity of households to repay mortgage debt. This left taxpayers holding a large portion of the risk given the implicit government guarantee backing the obligations of government sponsored enterprises (GSEs) operating in the housing sector. Therefore, US Congress adopted some principles of reform to ensure taxpayer protection, investor return, and consumer cost and access to credit are kept in balance. Some of the principles are as follows:

- Preserve the 30-year, fixed-rate, pre-payable single-family mortgage, as well as long-term financing for multi-family mortgages
- Attract global capital and preserve liquidity during times of economic stress through an explicit government guarantee for eligible mortgage-backed securities backed by single-family or multi-family mortgages
- Require the Guarantors to support an effective national affordable-housing strategy that helps meet the needs of low-income and underserved households and communities
- Support a competitive and diverse primary market for lenders of all sizes and business models
- Enable a robust, innovative, and purely private mortgage market to co-exist alongside the government-backed market
- Preserve existing multi-family financing executions and permit new options
- Establish a strong, transparent regulatory framework that promotes liquidity while protecting taxpayers
- Ensure that private capital assumes most of the credit risk.

Source: (Stevens, 2017[27]).

Notes

[1] For further information see: https://sustainabledevelopment.un.org/sdg11

[2] For further information see the Korean Times, 4 August 2017.

[3] The first Comprehensive Housing Plan was adopted in 2003.

[4] For further information see: http://ecursos.segeplan.gob.gt/recursos/downloads/04.pdf

[5] Information provided by MOLIT during the OECD study visit in September 2017. Housing Welfare Policy presentation.

[6] For further information see: Korea Land and Housing Corporation (LH) http://world.lh.or.kr/englh_html/englh_about/about_2.asp.

[7] Restriction of the computation ratio in cases of conversion into monthly rent in accordance with the housing lease protection act (current): 7% (base rate 1.75% x 4 times). www.korea.net/kpreanet/print.

[8] For further information see: (Schulze Baing, 2010[39])

[9] For further information see: www.helptobuy.gov.uk/shared-ownership/

[10] For further information see: Office of Policy and Research, US Department of Housing and Urban Development: www.huduser.gov/portal/periodicals/em/spring16/highlight3.html.

[11] For further information see: http://eastwestbank.com/ReachFurther/News/Article/How-Smart-Cities-Will-Change-the-Future-of-Urban-Housing and www.cnt.org/projects/rethinking-mortgages

[12] For further information see: http://eastwestbank.com/ReachFurther/News/Article/How-Smart-Cities-Will-Change-the-Future-of-Urban-Housing.

Bibliography

André, C. (2010), "A bird's eye view of OECD housing markets", *Economics Department Working Papers No. 746*, No. ECO/WKP(2010)2, http://www.oecd.org/workingpapers (accessed on 02 November 2017). [14]

Andrews, D., A. Caldera Sánchez and Å. Johansson (2011), "Housing Markets and Structural Policies in OECD Countries", *OECD Economic Department Working Papers*, No. 836, OECD, Paris, http://www.oecd.org/workingpapers (accessed on 27 November 2017). [3]

APRA (2014), *APRA outlines further steps to reinforce sound residential mortgage lending practices*, http://www.apra.gov.au/mediareleases/pages/14_30.aspx (accessed on 06 September 2017). [35]

CECODHAS (2013), *Study on financing social housing in 6 European countries*, CECODHAS European Social Housing Observatory, http://www.housingeurope.eu/file/217/download. [15]

Governa, F. and S. Saccomani (2009), "Housing and Urban Regeneration Experiences and Critical Remarks Dealing with Turin", *European Journal of Housing Policy*, Vol. 9/4, pp. 391-410, http://dx.doi.org/10.1080/14616710903357193. [23]

Government of Canada (2017), *Canada's National Housing Strategy*, https://www.placetocallhome.ca/pdfs/Canada-National-Housing-Strategy.pdf (accessed on 31 January 2018). [19]

Hilber, C. and W. Vermeulen (2016), "The Impact of Supply Constraints on House Prices in England", *The Economic Journal*, Vol. 126/591, pp. 358-405, http://dx.doi.org/10.1111/ecoj.12213. [8]

KDI School (2012), *Policy construction and supply of affordable housing in Korea*, KDI School, Seoul. [10]

Kim, J. (2016), "Why household debt held by Korean seniors is problematic: An international comparison", *Economics Bulletin*, Vol. 36/4, http://www.accessecon.com/Pubs/EB/2016/Volume36/EB-16-V36-I4-P203.pdf (accessed on 15 November 2017), pp. 2080-2093. [25]

Kim, K. et al. (2015), *Public Rental Housing Delivery System*, KRIHS, Sejong. [17]

Kim, K. and M. Park (2016), "Housing Policy in the Republic of Korea Asian Development Bank Institute", *ADBI Working Paper Series No 570*, http://www.adb.org/publications/housing-policy-republic-korea/ (accessed on 10 August 2017). [6]

Lim, S. (2006), *Housing Policy for Low-income Families in Korea, a Historical Overview*, http://www.academia.edu/14672315/Housing_Policy_for_Low-income_Families_in_Korea_a_Historical_Overview (accessed on 10 August 2017). [12]

López-Silva, M. et al. (2011), "Housing Finance in Mexico: Current State and Future Sustainability", No. Technical Notes No. 287, inter-American Development Bank, https://publications.iadb.org/handle/11319/5352 (accessed on 24 August 2017). [33]

Martin, C., H. Pawson and R. Van Den Nouwelant (2016), *Housing policy and the housing system in Australia: an overview Report for the Shaping Housing Futures Project*, UNSW Australia, http://shapingfutures.gla.ac.uk/wp-content/uploads/2016/09/Shaping-Housing-Futures-Australia-background-paper.pdf (accessed on 07 September 2017). [36]

MOLIT (2013), *Second Comprehensive Housing Plan (2013-2022).* [9]

MOLIT (2016), *Housing Policy Guidebook*, MOLIT, Sejong. [18]

MOLIT (2017), *Housing Welfare Roadmap*, MOLIT, Sejong. [11]

OECD (2011), *Economic Policy Reforms 2011: Going for Growth*, OECD Publishing, Paris, http://dx.doi.org/10.1787/growth-2011-en. [24]

OECD (2011), *How's life? Measuring well-being*, OECD Publishing, Paris, http://www.oecd-ilibrary.org/docserver/download/3011061e.pdf?expires=1512147246&id=id&accname=ocid84004878&checksum=5C00C6AD15832D0C57296AA1920C8973 (accessed on 01 December 2017). [28]

OECD (2012), *OECD Urban Policy Reviews, Korea 2012*, OECD Publishing, Paris, http://dx.doi.org/10.1787/9789264174153-en. [37]

OECD (2015), *OECD Urban Policy Reviews: Mexico 2015: Transforming Urban Policy and Housing Finance*, OECD Urban Policy Reviews, OECD Publishing, Paris, http://dx.doi.org/10.1787/9789264227293-en. [13]

OECD (2015), *How's Life? 2015: Measuring Well-being*, OECD Publishing, Paris, http://dx.doi.org/10.1787/how_life-2015-en. [38]

OECD (2016), *OECD Economic Surveys: Korea 2016*, OECD Publishing, Paris, http://pac-files.oecd.org/acrobatebook/1016141e.pdf (accessed on 08 December 2017). [5]

OECD (2016), *Urban Green Growth in Dynamic Asia*, OECD Green Growth Studies, OECD Publishing, Paris, http://dx.doi.org/10.1787/9789264266360-en. [20]

Park, D. and Q. Xiao (2009), "Housing Prices and the Role of Speculation: The Case of Seoul", No. 146, Asian Development Bank, https://www.adb.org/sites/default/files/publication/28239/economics-wp146.pdf (accessed on 08 December 2017). [7]

Park, M. (2013), *Housing policy*, Korea Research Institute for Human Settlements (KRIHS). [29]

Park, M. and S. Tae (2016), "Suggestions of policy direction to improve the housing quality in South Korea", *Sustainability*, Vol. 8, pp. 1-26, http://dx.doi.org/10.3390/su8050438. [31]

Park, M. (2017), *Public policies towards affordable housing in Korea*, Unpublished material, Paper pared for the OECD Housing Dynamics in Korea project.. [16]

Ronald, R. and M. Jin (2010), "Homeownership in South Korea: Examining Sector Underdevelopment", *Urban Studies*, Vol. 47/11, pp. 2367-2388, http://dx.doi.org/10.1177/0042098009357967. [4]

Salvi del Pero, A. et al. (2016), "Policies to promote access to good-quality affordable housing in OECD countries", *OECD Social, Employment and Migration Working Papers*, No. 176, OECD Publishing, Paris, http://dx.doi.org/10.1787/5jm3p5gl4djd-en. [2]

Schulze Baing, A. (2010), "Containing Urban Sprawl? Comparing Brownfield Reuse Policies in England and Germany", *International Planning Studies*, Vol. 15/1, pp. 25-35, http://dx.doi.org/10.1080/13563471003736910. [39]

SHF (2012), *House-price rent ratio.* [32]

Stevens, D. (2017), *Principles of Housing Finance Reform*, Mortgage Bankers Association, https://www.banking.senate.gov/public/_cache/files/51078e45-c3ea-49cd-95a2-d37c7b6ce75f/EAAB641A837ADCBDBEDC8D07FA54B095.stevens-testimony-6-29-17.pdf (accessed on 06 October 2017). [27]

The Conversation((n.d.)), *Australia's housing finance in seven charts*, https://theconversation.com/australias-housing-finance-in-seven-charts-57870 (accessed on 06 September 2017). [34]

UN-Habitat (2016), *New Urban Agenda*, http://habitat3.org/wp-content/uploads/NUA-English.pdf (accessed on 17 November 2017). [1]

Van den Noord, P. (2005), "Tax incentives and house prices in the Euro area: theory and evidence", *Economie internationale* 101, pp. 29-45. [26]

Williams, P. and C. Whitehead (2015), *Financing affordable social housing in the UK; building on success?*, International Union for Housing Finance, http://dx.doi.org/ISSN 2078-6328. [21]

Wilson, W., C. Barton and L. Smith (2017), "Tackling the under-supply of housing in England", No. Briefing Paper No. 07671, House of Commons, London, http://researchbriefings.files.parliament.uk/documents/CBP-7671/CBP-7671.pdf. [22]

Wilson, W. (2017), *Stimulating housing supply - Government initiatives (England)*, House of Commons, London, http://researchbriefings.files.parliament.uk/documents/SN06416/SN06416.pdf. [30]

3. Addressing Korea's urban challenges through urban regeneration and smart city solutions

This chapter examines Korea's urban challenges from the perspective of urban regeneration and smart city solutions. It assesses the strengths and weaknesses of the urban regeneration strategies to revitalise cities. It underlines the need to align labour market, business development, transport, inward investment and social policies to reinforce urban regeneration strategies and ensure sustainable outcomes for the long-term. Critically, this chapter discusses the links between housing policy and urban regeneration programmes as it stresses that housing policies require an integrated approach to build more inclusive cities. The chapter highlights the need for a long term thinking and local leadership in urban regeneration to be successful. Finally, the chapter analyses how Korea is using smart city technologies and strategies to build resilient, liveable and inclusive cities. It stresses Korea's international leadership on the area while acknowledging that could use smart city developments to promote service innovation. The chapter concludes with proposals to use smart city platforms for urban development.

3.1. Urban regeneration as a New Deal policy to revitalise cities

3.1.1. Rapid growth accelerated urban challenges in Korea

Rapid urbanisation and industrialisation in the 1960s set in train a parallel process of urban development and urban renewal in Korea. As national government created the basis for economic growth through key infrastructure investments it also sought to address housing issues through increased provision and improved quality (37.8% of housing in Seoul was classed as substandard in 1966). In the 1970s, the rate of urbanisation was 40-56% to support the rapid expansion of the economy which had an average growth rate of 10.3% and national government adopted a 10-year plan to build 2.5 million homes. In the 1980s, economic growth and housing shortages continued and accelerated the emergence of urban development programmes. The 1980s also marked a new approach to urban development, triggered by the 1986 Asian Games and the 1988 Olympic Games which led to increased demand for more long-term plans and for greater community involvement in development and renewal projects. The 1990s were characterised by decentralisation, regional economic blocks for polycentric development, the expansion of the capital region, urban competitiveness and the expansion of public transport and logistics.

The 21st century marked a further shift. Quality of life and sustainable development became priorities as national government pursued the Balance-Green-Welfare agenda through the 4th National Territorial Comprehensive Plan. Urban and housing renewal programmes were accelerated until the 2008 global financial crisis. Stagnation followed and the next decade has been characterised by the onset of low growth at 2.8% and changing demographics. As in other countries, the crisis has led to an increased focus on urban regeneration and community participation. Since 2017, the national government has sought to accelerate efforts to arrest decline in urban areas, reduce disparities and advance an agenda of inclusive growth.

3.1.2. A new context for Korean urban regeneration

Urban regeneration in Korea has historically focused on housing provision to meet the demands of rapid urbanisation. However, the government has increasingly recognised the need for a more integrated approach to respond to the more complex challenges of social inclusion, job creation and economic revitalisation. The 2013 Special Act on Urban Regeneration marked a critical shift towards inclusive and integrated approaches. The Act defines urban regeneration as the: "economic, social, physical and environmental revitalisation of a city which is declining due to depopulation, change of industrial structure, indiscriminate expansion of cities, deterioration of the dwelling condition, etc., by strengthening the local capacity, introducing and creating new functions, and utilising the local resources" (Article 2).

The Act marks a greater shift towards national and local governments working in partnership to create a more integrated framework for urban regeneration. The new framework comprises national guidance, a strategic plan and an activation plan which overarch the two thematic strands: economy and community. The Economy-based Activation Plan focuses on creating new urban functions and employment opportunities through links with core national infrastructure. The Community-based Activation Plan promotes community engagement through smaller-scale improvements to living conditions, local infrastructures and through the promotion of local small businesses. The overarching vision is the recreation of competitive cities to achieve personal wellbeing underpinned through four main policy areas:

- Regeneration-focused strategy through the reorganisation of the Urban Planning Law, the mixed use of land in the inner city and upgrading the urban environment
- Expansion of government funding on urban regeneration across government departments and the expansion of the regeneration budget by the Ministry of Land, Infrastructure and Transport
- Financial support and the mitigation of regulation through the creation of a public fund, mitigation of architecture and planning regulations and greater utilisation of public property
- Reinforcement of local competency and community revitalisation through co-operative associations and social enterprises, community capacity building and adopting cutting edge technologies (smart city).

The Act led to the Basic Policy on National Urban Regeneration Projects and the selection of the 1st priority areas in 2014. 13 areas were designated to implement 2 urban economy projects and 11 community projects. National government has confirmed investment of KRW 1.2 trillion in collaborative projects and private investments as of March 2015 and KRW 6-25 billion per local government up to 2017.

The new administration that started in 2017 has led to an even greater emphasis on urban regeneration, strengthening the Act through a five-year Urban Regeneration New Deal which will designate 100 projects supported by an investment of KRW 1 trillion.

Box 3.1. Urban regeneration: A proven catalyst for change

With its origins dating back to the 19th century, urban regeneration has been a critical mechanism to reduce disparities, arrest decline and create shared opportunity in cities by aligning social, physical, economic and environmental actions. Social reformers seeking to address urban poverty, public health and the slum dwellings which marked urban development in the 19th and early 20th centuries led to a focus on housing which continues to remain relevant and necessary today. Post World War II housing shortages followed by large-scale industrial restructuring, subsequent economic downturns and the 2008 economic crisis have exacerbated the need for ongoing urban regeneration interventions and draw attention to the complex nature of the problems it seeks to address.

Urban regeneration is by nature a long-term intervention which yields sustainable and meaningful results over time. Effective urban regeneration is an integrated process that works over cycles. Electoral cycles (3-5 years), business cycles (12-15 years) and funding cycles which can range from 1-20 years all impact upon outcomes and can create varying degrees of uncertainty to already complex issues (OECD, 2013). Urban regeneration is an ongoing process for cities; it is what makes them dynamic and resilient.

Urban regeneration activities work particularly by contributing to the "investment driver" in cities, especially in making urban property markets more attractive to external investment, more flexible and adaptable. They also encourage agglomeration economies in cities by fostering better conditions in which businesses can cluster, and by drawing together a larger labour pool to serve one location (usually a revitalised city centre and business district). Regeneration programmes encourage new urban governance, and better joint working in cities, to tackle the key obstacle of co-ordination failures, often through new forms of leadership. By enhancing the investment driver, supporting agglomeration, and by tackling co-ordination failures, urban regeneration interventions can increase the growth rate of city and regional economies.

Pursuing an integrated approach means that economic, social, environmental, spatial, and institutional factors are interdependent. In urban regeneration these elements have to be combined in purposeful ways that often require "whole of government" and "multi-sector partnership" approaches. National governments often set the framework conditions and provide substantial funding for regeneration programmes, but it is at the sub-national level that delivery and implementation take place. Vertical co-ordination between tiers of government, as well as horizontal across government departments and sectors, is fundamental to realising successful outcomes. (OECD, 2012).

Source: OECD (2013, 2012).

3.1.3. Delivering the Urban Regeneration New Deal

Housing remains a core component of the "New Deal" which will operate at different spatial scales and allow for 57 typologies of intervention to respond to local needs. Projects will focus on: urban renewal, low-rise residential areas, distressed station areas, residential environments in rural and suburban areas, government-owned property and creating innovative places (Box 3.2). The system has been designed to allow for greater collaboration between levels of government and local stakeholders. National government assumes a supportive role to unlock local growth potential and to build local capacity.

Box 3.2. The Korean regeneration planning system

State Level Urban Regeneration Policy: Assigned by MOLIT, reviewed by Special Committee and approved by the President.

Regeneration Strategy Plan: Assigned by Mayors every 10 years, stakeholder engagement, selection of priority areas.

Regeneration Promotion Plan: Assigned by Mayors or heads of government, delivered through an implementation plan designed around two programme headings:

The Urban Economy Programme will:

- Connect to the city long-term economic development plan
- Link with large-scale urban infrastructure renewal and development
- Review finance
- Create direct ripple effects on adjacent areas
- Minimise development risk.

The Community-based Regeneration Programme will:

- Take a neighbourhood-level approach
- Encourage the participation of diverse groups and individuals
- Make comprehensive improvements to soft and hard frameworks
- Take a long-term approach.

Adopting such a tailored approach has proved successful in other OECD countries such as the United Kingdom. The benefits of such an approach are that initiatives can be targeted to local needs and developed to become integrated in the existing local development system.

The broad nature of the New Deal will enable Korean cities to tackle issues such as:

- Improving slum dwellings through the Sae-teul Village Projects for City Slums. 68 projects receive KRW 5 billion to renovate housing stock, revitalise communities and create local jobs.
- Creating community facilities and employment training centres such as in Chunan-Si.
- Creating new communities through increasing housing density during renovation projects, transforming low-rise building into high-rise with the goal to create 20 000 homes.
- Supporting local businesses and creating new economic hubs.
- Working with universities to create student accommodation.

Each initiative will be underpinned by rigorous ex-ante and ex-post evaluation through the enabling framework created by MOLIT and overseen by supporting agencies.

Creating an enabling framework for urban regeneration

National government has created an enabling framework to support the programmes of the Urban Regeneration New Deal through two dedicated bodies. The Urban Regeneration Assistance Organisation (URAO) supports national and local governments through evidence-based policy and regulation, evaluation, project management, guidelines, consulting and training. The URAO will also support the Urban Regeneration Support Centres (URSC) whose role is to support local governments. The URAO works alongside Korea Land and Housing Corporation (LH) and the Korea Research Institute of Human Settlements (KRIHS) and has benefitted from USD 560 million from central government through a match funding system. The URAO currently support seven economy-based projects in Pusan, Chungju, Seoul, Daegu, Incheon, Daejun and Buchun and a further 29 neighbourhood-based projects throughout Korea.

This approach will play a critical role in ensuring that all plans and projects associated with the Urban Regeneration New Deal are evidence based, relevant to the local needs and build delivery capacity at the local level. Whilst other member countries have created institutions which support one or more of the tasks of the URAO, few take such a comprehensive approach.

In addition, Urban Regeneration Support Centres have been created in all cities participating in Urban Regeneration New Deal programmes. The centres comprise residents, community leaders and specialists to deliver targeted assistance and ensure that the projects become embedded into the local economy.

Effective urban regeneration demands robust ex-ante and ex-post evaluation. The system in Korea has been designed to ensure that priority areas are selected on evidence-based criteria and the URAO is tasked with evaluating projects. Sharing outcomes across the designated projects and adapting strategies when needed will ensure more sustainable outcomes and help strengthen local competencies for urban regeneration.

3.1.4. National government partnering urban regeneration

Throughout OECD member countries national governments play critical roles in determining regeneration policy, programmes and resources. This does not imply that all interventions are top down. More than four decades of intervention has enabled national governments across OECD member states to develop nimble and flexible programmes. However, since the 2008 financial crisis recession and the subsequent financial services bail-outs many national governments have faced reduced resources and increased dilemmas over how to redistribute dwindling tax revenues. The OECD report *New Growth and Investment Strategies (2013)* noted that "in the period leading up to the [2008] crisis there was a proliferation of different initiatives by national governments, not all of which were well absorbed or utilised by local actors. In the post-crisis world there is strong desire to rationalise such programmes around a common agenda for change and to find greater synergy of effort".

National governments adapt programmes over time and respond to changing economic contexts. Following the 2008 global financial crisis many national programmes have been adapted. For example, since 2010, the UK Government's approach to urban regeneration has become a vital part of the Government's approach to increasing local growth and competitiveness and building a strong and balanced economy. The current emphasis is on a place-based approach to regeneration that builds on the particular strengths of different places to drive growth and addresses the factors that hold them back" (Thorpe 2017).

Interventions such as the UK City Deals are creating long-term support mechanisms which at a time of fiscal restraint are proving to be critical enablers of local growth and job creation (Box 3.3).

Box 3.3. National priorities for urban regeneration in the United Kingdom

- Agreeing place-based approaches to driving economic growth, regeneration and housing development – including pan-regional models such as the Northern Powerhouse and Midlands Engine designed to boost economic growth and competitiveness in areas outside London and South East England.
- Creating the conditions for local growth through a competitive, deal-making approach which offers incentives such as the Local Growth Fund that supports successful growth projects and the creation of Enterprise Zones that provide tax breaks and government support in designated areas.
- Empowering strong and accountable local decision-making and giving a voice to the private sector through Local Enterprise Partnerships (partnerships between local authorities and businesses), elected Mayors for Combined Authorities/city regions. The latter provide a formal structure for collaboration between local authorities on joint regeneration and transport projects.
- Devolving and decentralising powers and functions to local areas, for example through Devolution Deals which devolve powers and spending from central government to consortia of local authorities.

Source: UK Urban Regeneration Policy for Competitiveness: A Government Perspective. Keith Thorpe, Cities and Local Growth Unit, Department for Communities and Local Government, United Kingdom, 2017.

Social rental housing to be provided through urban regeneration programmes

Korea's housing policy is linked to urban renewal. This is in line with the OECD and UN-Habitat approach of positioning housing at the centre of sustainable urban development. This allows shifting from a basic construction of houses to a more holistic approach that integrates urban planning and urban finance and puts people at the centre of urban development. Indeed, the Korean government has been making efforts to integrate the housing policy with urban planning and urban regeneration since the late 1980s when the "Two Million Housing Drive" (TMHD) was incorporated with new town developments surrounding the Seoul Metropolitan Area (Kim and Park, 2016). Although the current administration will also provide public rental housing, it is expected to be more consolidated with urban regeneration in a smaller and more incremental way compared to the previous initiatives such as the TMHD. These efforts involve improving existing houses and building new ones.

Currently, Korea's housing policy aims to ensure stable sustainable housing for low-income households through greater supply of public rental homes. For that, the current administration intends to supply 170 000 units annually for public rental housing. Of those, 70 000 units will be built linking housing with urban regeneration objectives (reconstruction of old public buildings); 60 000 units will be purchased (remodelling or reconstructing after purchasing old homes) and then rented to young adults and newlyweds; and 40 000 units will come from public assistance housing by promoting private rental housing with enhanced public value, regulating rents for the early phase of rentals and making stricter requirements for tenants. 30% of multi-family units in the country are 30 years old or more and require upgrading, retrofitting and renovation. "Happiness Housing" programme is in line with the urban regeneration policy because the government utilises public-owned land to produce "Happiness Housing" units as well as to link urban functions to industrial activities. By incorporating the production of "Happiness Housing" with urban regeneration, the government expects to produce a synergy effect and support the young generation by providing them with opportunities to reside in affordable and decent houses with a convenient access to employment locations and other public facilities.

Improving access to affordable housing in Korea is linked to improving urban planning and urban regeneration objectives, promoting a competitive and responsive housing market, as well as dealing with the demographic changes (ageing population). In other OECD countries, objectives for the social rental sector, for example, include reducing its construction and running costs (Denmark); improving its regulation (the Czech Republic); or enabling a more diverse range of providers (New Zealand) (Salvi del Pero, Adema, Ferraro, & Frey, 2016, p. 27). The example of HafenCity in Germany demonstrates how the city of Hamburg aligned with governmental and non-governmental partners to integrate affordable housing into the regeneration framework for the port area and neighbouring sites. What began as an ambitious plan to regenerate the port has become emblematic of the city's commitment to inclusive growth and an example of how projects evolve and take on new roles in cities.

Box 3.4. Regeneration and affordable housing in Hamburg, Germany

HafenCity is emerging as one of the largest city centre development areas in Europe, currently hosting over 10 000 jobs but with the potential to support up to 45 000 jobs. Public investment of EUR 2.4 billion, much of which was financed from land sales, has catalysed over EUR 8.5 billion of private investment. With the development process of HafenCity, a 1.5km^2 harbour and industrial site is effectively expanding the city centre by 40%. The urban development principles of HafenCity masterplan seek to add density, quality, and liveability to the site's public spaces, 7 000 homes (including affordable homes) and 45 000 jobs representing about 4% of the city's labour force.

The "Alliance for Homes" between the Senate, associations of the housing industry and the municipal housing company has set the specific objectives for an inclusive housing market, including not only the 6 000 homes per year target, but also greater flexibility in social housing provision, and special housing support for homeless and disabled people. Senate districts support the objectives by ensuring a faster approval process and the provision of affordable urban land. This has had an impact on the social mix in the major new development sites such as HafenCity.

Source: OECD (2015).

Urban Regeneration in Seoul: Smart and inclusive

The Seoul Metropolitan Government has strong competences in urban regeneration. The rapid development of the metropolitan area demanded an ongoing strategy that focused on economic revitalisation and housing need. Since the global financial crisis, the emphasis has shifted to ensure that regeneration also takes into account the needs of local communities and engages citizens in shaping the future. Seoul has advanced an agenda which the national approach reinforces. Working in partnership with national government the Seoul Metropolitan City Regeneration Centre was created in 2017 to serve as a co-ordination body for the Urban Regeneration Committee, establish major policies for urban regeneration, support project implementation, provide on-site support and community engagement. The Centre builds on the well-established approach to urban regeneration in the city which seeks to promote inclusive growth through urban regeneration. The Centre is engaging with 131 urban regeneration projects currently underway. The approach enables customised responses, providing targeted expertise.

The Centre, like others throughout the country, will play a critical role in delivering the Community-based Programme. Area-based neighbourhood initiatives, such as those supported by the Urban Regeneration New Deal have a well-established history throughout OECD countries. In cities seeking to address social exclusion or promote inclusive growth, the neighbourhood is often the most appropriate level and it has become increasingly apparent that success or failure is highly dependent upon social capital. Typically, the idea of social capital is associated with relations in civil society. Social capital is built in families, local communities, neighbourhoods, voluntary associations and firms.

The Urban Regeneration Support Centres place significant emphasis on the engagement of local residents and community leaders. This approach reinforces commitments to inclusive growth and signals a renewed emphasis on citizen engagement, which in turn can strengthen social capital, which will be critical for many of the neighbourhood initiatives. However, when area-based approaches towards excluded communities are adopted, there is still a need to develop mechanisms which link them strategically to the economic and social mainstream of the wider urban and regional areas.

The Urban Regeneration New Deal Programme and many of the initiatives pursued by Seoul Metropolitan Government seek to redress urban decline. As cities go through processes of regeneration, neighbourhoods change. Some prosper as processes of gentrification take place, while others deteriorate. OECD work over the last three decades demonstrates that distressed urban areas are commonplace and are often areas with strong local identities. Research continually highlights the fact that the neighbourhood environment has important social consequences. One of the most significant factors undermining local confidence is a strong sense of physical deterioration, hence the reason that many regeneration projects have concentrated more on physical urban renewal. Older, historic buildings are fundamental to residents' sense of place and the loss or decline of such "landmark" buildings leads to acute feelings of lost heritage, pride, status and identity. Similarly, new symbols emerge through architecture and urban design which reinvigorate communities and reflect neighbourhood changes. Because regeneration tends to take place at the micro level, thought must be given to ensuring that new spaces interact with the existing urban fabric.

The Seoul Metropolitan Government recently opened four new local regeneration offices in areas that have distinct cultural and economic identities and have experienced long-term decline. Each will oversee the renovation of the physical fabric of the area as well as enable economic regeneration. The focus is on cultural renewal utilising local assets with the aim of creating local jobs, improving well-being and housing opportunities. The Changsin and Sungin areas seek to preserve the historic fabric of the garment sector and maintaining the small business base whilst developing cultural heritage and capacity within the community.

Engaging citizens in urban regeneration is widely recognised as critical to the overall success of programmes. The national framework requires citizen engagement and Seoul has been pioneering in its approach to engage citizens at all stages of the development process.

Box 3.5. Citizen engagement in urban regeneration in Seoul

To support urban regeneration a 10-year plan, "2025 Urban Regeneration Strategy", was created in the course of a year (from March 2015 to December 2015). The Plan is underpinned by the "Urban Regeneration Revitalization Plan" which covers thirteen areas in Seoul as part of the master plan for the sustainable urban regeneration initiative. In the implementation stage, over 50 civilian experts selected as "conflict mediation co-ordinators" were sent to "conflict-ridden" development areas. They monitored these areas over 500 times throughout the year to provide customised solutions and decisions on the progress. Moreover, alternative projects were sought with the focus on preserving regional values, including the communities themselves, cultural assets, and natural landscapes. In addition, the Seoul Metropolitan Government (SMG) bought and renovated anchor facilities for the regeneration/revitalisation areas and made them available for use as bases for local residents' economic, cultural and social activities free of charge. The SMG also provided support to help the residents achieve economic self-sufficiency in operating the facilities, thereby laying the basis for the formation of sustainable and self-sufficient communities.

19 areas received support for implementing resident-led initiatives involving meetings with about 1 600 residents. In addition, 140 education and training classes were provided annually to over 3 000 residents in regeneration areas to strengthen their capacity for self-sufficiency. Educational and training programmes designed to discover and foster "regeneration activists" produced over 120 regeneration activists every year, who were dispatched as mentors to assist the residents of regeneration areas. To establish a sustainable and self-sufficient economic basis, the SMG also provided consulting services on the development of products that represent regional characteristics.

Through these efforts, 53 neighbourhood enterprises and co-operative associations in 23 areas received support, including joint marketing events to promote their products, as a means of establishing the basis for the residents' self-sufficient economy. Moreover, the SMG developed a comprehensive diagnosis and monitoring system for regeneration projects and enhanced their implementation through systematic management, comprehensive evaluation, and feedback. For the successful implementation of the regeneration projects, the SMG's Urban Regeneration Headquarters invested KRW 195 billion in such projects in 2016, and KRW 231 billion in 2017.

Source: SMG, 2017.

Strategies are fundamental for regeneration

The 2013 Act and the 2017 Urban Regeneration New Deal recognise the need for robust and aligned regeneration, economic and urban development plans and strategies. City governments and partners often control land use planning through land use plans and zoning regulations, but may not control other aspects of administration and investment in the city which means that regeneration strategies are a means to use spatial tools to shape and influence other parts of society, the economy, and government. Regeneration is a long-term process which requires the alignment of physical, social, economic and environmental policy, interventions and delivery mechanisms. The regeneration strategy can become a vehicle for breaking down silos across the public sector as well as being an effective mechanism to engage different sectors. Cities such as Seoul have created long term strategies which are underpinned by site specific plans. National government is further supporting cities and local governments through the URAO.

In terms of urban regeneration, there are gradual cyclical shifts from focusing on spatial and environmental dimensions to accruing stronger interventions in market economies and with social and institutional development. A regeneration plan is a means to define both the development path and also to assess the arrangements that will bring it about. Regeneration strategies have a spatial character but are designed to use space to integrate otherwise separate interventions. Equally, because they aim to be long term in nature they often require multi-party sign off and governance even if leadership comes from a smaller group. It is important, therefore, to have some participative over-sight on the strategy. The idea is that it should command enough consensus that it would be able to continue even if the party in power changes. Regeneration plans are likely to become more important in the programme areas as the projects reach the end of their life. Cities will need to create enabling environments to maintain the momentum of outcomes; the approach taken in Seoul is an approach that could be used elsewhere.

The importance of building a common agenda and vision for the future is critical for several reasons. Firstly, the context in which most development and regeneration strategies are produced is not promising. Usually a crisis or threat of some kind is present. This means that frequently these are times when the more mobile portion of a local population tends to move away and find a more attractive location with better life chances. At the same time, many choices are faced in how to calibrate a different future and these choices must be subject to some agreement and ownership if they are to be pursued with any convictions. Strategy is ultimately about building common purpose between the people and organisations who want to make regeneration happen. In Seoul, citizen and stakeholder engagement play critical roles in the regeneration process. The city uses traditional methods as outlined earlier through the "conflict mediation co-ordinators" but increasingly relies on its smart city platform to engage citizens.

At the same time, strategy is also testing ideas against external evidence and challenge. This often means assessing whether the aspiration and vision are really achievable. Questions it should answer are: is there "demand" for what the place wants to be and can it be attractive and competitive in the areas it wants to specialise in. Strategy recognises that many parts of the local economy have to be won through the contest of competition, so it serves both to educate about what the opportunities and competition are, and also to motivate communities to recognise the need to compete and the means to do so. Turin is an example of a city that has successfully brought together a broad spectrum of local actors around the task of regeneration and competitiveness over the past two decades. The Associazione Torino Internazionale first pioneered a strategic consultative approach to planning in 2000, and again later in 2006. Since the global financial crisis, the city has had to re-assess the structural deficiencies in its development model, and in 2012, in collaboration with the OECD LEED Programme, it re-galvanised around the task of a third strategic plan.

Strategies can aid confidence building and as strategic choices are made, communities consider how to use assets and opportunities fully to embrace change. Strategies often identify opportunities and catalysts and consider how to make the most of them. They are "Integrated Plans" and provide a means to see linkages between different aspects of city development and to understand complex phasing and sequencing issues and critical paths to success. For example, regeneration plans often show links between land use, transport, housing, and environment, or between education, skills, economy, and productivity, or between planning, branding, and promotion. For both the economy-driven and neighbourhood-focused aspects of the Urban Regeneration New Deal each of these aspects will be important at different phases of the projects.

3.1.5. Financing urban regeneration: Thinking long term

The Urban Regeneration New Deal is a five-year initiative which benefits from substantial investments by national government. Korean cities such as Seoul also allocate significant budgets for urban regeneration. In 2016, the city invested KRW 195 billion rising to KRW 231 billion in 2017. Across the OECD multiple actors and stakeholders finance urban regeneration including international financial institutions, national, regional and local governments, foundations/NGOs and the private sector (developers and investors). Finance is often provided through a diverse range of mechanisms which can include direct transfers and loan arrangements. Regeneration projects frequently rely on multiple funding streams over varying time frames which can affect outcomes, particularly when external shocks take place.

The global financial crisis is a case in point as it has significantly impacted public budgets and thus regeneration efforts in many cities (OECD, 2009; OECD, 2013; UCL, 2015). Fiscal restraint in many OECD countries has reduced both the size of transfer payments between higher tier and local governments, and in many cases local governments are being asked to undertake a wider range of activities with fewer resources, although in some cases local governments are provided with the freedom or opportunity to utilise new revenue-raising instruments. Overall, many local governments are poorer and the scope to use new instruments or to mount public and private funded urban regeneration is limited by the weaknesses in demand from private capital. Consequently, the major opportunity for urban regeneration often lies with skilful use of public budgets to achieve transformative investments and changes in addition to achieving efficient service delivery (OECD, 2013). The Urban Regeneration New Deal could consider such an approach but experience from other countries indicates that longer-term finance and investment will need to be considered for better results.

Many cities contain substantial public assets in the form of real estate, facilities, or other amenities which can be an opportunity for urban regeneration initiatives. Urban areas in particular were the centres of gravity in the industrial and pre-industrial eras, and their assets have accumulated over time. Public assets are an increasingly important mechanism in developing investment strategies which respond to broader economic geographies and respond to different needs. Seoul pursues this approach to underpin the 2025 Regeneration Plan and other cities in Korea may need to become entrepreneurial in the use of their assets to attract private sector investment. Leveraging local assets to create long term investment portfolios will enable cities to truly integrate the Urban Regeneration New Deal projects into the overall economic fabric of the cities where they are located.

It is a key task of city and regional development activity to make cities and regions both more "investable" and more "investment ready". "Investable" in that they need to clearly demonstrate how good returns can be made on investments in their territory and be ready to help make those deals attractive. "Investment ready" in that they must become involved directly with measures to stimulate a strong deal flow of good quality propositions for financiers to evaluate. Urban regeneration, as proposed through the economic and neighbourhood pillars of the Urban Regeneration New Deal, represents significant investment by the public sector which is attracting private sector investment and helping shape new local economies. However, funding is limited to a five-year time frame which means that institutional and commercial investment will need to be secured to support locally-focused financial instruments and assets. The key to most progress is a new relationship with the private sector. Not just public-private partnerships, but a more advanced means to shared risks, costs, returns, and the stewardship of assets.

Through its collaborative governance arrangements, metropolitan investment and integrated approach to urban regeneration, the Greater Manchester Combined Authority, in the United Kingdom, has skilfully collaborated with national government, the European Union and the private sector. It has created a long-term investment framework for urban regeneration which builds on a long series of systematic interventions over several decades.

Box 3.6. Integrated finance across the metropolitan area in Greater Manchester

In 2009, the **Greater Manchester Fund** was set up, which required the 10 local boroughs to invest over GBP 1 billion on joint transport projects such as the Metrolink light rail system. Shortly afterwards, the Association of Greater Manchester Authorities, in conjunction with other north west partners, were chosen to lead a North West Evergreen Fund. Evergreen is a GBP 300 million fund, comprising EU JESSICA Funds, pension fund investments and other private capital.

The investment capacity of Greater Manchester was further enhanced through the Regional Growth Fund and Growing Places funding awards of GBP 100 million with which Greater Manchester successfully developed a unified **Investment Framework** which prioritised a pipeline of commercial and physical projects according to measurable impact. This assembly of funding streams (totalling some GBP 170 million) has enabled the region to focus on effective resource management and growth optimisation. The commitment to collective investment decisions that apply across more than one cycle of development and which do not benefit all authorities equally, was a clear indication of the belief in **pooling for the greater good**. By 2015, the suite of GM Funds has committed in excess of GBP 160 million and delivered in excess of **8 000 jobs** with ambitions to create further complementary funds from the 2014-20 ERDF Programme.

This paved the way for Greater Manchester's landmark "**City Deal**" with the national government. The centrepiece of the Deal is a highly innovative mechanism for the city region to "earn back" part of the national tax revenues generated by the joint investment. The Earnback model allows the 10 authorities to recoup up to GBP 30 million a year from central government from raised business rates, on a payment-by-results basis. **These funds are then recycled and reinvested.**

Leaders have also actively sought to attract investment capital in order to create jobs. The GBP 800 million Airport City, located within Greater Manchester Enterprise Zone is the city region's premier development opportunity marketed internationally, especially to China. Enterprise Zone designation in the highest value-added part of the metropolitan area **enables the benefits of growth to be shared by deprived communities through investments which target the specific needs of those communities**.

In addition, leaders have built a constructive relationship with Abu Dhabi United Group, the investment company that owns Manchester City Football Club. This has enabled progress to be made in Manchester Life, an important new regeneration partnership for the city that will build **6 000 homes** over 10 years. Up to GBP 1 billion is being invested, with the Abu Dhabi private equity company citing the City Council's vision and track record for regeneration as a major incentive. The company is also a key investor in the regeneration of East Manchester, playing a key role in the social and economic transformation of the most deprived area in the city which builds on the 2002 Commonwealth Games legacy.

Source: New Growth and Investment Strategies, OECD, 2013; Local Economic Leadership, OECD, 2015.

3.1.6. Urban regeneration needs local leadership

A key lesson from the recent global economic crisis is that in the future, leaders of local economies will continue to be faced with challenges that cannot be resolved using their formal authority and powers alone. They therefore need to be accomplished innovators, who can come up with new approaches and tools to address the system weaknesses that they face. They also need to be adept at influencing and persuading other stakeholders, so as to align resources and efforts, and to make space for their innovations. They need to become expert in sharing, listening and networking, in order to learn about and adopt successful tools and platforms developed elsewhere. They may need to adapt, adjust and implement the innovations of others, and they will certainly need to be skilled at planning for the future and anticipating challenges wherever possible, so as to be able to implement innovations before (or as) they are needed (OECD, 2015).

Leadership has a critical role to play in both urban regeneration and inclusive growth. The Mayor of Seoul's commitment to these mutually reinforcing agendas is also evident in other cities. In Hamburg, the leadership agenda has embarked on a long-term strategy of socially responsible growth. Fiscal prudence has been the hallmark of the Mayor's leadership which has underpinned confidence in other inclusive growth policies. Similarly, local leaders in Amsterdam stand out for the strong case they have put forward in favour of immigration, inclusion and in defence of tolerance. Each has argued that the challenge of integration is one of economic growth and job creation, and not only about cultural or religious identity. In addition, the OECD's Champion Mayors for Inclusive Growth Coalition, which includes the Mayor of Seoul, is helping shape a new global dialogue.

Box 3.7. Inclusive Growth in cities and the Global Coalition of Champion Mayors at the OECD

Across the OECD, the average income of the richest 10% of the population has grown from 7-10 times that of the poorest 10% in a single generation. But inequalities are not just about money: they affect every dimension of people's lives and well-being, such as life expectancy, education outcomes, and job prospects.

In 2012, the OECD launched the Inclusive Growth initiative as a response to a widening gap between the rich and the poor. The OECD defines Inclusive Growth as "growth that creates opportunities for all segments of the population to participate in the economy and distributes the dividends of increased prosperity fairly across society" (OECD, 2014). The OECD takes a multidimensional approach, going beyond income to take into account a range of well-being outcomes and policy domains.

Inequalities can be even more acute in cities. According to OECD evidence:

- Income inequality tends to be higher in cities relative to their respective countries (in 10 out of 11 OECD countries surveyed). This is because cities have a wider polarisation of high and low skills and top earners capture a higher share of total income (OECD, 2016a).
- Income inequality also tends to be higher in larger cities.
- Inequality goes beyond income, affecting every dimension of an individual's life, such as employment opportunities, health and education outcomes. For instance, in London (United Kingdom) and Baltimore (United States), life expectancy can vary by 20 years across neighbourhoods.
- Moreover, income inequality has a clear spatial dimension, with the persistence of neighbourhoods of concentrated wealth and poverty. OECD research found that the most income segregated cities in the Netherlands and France are at comparable levels to the least segregated cities in the United States.
- Even in the same country, income segregation can vary across the cities depending on region-specific factors such as labour productivity, the degree of spatial decentralisation, and demography as well as the level of wealth.

In recognition of the key role of cities in tackling inequalities, the OECD created a Global Coalition of Champion Mayors for Inclusive Growth in March 2016. Together, Champion Mayors delivered the *New York Proposal for Inclusive Growth in Cities,* the *Paris Action Plan for Inclusive Growth in Cities*, and the *Seoul Implementation Agenda,* which outlined a series of commitments and policy priorities, along four main pillars: 1) Education; 2) Labour markets; 3) Housing and the urban environment; and 4) Infrastructure and public services. Across these four pillars, a number of cross-cutting themes have emerged as strong priorities among Champion Mayors, including: urban regeneration, the integration of migrants in cities, the nexus of climate change and inclusive growth strategies, and health inequalities in cities.

Source: OECD (2014), All on Board, OECD Publishing, Paris; OECD (2016a), Making Cities Work for All; OECD (2016b), New York Proposal for Inclusive Growth in Cities; OECD (2016c), Paris Action Plan for Inclusive Growth in Cities; OECD (2017) Seoul Implementation Agenda for Inclusive Growth in Cities.

Regeneration also demands broader coalitions of leaders from civil society and the private sector. The Urban Regeneration New Deal commits to raising local capacity and engaging residents and stakeholders to shape and lead the programmes. This approach has been tested elsewhere. Local economies benefit from strong, integrated civic leadership driving a local development coalition. Civic leadership encompasses all leadership activity within a given locality that serves a public purpose (Hambleton, 2011). Civic leaders hail from a wide range of bodies, as representatives of NGOs and community-based organisations, religious groups, trade unions, universities, arts institutions, charities, social networks or community volunteers. The distinguishing feature of civic leadership is that it is place-based: that is civic leaders are concerned about focusing on the needs of a place as a result of loyalty and civic identity. Often its contribution is to leverage collective leadership to assemble a fact base, build consensus for action around a limited set of issues (e.g. regeneration, education, services, and infrastructure), incubate programmes in strategic areas, and attract attention from local and higher tier governments (OECD, 2015).

3.1.7. What next for Korea?

The Urban Regeneration New Deal marks a change in approach to delivering urban regeneration in Korea. The 2013 Act laid strong foundations and the Urban Regeneration New Deal adds momentum to create a more integrated system which aligns people and place. It is too early to assess or evaluate the full impact of the approach but based on understanding what has worked elsewhere and what the successful pillars of urban regeneration are the approach may contribute to national and local commitments towards inclusive growth. Areas which may need further consideration to reinforce the Urban Regeneration New Deal are as follows.

Consider the long term

Urban regeneration is by its very nature a long-term process which requires national and city governments to also think and plan for the long term. The Urban Regeneration New Deal is a five-year initiative which may require additional support to create sustainable outcomes and bring about lasting change. National and city government partners should consider how other policies and interventions can reinforce the Urban Regeneration New Deal. To create a truly integrated process this will mean aligning welfare, health, skills, education, employment, transport, investment and business development agendas in a similar way to the realignment of urban regeneration and housing. A whole-of-government approach will accelerate outcomes, facilitate lasting changes and future proof projects beyond election cycles to take into account investment and regeneration life-cycles.

Align investments

Throughout the life of the Urban Regeneration New Deal, significant investments will be made by national and city governments. To reinforce these substantial investments other related public-sector investment in the selected areas and their immediate environs could be evaluated as a means to ensure that public funding is used to its most effective ends. This could be particularly important as the projects mature and need to create long term business plans. Furthermore, cities contain substantial public assets in the form of real estate, facilities, or other amenities which can be an opportunity for urban regeneration initiatives. Public assets are an increasingly important mechanism in developing investment strategies which respond to broader economic geographies and respond to different needs and Korean cities could further explore how local asset bases can reinforce regeneration efforts.

Building the evidence base

Urban regeneration requires careful planning and organising, based on evidence and analysis, and consideration of different options. Building an effective and rigorous evidence base against which programmes, policies and actions can be developed and monitored is an essential feature of effective urban regeneration and economic development. This requires robust and diverse data collection, economic intelligence gathering across economic geographies to monitor economic growth, labour and capital productivity, employment growth/unemployment reduction and business base scale and diversity. Knowing which economic indicators will be used to judge the success of the plans and policies would follow and should be used to judge investment priorities. The URAO are committed to working with the selected projects to help build the evidence base and to evaluate each project. This approach will be critical and allow for adjustments when needed but each of the local authority areas should be involved in the process to help build local capacity and to mainstream evidence-based approaches.

Housing as a catalyst for urban regeneration

Housing-led regeneration has a long and established history in Korea. Housing remains a priority for national government and MOLIT has aligned housing and urban development funding as well as creating new measures to address housing need and affordable housing challenges. The Urban Regeneration New Deal, through its diverse range of interventions including the "Public Housing and Facilities Model", proposes a number of incentives to renovate and transform residential buildings. Investors will be eligible for low interest loans from the Korea Housing and Urban Guarantee Corporation to help with seed money and construction costs. This pillar of the Deal will support other measures aimed at promoting local growth and creating more competitive local areas and should be part of the city-wide regeneration plan and could become a viable model beyond the programming period.

Invest in capacity building

Increasing confidence and competence within local government to take on leadership and convening roles and to command the confidence of stakeholders engaged in regeneration will be critical. Large cities tend to have such capacity but smaller local and district authorities will need to strengthen their competences. The URAO and local Urban Regeneration Support Centres are critical elements to build local capacity and may need greater resources and competences along the way to maintain local momentum and strengthen outcomes.

Make the case for smart urban regeneration

2017 saw the launch of the Urban Regeneration New Deal and the Smart City New Deal. It is early days for each initiative but the foundations have been soundly laid. Making existing cities work more efficiently is an increasingly important part of addressing urban regeneration and housing challenges, especially with the use of big data. Compelling business cases will need to be made for smart rebuilding, or regeneration, of existing cityscapes, using smart technology and sustainable building materials and constructing denser housing, to revive deprived areas of cities. Urban regeneration plans will need to be smart and smart plans will need to demonstrate how they contribute to urban regeneration.

3.2. Smart cities driving change through innovation.

3.2.1. 1. Understanding the smart city

In an increasingly urban world, smart city technologies and systems have rapidly evolved to create a global movement which applies ICT and innovation to enable cities to become more resilient, liveable and inclusive. Smart cities emerged as the global financial crisis was changing the economic, political and social landscape of cities. Becoming smart was also seen as an opportunity to mitigate against the negative consequences of rapid urban population growth and urbanisation through citizen engagement or private-public partnership platforms. The notion of the smart city originates from various urban definitions, which have evolved consecutively from "information city" and "digital city", to "ubiquitous city (U-City)", "intelligence city" and "knowledge-based city". The smart city aims to: 1) improve the quality of life of citizens; 2) enhance the city's effectiveness; and 3) create new values (NIA, 2013; KISA, 2015).

Whilst no standard definition exists for the concept, a shared global understanding underpins approaches pursued by supranational bodies, national and local governments and the private sector, for example:

- "The concept is not static: there is no absolute definition of a smart city, no end point, but rather a process, or series of steps, by which cities become more 'liveable' and resilient and, hence, able to respond quicker to new challenges." Department of Business, Energy and Industrial Strategy, UK Government.
- "A smart city is a place where the traditional networks and services are made more efficient with the use of digital and telecommunication technologies, for the benefit of its inhabitants and businesses." EC Digital Agenda for Europe: Smart cities.
- IBM defines a smart city as "one that makes optimal use of all the interconnected information available today to better understand and control its operations and optimise the use of limited resources".
- Cisco defines smart cities as those who adopt "scalable solutions that take advantage of information and communications technology (ICT) to increase efficiencies, reduce costs, and enhance quality of life".

The concept of a "smart city" was proposed by the Ministry of Land, Infrastructure and Transport (MOLIT) through the New Urban Agenda at Habitat 3 in 2016. The New Urban Agenda now commits to: "...adopt a smart city approach, which makes use of opportunities from digitalisation, clean energy and technologies, as well as innovative transport technologies, thus providing options for inhabitants to make more environmentally friendly choices and boost sustainable economic growth and enabling cities to improve their service delivery."

Smart cities have become a global market

The rapid development of smart cities since 2010 was also driven by ICT, including the Internet of Things (IoT), big data, artificial intelligence (AI), self-driving cars, drones, virtual reality (VR) or augmented reality (AR) devices, and smartphones. While such a phenomenon has resulted in a rapid increase of energy consumption levels especially among non-OECD countries, it is simultaneously predicted that the global smart energy market will more than double from USD 1.8 billion in 2010 to USD 4 billion by 2020 (BP, 2014). Furthermore, along with the technological developments, the word "platform" has dominated the recent smart city literature that fosters new product and service developments for various stakeholders, including citizens, city officials, private companies and start-ups. Smart cities have become regional innovation platforms, or systems to solve urban problems through an innovative crowdsourcing approach.

Smart city technologies and systems have become valuable global assets. As more cities adopt the smart city concept to foster urban innovation, the smart city market is estimated to grow from USD 312 billion (2015) to USD 758 billion (2020) - at an estimated Compound Annual Growth Rate (CAGR) of 19.4% (Markets and Markets, 2016). Approximately 150 of the 4 037 cities with 100 000 or more inhabitants are early adopters in the process of constructing a smart city. Among different regions, the Asia-Pacific region is expected to grow with the highest CAGR. Furthermore, Markets and Markets (2016) states that IoT within the smart cities market will reach USD 148 billion by 2020 (23.2% CAGR). According to the research study conducted by Nikkei BP, 84% of 208 smart city projects facilitated worldwide are conducted by five major cities in Europe, China, the United States, Japan, and South Korea (Korea).

As a result, national governments are increasingly recognising the net worth of smart cities and the contribution that they can make to economic growth. Capturing value from national programmes is a priority for many governments pursing the smart city agenda. It is increasingly common for countries to have strategies which assess the global market potential for sectors involved in smart city solutions. The United Kingdom, for example, drawing on research carried out by Arup based on the UK's share of OECD tradable services, conservatively estimates that it should aim to secure 10% of this global market, worth USD 40 billion per annum (UK Government BEIS, Smart Cities Background Paper 2013). Similarly, the Dutch Ministry of Economy has analysed the market opportunities for Dutch companies in its report *Smart Cities in South Korea* and is developing its strategy accordingly. Capturing the value of the sector will require specific actions by governments. Korea has prioritised the global market for smart cities since 2009 with the aim to "drive U-City industry as a new growth engine and to bolster an entrance in the overseas market" (KRIHS, p42) and continues in 2017 with the clear ambitions to:

- Contribute to international society by offering smart city solutions to developing countries, which have rich urbanisation demand and urban problems, and their corresponding cities.
- Establish executive plans and promote relevant business in co-operation with the World Bank and the Korea Land & Housing Corporation.
- Establish a multilateral system by setting up a long-term future vision and exploring investable core businesses.

3.2.2. Different global responses to a common agenda

Most smart city initiatives in the North American region are focused on open data movement including transportation and energy, delivered through a range of federal, state, local and private initiatives. To accelerate a smart transition in the United States, the Smart Cities and Communities Task Force, a body under the Networking and Information Technology Research and Development (NITRD) Program now co-ordinates federal action and partnerships with academia, industry, cities, communities, and other government entities to enable cities/communities of all types in accessing networking and information technologies and services. This recent innovation ensures that federal initiatives such as the Department of Transport Smart City Challenge, Green Bonds and loan guarantees by the Department of Housing and Urban Development operate in synergy with state and city initiatives.

Similarly, in Canada, federal, state and city governments are pursuing smart agendas. Infrastructure Canada recently launched the Smart Cities Challenge, which is a pan-Canadian competition open to communities of all sizes, including municipalities, regional governments and Indigenous communities. The Challenge encourages communities to adopt a smart cities approach to improve the lives of their residents through innovation, data and connected technology. Three initiatives will be selected to receive federal funding, with the requirement that projects are scalable and replicable.

Smart city initiatives in the Asian region have focused on efficient city maintenance and control, such as traffic management and crime prevention using CCTV as a visual sensor. The cities are constructed with collaborative public or private partnerships which are driven primarily by the central government. Furthermore, Asian cities are implementing smart city strategies in new development areas. Cities in this region are supported by strong national initiatives, and the degree of development is very extensive (Chang et al., 2015). The Chinese government announced that it would establish 320 smart city projects by 2015 and invest CNY 2 trillion (USD 33 billion); India's Prime Minister, Narendra Modi, has announced the plan to establish approximately 100 smart cities. Developed countries tend to adopt urban regeneration strategies for revitalising original cities, through concepts such as "resilient cities" or "circular economy", while developing countries establish new cities for new economic development.

The Europe 2020 Strategy launched in 2010 focused on "smart" technological solutions that could help deliver more sustainable and inclusive growth and paving the way for an integrated approach to smart cities throughout the Commission and its financial arms. Funding programmes such as the European Regional Development Fund (EDRF) will allocate EUR 16 billion to promote sustainable urban development for the 2014-20 programming period. These funds will enable local authorities to pursue smart city development. Horizon 2020 similarly allocates substantial funding for smart city projects (EUR 92.32 million in 2014 and EUR 108.18 million in 2015). In 2011, the EC launched the Smart Cities and Communities European Innovation Partnership (EIP) which is a critical platform for research and innovation. In 2013, EUR 365 million was awarded to demonstration projects. The European Commission (EC) facilitates an integrated process of establishing smart city protocols and specific interdisciplinary research projects are carried out individually on a country and city basis.

Explicit links to inclusive growth and the role of smart solutions and technologies to tackle poverty and to promote sustainable urban development are embedded into programming frameworks for other IFIs and Development Banks such as the Asian Development Bank (ADB). The ADB's Future Cities Programme, for example, has allocated USD 2 million in technical assistance to five cities to develop smart city knowledge and good practices targeting pro-poor initiatives. Korea has partnered a number of development bank initiatives.

3.2.3. Korea has been a world pioneer of smart cities

Korea has pursued smart city programmes since the early 2000s and became an early pioneer in the adoption of the concept of the smart city. In 2008, the Act on the Construction of Ubiquitous Cities (U-City Act) was passed. The U-City Act focused on infrastructure, technology and services with the aim of improving competitiveness and quality of life. The U-City concept is an evolution of the shift towards National Geographic Information Systems which emerged in the mid-1990s, paving the way for the Urban Information Systems Project (UIS) which sought to create an integrated system for utilities. UIS development strategies and the emerging field of ubiquitous computing gave rise to the U-City (KRIHS, 2015).

U-Cities offered solutions for urban problems and were seen a driver of competitiveness. MOLIT released the first U-City Comprehensive Plan in 2009 with the aim to 'drive U-City industry as a new growth engine and to bolster an entrance in the overseas market' (KRIHS, p42). Korea aimed to draw on its strong domestic technology base to position itself to benefit from a rapidly expanding global market. The budget allocation for the five-year Plan was KRW 490 billion, KRW 350 billion of which was allocated to nurture U-City industries and to create U-Services.

The first U-City was launched in the Hwasung-Dongtan area and by the end of 2012 some 50 projects had already been implemented. The initial focus was on new towns but just as technology evolves at a rapid pace, national and municipal governments have continued to innovate and evolve into developing smart city projects nationwide using its strong ICT infrastructure. Driven by the Ministry of Land, Infrastructure and Transport, U-City projects have progressed rapidly with the construction of new cities, such as Songdo and Dongtan. The national goal was to combine and converge between new ICT and urban infrastructures in various areas including transportation and public facilities. Along with such infra-focus smart city developments, the Ministry of Science, ICT and Future Planning also pioneered the next generation of smart city initiatives in 2015, by implementing new ICT concepts such as IoT, big data and cloud computing in new test-bed sites across Busan, Goyang and Daegu. Recently, SK Telecom - the biggest mobile operator in Korea - completed nationwide deployment of Low Power Wide Area Networks for IoT. Korea's new concept of the smart city is "Implementation of Open Infrastructure, Ecosystem and Platform" where anyone can participate through an IoT open platform.

Table 3.1. Smart City Budget Allocation Since 2009 (KRW million)

Project	Funding	2008	2009	2010	2011	2012	2013	2014	2015	2016	2017
Pilot U-City Designation and Assistance	Central Gov		6 000	4 000	4 900	4 300	3 900				
	Local Gov		6 000	4 000	4 900	4 300	3 900				
Building Basis of Integrated Platform for Smart City	Central Gov								600	600	3 600
	Local Gov								600	600	3 600
Human Resource Training for Smart City	Central Gov		1 772	2 800	2 500	2 100	1 890	1800	1 400	980	980
U-Eco City (R&D)	Central Gov	8 885	10 438	21 944	17 863	9 559	6 564				
Developing Intelligent Urban Information System (R&D)	Central Gov						1 900	3300	4 389	2980	2 804
National Strategy Project (R&D)	Central Gov										400

Note: The term "Ubiquitous City, U-City" was changed to "smart city" following the amendment of the Act on the Construction, etc. of Ubiquitous Cities to the Act on the Creation of Smart Cities and Promotion of Industries in March 2017.
Source: MOLIT, 2017.

3.2.4. The Fourth Industrial Revolution creating a new imperative

The Presidential Committee on the Fourth Industrial Revolution of Korea is accelerating the creation of the "smart city" concept to become a broader mechanism to benefit society. For example, a special sub-committee for the smart city and mobile health care sectors will address various social problems in cities based on wired and wireless communication networks and nationwide Internet of Things (IoT) networks, which are strengths of Korea, and create high-tech cities by converging artificial intelligence (AI) and big data.

In the smart city context, the Fourth Industrial Revolution influences not only the industry itself, but also the form and function of entire cities. Intelligence information technologies, including IoT and AI, are anticipated to enhance the quality of citizens' lifestyles by enabling cities to distribute their resources efficiently and resolve urban problems. The concept of smart cities in the Fourth Industrial Revolution continuously evolves into an open innovation ecosystem – as the driving force in human and social capital production – through Public-Private-People-Partnerships (4P) in converging the latest ICT and urban infrastructure. Ultimately, the smart city is the next-generation city designed to resolve urban problems by enabling citizens to use intelligent services based on hardware and software infrastructures. In Korea, the smart city can be defined as a regional innovation system, or platform, on which citizens, government officials, private sectors, and other diverse stakeholders may utilise ICT altogether to resolve various urban problems including transportation, environment, energy, and urban infrastructure, as well as to discover and develop new growth engines.

The government will move ahead with the Smart City New Deal project by selecting and supporting a place where early performance can be created when holding the "2017 Urban Regeneration New Deal" contest. The chosen city will become a model for other local governments. In addition, the government is planning to integrate existing smart city-related work that has been promoted by the central government, local governments, and the private sector into a platform to enhance smart cities' accomplishments.

In 2017, MOLIT stated:

> We commit to adopt a smart city approach, which makes use of opportunities from digitalization, clean energy and technologies, as well as innovative transport technologies, thus providing options for inhabitants to make more environmentally friendly choices and boost sustainable economic growth and enabling cities to improve their service delivery. Smart cities are a tool for solving urban problems and improving the quality of life by applying ICTs and new technologies to cities (MOLIT, 2017).

3.2.5. Korean cites leading the way internationally

Smart City Key Trends

Increasingly, Korean smart cities are using international benchmarking as a means to exchange knowledge, remain competitive and to adapt framework conditions. For the purpose of this report, a comparative assessment led by Yonsei University focused on 10 smart cities: Amsterdam, Barcelona, Busan, Helsinki, London, New York City, Paris, San Francisco, Seoul, and Singapore. The University analysed 676 applications and web services, 116 infrastructure services, and 238 projects across the 10 cities.

Eight key trends of global smart cities emerged from this analysis and demonstrate how the cities are constructing their own regional innovation systems and the implications for future smart city development in Korea and elsewhere. The eight key trends of global smart city development are:

4. Service innovation
5. Urban sustainability
6. Urban intelligence
7. Urban openness
8. Infra-integration
9. Smart city governance
10. Urban innovativeness
11. Collaborative partnership

1. Service Innovation

Service innovation refers to service diversity and interoperability. By analysing 676 identified applications and web services in the 10 smart cities, services can be classified into ten service types, among which 1) Transportation (28.3%); 2) Culture, Tourism and Recreation (18.5%); and 3) Health and Social Services (10.4%) were the most prevalent. The three service types account for more than half (57.2%) of all services.

For service innovation, London, Seoul, and New York City are the three leading cities in service diversity, providing applications and web services. London leads service innovation by producing a wide variety of services – in 2008, the city launched the "Smart London Innovation Networks" and "Tech City UK" projects to invigorate its ICT and start-up ecosystem. Co-operative smart city projects by organisations have provided opportunities for start-up growth, thus leading to an active innovation ecosystem. The tech sector in London now generates over GBP 13 billion.

Although not a leader in service innovation, Busan demonstrates service innovation that reflects its regional characteristics. As a tourism city of Korea, a substantial 26% of its services pertain to the Culture, Tourism and Recreation category. Typical tourist information services include mobile applications. Busan also provides public administration services such as "120 Call Centre Mobile App".

2. Urban Sustainability

The smart city aims to solve numerous problems such as energy, environment, and social welfare caused by urbanisation and growth in urban populations, thus enhancing urban sustainability and the quality of citizens' lives. The 10 smart cities have all adopted cutting-edge ICT to enhance urban sustainability with most infrastructure-based services focused on controlling energy (61.0%), waste (19.0%), and air quality (10.0%).

For example, Helsinki is home of "ZenRobotics", a world-leading supplier of an AI-based robotic waste separation system. The robotic infrastructure increases the efficiency of waste separation, while simultaneously lowering energy consumption as well as labour and landfill costs. Barcelona operates a smart irrigation system, in which sensors determine the degree of irrigation that each of the city's districts requires. The sensors also monitor precipitation and humidity levels to save approximately 25% in water usage. In Amsterdam, the "Tree Wi-Fi" visualises information on air pollution levels, collects real-time measurements of air pollution in districts, and represents the pollution statuses as different coloured lights. The "Ring-Ring" is a platform service for cyclists in Amsterdam, operated by a private enterprise through which the municipal government grants points to citizens based on the distance travelled by bicycle; points are exchangeable between users and with the government in return for social and financial benefits.

3. Urban Intelligence

Urban intelligence in smart cities is the provision of intelligent services based on new technologies such as IoT, big data, and AI to solve various urban problems. Intelligent services involve real-time big data analysis of diverse spatial, environmental, and criminal data collected using a variety of IoT sensors. Smart cities are beginning to improve the urban environment by increasing efficiency in urban maintenance, as well as converging real-time urban data with intelligent infrastructure that brings service innovation. Analysis on the 10 cities shows that the majority are facilitating urban intelligence through application and infrastructure-based services that employ emerging technologies: 53.8% of all smart city services utilise either or both IoT and big data. A large proportion of the intelligent services based on new technologies target Energy and Environment (37.0%) and Transportation (16.0%).

All 10 cities aim to provide new means of intelligent services by combining and utilising emerging technologies effectively. London and Barcelona have implemented smart lighting systems which perform various smart city-related functions. Sensors in Barcelona's street lights collect atmospheric and traffic data to improve the environment and ensure public safety. Similarly, London has installed 12 000 LED street lights through the "Smart Light Platform" project, which collect parking and noise-related data additionally to decrease operating costs while increasing service stability. The "Smart Light Platform" will serve as a platform for forthcoming IoT applications. Another intelligent service in Barcelona is the smart parking system. Introduced in 2013, the city's smart parking relies on sensors which are deployed around the central district to identify available parking spaces and notify citizens in real-time through a mobile application. As well as reducing traffic congestion the service generates USD 50 million revenue from parking fees annually.

4. Urban Openness

Urban openness is the open innovation environment of smart cities that employs citizen-centred innovation for effective service development and has two main features: civic engagement and open data.

4.1 Civic engagement

Smart civic engagement began with what can be described as the *Participation* phase whereby citizens were invited to vote on proposed smart city services or ideas; this evolved into the *Idea Suggestion* phase whereby cities engaged citizens more directly through mechanisms such as smart city "ideas contests". From this emerged the *Co-operation* phase, whereby citizens participated in smart city communities operated by public or private sectors; from this could emerge a culture of *Co-creation* where smart cities co-operate with citizens to produce smart city solutions based entirely on voluntary civic engagement. Smart city services are forecast to evolve into citizen-centred services using civic engagement platforms. Analysis reveals that most of the services provided by the 10 cities provide information to citizens unilaterally or, at best, allow citizens to partially share information. Among the 676 applications and web services analysed, citizen-participatory services – either partially or fully – account for 33.3% of all services, out of which 9.3% of the services provide a "real civic engagement" platform for citizens. However, at present the majority of smart city services deliver information unilaterally (66.7%).

To promote urban openness, citizen-oriented open innovation platforms contribute concurrently to engaging citizens in solving urban problems and the creation of new social values. Under the "Green Watch" project in Paris, approximately 200 participants were given smart devices containing two environmental sensors. Each device measured ozone and noise levels throughout the participants' daily routines, which subsequently reduced environmental monitoring costs. Barcelona has developed a similar product, "Smart Citizen Kit", to measure air pollution levels and enables policy makers to use the accumulated data to support decision-making processes. Amsterdam operates "Peerby", a mobile application and sharing platform where citizens may rent unused household tools from neighbours and is part of the "Sharing City Initiative", to create a sharing economy and build trust among citizens.

4.2 Open data

As the fundamental source of smart city innovation, diverse open data is expected to be the most significant infrastructural resource in constructing a data-driven smart city in the Fourth Industrial Revolution. Of the municipal open data portals from the 10 cities Singapore is the most developed (11 587 datasets), followed by Seoul (4 479 datasets) and New York City (1 484 datasets). *Nonetheless, a cautious distinction must take place between the quantity and quality of open data.* Although Singapore ranks 1st in the number of open APIs, the number of open APIs will not be a major issue in the future as the world's leading smart cities are now committed to disclosing their urban data to the private sector.

London and New York City are particularly strong in urban openness, in terms of the diversity of open government data sets. As the trend continues, the quality of open data will become crucial in determining smart city development. The quality of open data will be influenced by three factors: 1) Diversity of open data (how various types of open data are offered to citizens and private sectors); 2) Open data utilisation (how innovatively open data is utilised through data conversion and integration); and 3) Open data platforms (how different stakeholders co-ordinate through the open data platforms).

The notable smart cities specify the characteristics of open data in driving urban openness. Singapore's integrated data portal website possesses more than 11 000 open data sets, pivoting around 70 public organisations. The city provides generic open data sets mainly in the fields of economy, education, environment, health, infrastructure, demographics, etc. In comparison, London's official "London Datastore" enables users to access useful living information that may be utilised across the city – the city discloses data such as traffic count during rush hours, crime rates, and disaster areas. London has further developed smart city services based on more than 80% of its 990 data sets.

5. Infra-integration

Infrastructure integration (infra-integration) generates higher-standard network effects, by supporting smart city planning and establishing connections across cities. The expansion of smart city services must be preceded by the creation of a centralised, integrated infrastructure; it is thus expected that smart cities will accelerate the development of "cyber-physical systems" that retain efficient urban management capabilities. Evidence from the cities reveals that building smart city infrastructure is often dependant on strong local political leadership and commitment, the support of national governments and private sector initiatives. Smart cities in the Asian region aim to create new industrial economies through a holistic approach, as well as to leverage advanced e-government infrastructure. Most infrastructural initiatives are driven by central governmental. Meanwhile, the North American region focuses much more on information accessibility or on specific themes (i.e. transportation, energy, and open data). European cities' initiatives are particularly effective at building soft-aspects of infrastructure through public-private partnerships, with a focus on civic engagement initiatives to facilitate "smart citizens".

Busan aims to provide an open infrastructural ecosystem in which citizens and private organisations may participate actively through an IoT-based open platform. The city's smart city goal is to devise new ideas and business models to promote and revitalise the local economy. Busan's open platform follows the oneM2M international standard to guide data analysis and disclosure procedures in order to encourage international citizens and private firms to participate freely, leading to collaborations with smart cities around the world. Busan is currently in the validation process of 26 IoT-based services regarding "smart parking", "smart street light", "smart crosswalk", and "smart building" to ultimately extend coverage to the entire city.

In terms of infra-integration, Singapore's 10-year "Intelligent Nation 2015 (iN2015)" masterplan has established ICT infrastructure to provide a broadband connection service usable anywhere on any device. The city's consecutive "Infocomm Media 2025" masterplan sets out to create a globally competitive ICT and media ecosystem. Singapore has made infrastructure establishment its foremost task, and correspondingly accumulates data from its "Heterogeneous Network (Het-Net)" project. Data is transferred to aggregation gateway (AG) boxes which are composed of sensors transmitting data to governmental institutions. Examples of services include the intelligent transportation system and the sensor-based water and sewage maintenance system, which are both referred to as world-leading cases of well-established infrastructures.

6. Smart City Governance

Smart city governance is based on the concept of effective and efficient intra-city governance systems for smart city construction. The process of smart city realisation demands a number of aligning factors including, but not limited to: 1) Smart City Leadership; 2) Dedicated Smart City Organisation; 3) Smart City Vision and Strategy; and 4) Municipal Act or Legislation.

Firstly, the 10 cities demonstrate strong leadership from mayoral and senior management teams to achieve their smart city vision. In general, leadership support is driven by the city's chief technology officer (CTO) or chief information officer (CIO); leading smart cities have also created new high-level positions such as chief innovation or data officer. Secondly, most of the cities have established a dedicated organisation to support smart city development within the region. Various dedicated organisational forms exist externally or internally to deliver action plans, initiated by either third-party organisations or departments that are dedicated to support the municipal government. Dedicated new organisations often faced challenges in co-ordinating and co-operating with other cities' departments, often due to the lack of human resources or strong governance structures to support smart city initiatives. On the other hand, Asian and North American smart cities are often more driven by a centralised municipal government. Thirdly, smart cities in global regions establish visions and strategies in defining a smart city roadmap, with each region displaying unique approaches. The European smart cities (i.e. Amsterdam, Barcelona and London) share a holistic view of city-wide master planning to implement their smart city strategy, and monitor their progress using key performance indicators (KPIs). Cities in the North American region take a more piecemeal approach in implementing urban functions to support the cities' smart city strategies, rather than designing a comprehensive strategy. Lastly, institutionalising smart city planning and development with municipal acts and legislation is another key driver of propelling smart city governance. Korea has already promulgated the "U-City Act" since 2008, which is currently under amendment as the "Smart City Act". Smart city planning and development in both the Asian and North American regions are developed by the centralised government; in comparison, smart cities in Europe possess relatively fewer cases regarding acts that directly pertain to smart city planning.

Smart city development for Amsterdam, Seoul and Busan, for example, is driven by the CIO and CTOs who collaborate with other city departments to establish an appropriate governance structure, aligned with an effective planning, development and implementation process. Seoul has recently published a municipal act for IoT city planning in 2016, while other cities or nations also provide guidelines (e.g. IoT guideline for New York City, or "PD8101 Smart Cities Planning Guidelines" from the British Standards Institution). New York City established a department solely responsible for promoting the smart city project; and from 2015, with the Mayor's Office of Technology and Innovation (MOTI) at the centre, the city initiated the "Building a Smart + Equitable City" strategy. MOTI has attempted to enhance network service to strengthen connections within the city and to reduce digital divide. It installed kiosks that are equipped with

"Link NYC" technology to provide free Wi-Fi. As of this year, 400 kiosks are installed across the city with plans to increase this number to 500 by the end of the year, and ultimately, to 7 500 kiosks by 2024. To carry out its' five-year ICT plan, San Francisco has established the Committee on Information Technology (COIT) for public open-data policy and IT infrastructure expansion. In 2009, San Francisco launched the first public data policy in the United States, requiring all departments to register data on "Data SF (San Francisco Data Portal)".

7. Urban Innovativeness

For urban innovativeness, smart cities adopt technologies and methods that have not been previously utilised to build new start-up and living lab ecosystems by discovering, developing and commercialising new services. Cities seek to improve their urban innovativeness by generating new economic assets and expanding on open innovation ecosystems. A key finding from the cities is the importance of soft-aspects (i.e. civic government) of smart city elements for constructing a sustainable smart city ecosystem. In general, numerous smart city initiatives are dedicated to building new social and human capitals to create new economies. Living labs – where the smart city users or citizens become the principal actor in smart city innovation activities – are operated in several European cities such as Amsterdam, Barcelona, London, and Paris. In particular, Europe has successfully established the European Network of Living Labs (ENoLL) for cities to collaborate and share knowledge with one another. Living labs promote innovation activities by various smart city stakeholders to achieve user-driven open innovation. The five types of living labs are as follows: 1) utiliser-driven; 2) enabler-driven; 3) provider-driven; 4) user-driven; and 5) community-driven. Another dimension of urban innovativeness is the competitiveness of start-ups. In general, a start-up refers to a new venture corporation that has innovative technology and ideas; it introduces a new paradigm in business, and acts as a leader in propelling the city's innovativeness. The 10 cities are accelerating their efforts to expand start-up ecosystems through new platforms, strengthening mentoring, and improving the general start-up environment.

London has recently shown significant growth in urban innovativeness. In 2011, the UK government implemented "Tech City UK" in London to support start-ups, and enforced policies in constructing and supporting start-up clusters, leveraging London's financial industry. The "Smart London Innovative Network" project provides start-ups with growth opportunities from collaborations with other smart cities. In Amsterdam, a total of 11 living labs and civic community programmes including "IoT Living Lab", "Amsterdam Smart Citizens Lab", and "Transform City" conduct pilot tests and projects on a reduced scale to establish sustainable transportation and environmental infrastructure for carbon reduction. Paris focuses largely on locating and supporting start-ups through several entrepreneur support organisations, including "Paris Incubateurs" and "NUMA". As a start-up support network established by over 300 start-ups, "NUMA" is now a global start-up incubation centre that has expanded globally including Barcelona, Moscow, and Mexico. Paris has the second-largest number of start-ups among European cities after London, as well as the second-largest number of living labs after Amsterdam. The ongoing efforts to construct a start-up ecosystem in Paris have been instrumental in building a technology-based start-up ecosystem to enhance urban innovation.

Cities in the North American region – San Francisco and New York City – have founded a larger number of start-ups compared to other cities across the globe. This can be attributed to the Silicon Valley effect in San Francisco, as well as the so-called "Silicon Valley of the East" or "Silicon Alley" of New York City, which have vibrant start-up ecosystems. San Francisco is dominated by new entrepreneurs in the region; considering that 1 146 start-ups have registered in 2016 alone and that various IT R&D projects are currently being executed within the municipal area, it is suggested that San Francisco retains the potential to evolve into a market-oriented organic smart city platform and ecosystem.

Asian smart cities are shifting progressively towards urban innovativeness. Singapore is a city-state with an abundance of start-ups in the Asian region. The city-state owns "Government Digital Service (GDS)", a start-up incubating space that has become the centrepiece of start-up facilitation in the surrounding regions. Seoul and Busan are home to a relatively small number of start-ups in comparison to North American and European cities. To address this, the Korean government has launched a national initiative to transform the start-up funding system from financing to investing, by facilitating angel investors, institutionalising crowdfunding, and creating new funding mechanisms. Accordingly, Seoul has begun to transform the traditional Bukchon district into an IoT living lab since 2015, with plans to implement various IoT services and technologies to develop an IoT-based smart city ecosystem by 2020. Bukchon IoT test-bed provides 17 services in tourism, safety, transportation and environment. The services are now being piloted in the districts of Hongdae, Sinchon and Gangnam to expand the IoT test-beds to the entire city by 2020.

8. Collaborative Partnership

Collaborative partnership is a co-operation system that stimulates smart city services and infrastructure development through diverse co-operative partnerships within and between cities. Public-private partnerships currently play a critical role in the development of smart cities and private sector investment is critical in London (74.5%), Helsinki (58.9%), and Singapore (58.9%). However, an emerging smart city trend is 4P (Public-Private-People Partnership) which extends the traditional public-private partnership approach to include citizens.

The types of inter- and intra-collaborative partnerships vary across cities, due to the involvement of internal or external government agencies (e.g. National Police Agencies or National Weather Forecasting Centre), or the private sector. Another emerging smart city trend is the foundation of city-to-city (C2C) collaboration among smart cities around the globe. In the Fourth Industrial Revolution, cities share their know-how and resources through open platforms. Cross-border data flows enable the cities to create new values through data flows transcending national borders, realising global economies of scale. Subsequently, global smart cities are established through external C2C co-operation. Such collective movements bring more sustainable, innovative and integrated solutions to achieve a "data-driven smart city", through IoT infrastructures and the improvement of citizens' urban lives.

In the EU, the predominant type of collaboration is in building common infrastructure (i.e. open platform and infrastructure standard) as well as C2C programmes (e.g. C2C hackathon). The C2C urban platform creates a co-operation network for sharing and solving joint problems across six cities in Europe including London, Milan, and Lisbon. The EU prepares common standards and interoperability for platforms with approximately 40 enterprises, considering economies of scale. Additionally, 57 cities in the EU develop innovation capabilities and enforce policies through co-operation. One of the leading C2C projects is "CitySDK" with Barcelona, Amsterdam, Helsinki, and five other European cities, to provide an "open source" toolkit for developers and increase scale-up for start-ups with other partnership cities. Under collaborative initiatives,

Barcelona and Amsterdam are also working on 11 and 12 C2C projects respectively and are outreaching to other global regions.

London is the most active in the development of various services and infrastructures through private finance. London's citizens can participate as developers and as investors through the crowdfunding platform "Funding Options" and participate in sharing economy services such as sharing parking space "Justpark" or living space "Cityflatpals" to promote sustainable living. Seoul also has been moving away from its public-led system towards more civic engagement. Seoul has constructed "Citizen Communication" governance by establishing the following services: an online civil policy suggestion platform "Chun-man-sang-sang Oasis", citizen-centred city lifestyle survey "mVoting", and smart service desk. In addition, the city has been using the term "Connected City" rather than "Smart City". Busan built a strong public-private partnership to implement a IoT-dedicated network. Currently, as a form of industry-university-institute collaboration, 40 different private and public organisations, including SK Telecom, Busan Information Promotion Agency (BIPA), Busan Metropolitan City, and Yonsei and Kyungsung Universities are developing a citizen engagement platform and smart city services in the IoT test-bed site.

3.2.6. What the ten cities reveal

The smart city could be considered as five independent platforms, from an "open data platform", to a "civic engagement platform", an "urban innovation platform", an "urban living lab and test-bed", and a "city-to-city (C2C) platform". The rapid growth of service innovation means that more integrated, diversified, and citizen-centred smart city services will be developed in the near future. Current analysis of the 10 cities indicates that the majority of services are distributed across three service types: 1) Transportation; 2) Culture, Tourism and Recreation; and 3) Health and Social Services. It has also been identified that some cities overlook public-driven smart city services that focus on public welfare. To address this imbalance, more needs to be done to enhance citizens' perception of experience in smart city services by building a balanced service portfolio consisting of services and projects across diverse categories. Smart city developments must promote service innovation through integrating and diversifying smart city services, and thus achieving a balance between the public and private sector-driven initiatives.

Critical for climate change

As public awareness about environmental issues continues to rise, most smart cities are exerting efforts to resolve environmental and energy-related problems to achieve zero carbon emissions and improve the sustainability of the urban environment. Nonetheless, several services developed on sensor-based urban infrastructures have yet to create an impact on citizens' behaviour towards climate change. In the case of Busan, environment and energy-related projects pivoting around urban infrastructure will be launched – including energy conservation for smart residential and commercial properties, as well as self-supporting urban smart agricultural zones. Besides initiatives focusing on infrastructure, smart cities must develop services that encourage direct civic engagement for increasing sustainability. Evidence from the cities suggests that smart city development in the future must break from the conventional, infrastructure-centred urban renewal towards a greater focus on energy conservation and begin to actively induce citizens' actions towards sustainability.

The next revolution

The prevalence of new technology in the Fourth Industrial Revolution will facilitate the collection and analysis of data by applying IoT, big data and AI technologies. The key agenda for smart city development will be the increase in urban intelligence through ICBM (IoT - Cloud - Big data - Mobile) technology used for managing the city and offering life intelligence services. To improve life for citizens by resolving future urban problems, smart cities must enlarge the scope of their technologies, taking the lead for other aspects of smart cities. Busan attempts to plan and substantiate ICT to accommodate urban intelligence through its global smart city test-bed construction business starting from Haeundae district, which reflects the city's tourist territorial characteristics. To scale-up its smart city business into the global network, Busan could further develop its smart city with a view to supplying resources to create value. This will provide a firm basis for the mainstreaming of new technology. In addition, it should secure diverse participation incentives for the acceleration of smart city development.

People-centred solutions

Urban openness pertains to establishing an open innovation environment through civic engagement platforms and open data network systems. Most smart cities are within the initial stage of smart city development in terms of urban openness. Efforts by some of the leading smart cities and growing interest by others shows the potential for greater civic engagement and data disclosure in the future. Smart cities are seeking solutions in acquiring high-quality urban data from diverse categories as well as maximising open data usage. As more data is accumulated and disclosed as usable open data, smart cities will establish specific international standards along with a universal data interface to accelerate the growth of open smart city big data platforms. Smart cities must acknowledge that inducing citizen participation at the co-creation level and enhancing the quality of open data are the preceding bases for securing urban openness.

Globally connected

Smart cities in different global regions have demonstrated contrasting approaches to achieve infra-integration, from a holistic approach driven by central government to civic engagement approaches through public-private partnerships. Some global smart cities have attempted to integrate urban infrastructure to a limited degree by expanding network infrastructures, building interoperability platforms, and constructing city-wide integrated data centres. As with Korea's LoRa network installation or Singapore's high-speed, cost-effective connectivity solutions using AG boxes, expanding network infrastructure will complement other smart city elements to bring extensive volumes of information.

Enabling interoperability among dissimilar smart city infrastructure devices and standard platforms within the city will be critical in increasing network effectiveness – this will ensure harmonisation among infrastructures and create a new standard for smart city development. Furthermore, the role of the city-wide integrated data centre will become a driving force to leverage new sets of urban data and capture new value from consolidating a variety of data sets. While data consolidation depends principally on mayoral leadership and relevant IT department support, the expected benefits of data centres will not only improve IT asset utilisation with reduced costs, but also provide new opportunities for the cities to become a data-driven smart city as a source of open big data innovation. Overall, constructing an interoperable IoT network to become a data-driven city will be the critical factor for enhancing infra-integration in smart cities of the next generation.

21st century governance

Smart city governance for smart city construction encompasses: 1) leadership; 2) dedicated organisation; 3) vision and strategy; and 4) municipal act and legislation. Strong leadership and commitment bring more innovative solutions to citizens and achieve balance between creating new economic opportunity and closing the digital divide. In addition, dedicated organisations must consider how willing their cities are in increasing their own absorptive capacity for smart city innovation, and must leverage departments and agencies of other cities as new technology-based services continue to emerge. Most cities do not have holistic views on smart city performance measurements and lack comprehensive indicators on civic engagement. Based on the benchmark smart city strategies, such cities must set KPIs to monitor their strategies with feasible roadmap actions. Lastly, legislation can set clear standards which could institutionalise smart city planning and development.

The core attributes for urban innovativeness are creating and expanding an open innovation ecosystem. Open innovation ecosystem is necessary for the future smart city in that it stimulates citizens' participation. Living labs and start-ups are the main factors that construct and expand open innovation ecosystem. Urban innovativeness of a smart city ecosystem will be driven more by civic engagement, through these factors based on civic entrepreneurship. Ultimately, the urban innovation cluster must be based on civic engagement through living labs and start-ups that are based on civic entrepreneurship.

Redefining partnership

The increasing growth of ICT both enables and requires collaborative partnership within and among smart cities. More innovations between smart cities are expected to be achieved by C2C co-operation and 4P partnerships based on crowdfunding to create smart city living labs with citizen participation at the centre. Additionally, citizen-private-public collaborative partnerships are crucial for acquiring public value and the effective supply of funds through the construction of smart city crowdfunding platforms. By utilising the benefits of global ICT, smart cities may execute scaled-up strategies and gain access to foreign markets through C2C collaboration networking. Currently, cities such as Seoul and Busan have a higher tendency to operate their smart city services depending on their public financing than other cities like London. This implies that these cities actively facilitate open data movements, yet do not have a strong correlation to private sector led service development. Although the types of collaborative partnerships vary across cities, increased collaboration will be the key to sustainable smart city development.

Global smart cities including Busan are in the process of achieving economic growth through efforts to "scale- up" the ecosystem and through the "local innovation platform centred on citizens' participation and living lab" making cities more resilient. In addition, co-operation between smart cities through global networking, 4P models, and C2C partnerships are creating economies of scale, building capacity and enabling knowledge exchange.

3.2.7. The implications for Korea

Smart cities in Korea utilise cutting-edge ICT infrastructures to effectively resolve urban problems such as transport, energy and environment, education, and health. Korea has taken the "U-City" approach since the early 2000s to construct an integrated urban environment that combines ICT with urban infrastructures, as a national initiative for research and development. As a result, Korea is now home to the world's leading smart city pilot cities and test-beds in terms of infrastructure integration. Diverse government policies to promote open innovation-based smart cities are currently being implemented, such as: civic engagement initiatives and living labs based on open urban innovation, the establishment of a start-up ecosystem, as well as utilisation of open data. In recent years, Korea passed the "Ordinance on Smart City Development and Management", which was a renewal of the earlier "Ordinance on Ubiquitous City Construction Projects" (Korea was the first country in the world to pass such legislation). Korea's efforts in preparing proactive and anticipatory policies for the rising demands of the smart city indicate the country's nationwide leadership in smart city development.

The digital information era of the Third Industrial Revolution was initiated with the concept of providing digital information services to citizens via web services or applications, focusing on "U-City", that maximises convenience in the perspective of urban management grafted onto ICT-based city infrastructures. In the era of the Fourth Industrial Revolution, diverse data and information, generated by the provision of user-oriented citizen participatory services based on smart city infrastructure, will become the driving force for urban innovation. Furthermore, considering regional characteristics, the cities themselves are expected to realise a data-driven smart city as an integrated urban innovation platform.

As the future technologies leading the Fourth Industrial Revolution, including IoT, cloud computing, big data, AI, mobility, and Blockchain technologies, are progressively applied world-wide, yet another hyper-connected intelligent society will be created. In preparation, the Ministry of Land, Infrastructure and Transport (MOLIT) in Korea is taking various research initiatives to create data hub-centred smart cities over the next five years. Furthermore, MOLIT is constructing the citizen-centred smart city to align "Urban Regeneration", "Inclusive Growth" and "Technological Innovation". Aligning government policies and objectives in this way is helping create the Fourth Industrial Revolution, and the importance of smart cities in solving diverse urban problems is expected to rise not only for Korea, but also for other OECD member states.

Bibliography

AGMA (2014), *A Plan for Growth and Reform in Greater Manchester*, www.agma.gov.uk/cms_media/files/growth_and_reform_plan_final_4_apr_14.pdf (accessed on 17 December 2017).

Antalovsky, E. (2015), 'Reinventing Vienna'. Presentation, RPA International Advisory Committee, London, 17th March.

BP (2014), *BP Energy Outlook 2035, British Petroleum, Global*, www.bp.com/content/dam/bp/pdf/energy-economics/energy-outlook-2016/bp-energy-outlook-2014.pdf (accessed on 1 November 2017).

Caird S. (2017), *City approaches to smart city evaluation and reporting: case studies in the United Kingdom,* Urban Research and Practice, Routledge, London.

City of Hamburg (2014), *Green, inclusive, growing city by the water: Perspectives on Urban development in Hamburg.* www.hamburg.de/contentblob/4357518/data/broschuere-perspektiven-englisch).pdf (accessed on 1 November 2017).

Clark, G. and T. Moonen (2015), *Technology Real Estate and the Innovation Economy*, Urban Land Institute, London.

Clark, G. and T. Moonen (2014), *Urban Innovation and Investment*, Future Cities Catapult, UK Government Office for Science, London.

Clark, G. and G. Clark (2014), *Nations and the Wealth of Cities: A new Phase of Public Policy*, Centre for London, London.

Clark, G. and T. Moonen (2013), *The Ten Traits of Globally Fluent Metro Areas: International Edition*, Brookings Institution, Washington D.C.

Coletta, C., L. Heaphy and R. Kitchen (2017), From the accidental to the articulated smart city: the creation and work of smart Dublin, NIRSA, Ireland.

Department of Business, Energy and Industrial Strategy (2013), *The Smart City Market: Opportunities for the UK BIS RESEARCH PAPER NO. 13.*, UK Government, London.

Department of Business, Energy and Industrial Strategy (2013), *Smart Cities Background Paper,* UK Government, London.

Dudman, J. (2014), "Devo Manc: What powers will the new Greater Manchester mayor have?" *The Guardian,* November 3rd. www.theguardian.com/public-leaders-network/2014/nov/03/devo-manc-powers-greater-manchester-mayor (accessed on 15 November 2017).

Economist Intelligence Unit (2015), *Urban Infrastructure Insight 2015,* www.economistinsights.com/sites/default/files/Urban%20Infrastructure%20Insights.pdf (accessed on 21 November 2017).

European Commission (2013), *Using EU funding mechanism for Smart Cities,* EC, Brussels.

European Commission (2016), *Analysing the potential for wide scale role out of integrated Smart Cities and Communities solutions, final report,* EC, Brussels.

HafenCity Hamburg (2014), "Development Management and HafenCity Hamburg GmbH", www.hafencity.com/en/management/development-management-and-hafencity-hamburg-gmbh.html (accessed on 19 November 2017).

Han, Sang Ki (2015), "*스마트시티 도시별 추진 현황*" *[Current status of the smart cities],* Power Review, Vol. 2015/11, Korea Internet and Security Agency, Seoul, www.kisa.or.kr/public/library/IS_View.jsp?mode=view&p_No=158&b_No=158&d_No=291 (accessed on 4 December 2017).

IDB (2016a), *International Case Studies of Smart Cities, Songdo, Republic of Korea,* IDB, Washington D.C.

IDB (2016b), *The Road toward Smart Cities,* IDB, Washington D.C.

Kim, J. and M. Cho (2017), *Creating a sewing village in Seoul: towards participatory village-making or post-political urban regeneration?* Oxford University Press and Community Development Journal, Oxford.

Kleinman, M. (2016), *Cities, Data and Digital Innovation*, IMFG Munk School of Global Affairs, Toronto.

Korea Ministry of Land, Infrastructure and Transport (2014), *National Report for Habitat III: the Republic of Korea,* UN, New York.

KHRIS, (2013), *A Primer on Korean Planning and Policy: City Management and Urban Renewal*, PKPP 2013-0, KRHIS GDPC, Sejong.

Lee J., W. Sher, H. Lee, M. Mak and M. Ostwald (2015), *Strategic planning indicators: towards mixed-use developments supporting regeneration in Seoul.* GBER Vol 9 Issue 2. Seoul

Manchester City Council (2012), "City Centre regeneration Team - Economy, Employment and Skills Overview and Scrutiny Committee 8th February", www.manchester.gov.uk/egov_downloads/7_City_Centre_Regeneration.pdf (accessed on 4 November 2017).

Markets and Markets (2016), *Smart Cities Market by Solution and Services for Focus Areas - Global Forecast to 2020*, Markets and Markets, Global, www.marketsandmarkets.com/Market-Reports/smart-cities-market-542.html (accessed on 29 November 2017).

Ministerie Van Economische Zaken, *Smart Cities in South Korea,* Agentschap NL.

Moir E., T. Moonen and G. Clark (2014), *What Are Future Cities?,* Future Cities Catapult, UK Government Office for Science, London.

MOLIT (2017), "The Smart City New Deal", Power Point presentation, Sejong.

New Economy (2014), "Briefing 32: Fiscal decentralisation", www.neweconomymanchester.com (accessed 12 November 2017).

NIA (2013), "*해외 Smart City 열풍과 시사점*" *[Trends and implications of smart cities in the world], IT & Future Strategy,* Vol. 2013/11, National Information Society Agency, Seoul, www.nia.or.kr/common/board/Download.do?bcIdx=14878&cbIdx=25932&fileNo=2 (accessed on 1 November 2017).

OECD (2012a), "Delivering Local Development in Derry~Londonderry, Northern Ireland: Inclusive Growth Through One Plan", *OECD Local Economic and Employment Development (LEED) Working Papers*, No. 2012/15, OECD Publishing, Paris, http://dx.doi.org/10.1787/5k92s6tv9c0r-en.

OECD (2012b), *OECD Urban Policy Reviews, Korea 2012*, OECD Urban Policy Reviews, OECD Publishing, Paris, http://dx.doi.org/10.1787/9789264174153-en.

OECD (2013), *Delivering Local Development: New Growth and Investment Strategies*, OECD Publishing, Paris, http://www.oecd.org/cfe/leed/NGIS_final2.pdf.

OECD (2015a), *The Metropolitan Century: Understanding Urbanisation and its Consequences*, OECD Publishing, Paris, http://dx.doi.org/10.1787/9789264228733-en.

OECD (2015b), *Governing the City*, OECD Publishing, Paris, http://dx.doi.org/10.1787/9789264226500-en.

OECD (2015c), *Local Economic Leadership*, OECD Publishing, Paris, https://www.oecd.org/cfe/leed/OECD-LEED-Local-Economic-Leadership.pdf.

OECD (2016), *Paris Action Plan for Inclusive Growth in Cities*, OECD, Paris, https://www.oecd.org/inclusive-growth/champion-mayors/internationalandregionalevents/Binder2.pdf.

Russo, F., C. Rindone and P. Panuccio (2017), *European plans for the smart city: from theories and rules to logistics test case,* European Planning Studies, Routledge, London.

Shin, D. (2013), *Smart City: A Primer on Korean Planning and Policy,* KRHIS, Seoul.

Thorpe, K. (2017), *UK Urban Regeneration Policy for Competitiveness: A Government Perspective,* LHI Journal, http//dx.doi.org/10.5804/LHIJ.2017.8.2.033 (accessed on 4 December 2017).

UN (2014), *World Urbanization Prospects: The 2014 Revision*, United Nations, New York, https://esa.un.org/unpd/wup/publications/files/wup2014-report.pdf (accessed on 28 November 2017).

UN Habitat (2015), *Habitat III Issue Papers 21 – Smart Cities,* United Nations, New York.

UNECE, (2015), *United Smart Cities: smart urban solutions for transition and developing countries,* United Nations, New York.

Yu, J. and H. Kwon (2011), *Critical success factors for urban regeneration projects in Korea,* Science Direct, Elsevier.

Woo, Y. (2014), *Two tales of Housing-led Urban Regeneration Policy Network: The UK and South Korea,* International Planning Studies, Routle.

ORGANISATION FOR ECONOMIC CO-OPERATION AND DEVELOPMENT

The OECD is a unique forum where governments work together to address the economic, social and environmental challenges of globalisation. The OECD is also at the forefront of efforts to understand and to help governments respond to new developments and concerns, such as corporate governance, the information economy and the challenges of an ageing population. The Organisation provides a setting where governments can compare policy experiences, seek answers to common problems, identify good practice and work to co-ordinate domestic and international policies.

The OECD member countries are: Australia, Austria, Belgium, Canada, Chile, the Czech Republic, Denmark, Estonia, Finland, France, Germany, Greece, Hungary, Iceland, Ireland, Israel, Italy, Japan, Korea, Latvia, Luxembourg, Mexico, the Netherlands, New Zealand, Norway, Poland, Portugal, the Slovak Republic, Slovenia, Spain, Sweden, Switzerland, Turkey, the United Kingdom and the United States. The European Union takes part in the work of the OECD.

OECD Publishing disseminates widely the results of the Organisation's statistics gathering and research on economic, social and environmental issues, as well as the conventions, guidelines and standards agreed by its members.

OECD PUBLISHING, 2, rue André-Pascal, 75775 PARIS CEDEX 16
(04 2018 05 1 P) ISBN 978-92-64-29886-6 – 2018

www.ingramcontent.com/pod-product-compliance
Lightning Source LLC
Chambersburg PA
CBHW061217240926
51846CB00006B/1253